MASS COMMUNICATION
Issues, Perspectives and Techniques

MASS COMMUNICATION
Issues, Perspectives and Techniques

Jason R. Detrani
Associate Professor of Communications/Media Arts,
Broome Community College, State University of New York,
Binghamton, U.S.A.

Apple Academic Press

Mass Communication: Issues, Perspectives and Techniques

© Copyright 2011*
Apple Academic Press Inc.

First Published in the Canada, 2011
Apple Academic Press Inc.
3333 Mistwell Crescent
Oakville, ON L6L 0A2
Tel. : (888) 241-2035
Fax: (866) 222-9549
E-mail: info@appleacademicpress.com
www.appleacademicpress.com

> **The full-color tables, figures, diagrams, and images in this book may be viewed at www.appleacademicpress.com**

First issued in paperback 2021

ISBN 13: 978-1-77463-253-6 (pbk)
ISBN 13: 978-1-926692-95-1 (hbk)

Jason R. Detrani

Cover Design: Psqua

Library and Archives Canada Cataloguing in Publication Data
CIP Data on file with the Library and Archives Canada

CONTENTS

INTRODUCTION

The essence of journalism and mass communication has not changed throughout the past six hundred years. Whether it is a printer using a mechanical press to copy ink-based letters onto a paper medium, a photographer using chemical-based medium to record images on film, or a video maker using a digitally based camcorder to electronically capture moving images, all three processes share the same common link—the desire to convey something to a large number of people in the most expedient and efficient way possible.

Journalism is the investigation and reporting of events, issues, and trends to a broad audience. Although there is much variation within journalism, the ideal is to inform citizenry. Besides covering organizations and institutions such as government and business, journalism also covers cultural aspects of society such as arts and entertainment. The field includes jobs such as editing, photojournalism, and documentary. In modern society, news media have become the chief purveyors of information and opinion about public affairs, but the role and status of journalism, along with other forms of mass media, are undergoing changes resulting from the Internet.

One of the most important things that students must understand when studying mass communication or one of its many subfields (journalism, radio, television, filmmaking, photography, etc.) is the ability to differentiate between the "how" and the "why" of modern mass communication. While the technology used to convey that something has changed considerably over time (and will continue to grow and change in our near future), being able to understand and be understood as clearly and as successfully as possible always has been—and always will be—the ultimate goal. Understanding the many different facets of modern technological communication is merely the "how"; mastery and understanding of the need for that something to be conveyed is the "why".

At a time when almost limitless technology allows larger groups of people to access a more diverse field of information everyday, issues surrounding media quality, media ethics, and media effectiveness are just some of the big questions with which students must be concerned. These questions are not merely academic exercises meant for the classroom but larger concerns that students will face in their future careers—whether it is in the field of education as instructors; in the field of media production as journalists, videographers, filmmakers, photographers, and sound artists; in the field of multimedia technology research and design as electronic technicians and engineers; or in the field of global business as directors, managers, and leaders.

The many media of mass communication are relevant to the world today because they represent how the majority of people in the world remain in contact with each other. It is a field that is simultaneously both diverse and specialized. It is diverse in its reach and scope throughout today's global environment, across countless cultures and individual backgrounds. It is specialized in the technology it uses and in the essential knowledge and skill sets needed by those who make use of it and advance it forward.

With the instant gratification and expediency offered by the emerging fields of social media, social journalism, blogging, YouTube, MySpace, Facebook, and Twitter, increasing demand for new technology and new forms of mass communication will have a decisive impact upon both the consumers and producers of mass media. It is today's mass communication student that must adapt and function with each of the new technological changes that emerge from such a dynamic field of study. While we may now only be getting a glimpse of what the future of mass communication may be, the fundamental concept of mass communication—the ability to convey something to a large number of people in the most expedient and efficient way possible; to understand and be understood—always has been, and always will be the core of the process.

— **Jason R. Detrani**

Working with the Media

Shay Bilchik

Which Organizations Make Up the Media?

The term "media" refers to all means of mass communication in your community—news and nonnews, local and national. It is largely through these publications, broadcasts, visual displays, and advertisements that you and everyone in your community learn what's going on.

Media vary widely in how many people they reach. Your school newspaper, for example, reaches far fewer readers than a national newspaper or magazine. Different media organizations also have different goals. Your school newspaper reports on items of interest to you and your classmates, such as student elections, dances, and athletic events, while a major newspaper concentrates on stories of regional, national, and international importance.

News media include daily and weekly newspapers, television, radio, and news magazines. Other communications fall within the term "media," such as billboards; neighborhood and community newsletters; cable television (TV) providers; and posters, magazines, and newsletters.

Whatever their audience size, purpose, or affiliation, the media in your community reach and inform almost everyone. Partnerships with the media, therefore, will allow you to get your crime prevention message to individuals and organizations that help decide exactly what your community sees, hears, and reads.

There are so many messages to send, so many stories to tell, so many people to reach. The media offer direct and often immediate access to people in their schools, homes, and workplaces. They may even reach people driving in their cars as they listen to the radio or read billboard messages. Given the media's far-reaching effects, establishing lasting partnerships with newspapers, magazines, TV and radio stations, advertising companies, and other communications organizations is important in your effort to publicize your program and prevent crime.

How does Working with the Media Prevent or Reduce Crime?

By working with the media in your community, you help educate everyone—children, youth, and adults. You also build support for youth crime prevention. Using your connections in the media will allow you to get your message out in a very powerful way. Broadcasting a message on a local radio station, for example, may be much more effective than simply posting fliers in your neighborhood. While hundreds of people listening to radios at home, at work, in their cars—or even while jogging down the street—will hear the radio message, only those who happen to walk or drive through the particular streets in your neighborhood where fliers are posted—and who actually read the fliers—will receive the message.

You can use the media to inform the public about your efforts and your successes. The media can help you attract new volunteers and supporters and allow you to build partnerships with other community groups that can help. You never know where these relationships may lead. You may even receive some free publicity or sponsorship!

What does it take to Start Working with the Media?

First of all, you'll need to know exactly where to send information that you want printed, broadcast, or displayed. Call your local television station or community newspaper, and ask for the public affairs or marketing department. Find out if a specific reporter is assigned to cover your school or youth programs for the community newspaper. Your school's journalism teacher, athletic director, or principal can provide information on helpful media contacts. Parent-teacher association (PTA) officers are also good sources of information. Make sure to introduce yourself to the person in charge of collecting information for the PTA newsletter and find out how and when to submit an item to be printed in the newsletter. Ask the faculty sponsor or student editor of your school paper to include an article on your program in the next issue.

After getting to know media contacts and learning where to send information that you want to publicize, your group should work on clarifying the message that it wants to communicate. Think about the main points of your message. Are you promoting one program or addressing many activities? Are you calling for a specific action? Do you simply want the media to publicize your program or do you want to get the media involved directly as a program participant or an official sponsor?

As your group plans its work with the media, it should follow five critical planning steps:

- Develop a process.
- Reach out to a variety of media organizations.
- Start getting the word out.
- Keep media contacts lined up.
- Develop allies.

Step 1: Develop a Process

Spreading information about your program also requires developing a process for preparing and sending out media communications such as media advisories, press releases, and pitch letters. Follow these steps:

- Design a letterhead that highlights your organization's name, address, and telephone number; copy or print advisories and front pages of press releases onto this letterhead.
- Decide who will be your group's "point of contact" (the person whom reporters or other media representatives should contact) for a particular issue or story. Always provide the name and telephone number of the point of contact so that the media representatives can get answers quickly.
- Write media releases in the "inverted pyramid" style. This means the most important facts (who-what-when-where-how-why) come first. The less important facts come later; and the least important facts come last. Importance is defined by what the media and the public will find important, not by what your group

wants highlighted. Study news articles to see what type of information is usually emphasized. By following the "inverted pyramid" style of writing, you'll make sure that your audience or readers get the most important information first. You'll also make sure that readers who stop reading or listeners who tune out early receive the most crucial information. Don't bury the most important information at the end of a story or broadcast!

- Limit press releases to no more than two or three pages.

- Check spelling and grammar. Better still, have someone else proofread for you.

- Double space the press release, and print it on only one side of the paper.

- Fax or mail the release promptly, and make sure you've sent it to the most current media contact. Old news is no news, and news on the wrong person's desk is dead news!

Step 2: Reach Out to a Variety of Media Organizations

Remember: don't limit your media contacts to your community's daily newspapers and major TV and radio stations. Include your school's newspaper and PTA newsletter, your school system's publications, bulletins of religious organizations in your community, weekly newspapers, "magazine" sections of the Sunday newspaper, local calendars of events (often found in newspapers but separate from the daily news), youth center leaflets and message boards, and any other communication outlets in your community. Local talk shows are usually produced separately from the TV or radio news departments, so add them to your list of media contacts. Don't forget about Web sites, cable TV organizations, and supermarket bulletin boards!

Step 3: Start Getting the Word Out

Getting the word out about your program requires concentration, a significant time commitment, persistence, and—most important—a clear and powerful message.

Concentration

To keep your media efforts focused, assign one person or a small group of people to be your group's media representative(s) or spokesperson(s). As they will have the important job of communicating with media representatives on behalf of your group, spokespersons or media representatives must be responsible, well spoken, and easy to get along with.

Time Commitment

Form a media committee for your group and assign activities to all committee members so that no single person has too much to do. Even with a committee, however, writing up the following types of media releases is time consuming:

- Media advisories (notices of upcoming events that highlight why media should be interested).

- Press releases (stories that tell the "who, what, when, where, how, and why" of an event or activity that has taken place and provide interesting quotes or illustrations).

- Pitch letters (brief letters to media contacts that propose ideas for a story, especially one that is more in depth than a regular news item).

Time is also needed to fax or mail these items to the media; to determine your message; to select spokespeople; to collect photos, summaries, and fact sheets; to make followup telephone calls; to discuss story ideas with reporters, editors, producers, administrators, or advertisers; and to record all media coverage your program receives. Make sure your volunteers understand how much time and hard work it takes to secure great media coverage!

Persistence

Getting the media to cover your program also requires persistence. Explain to your volunteers the importance of introducing themselves to media representatives, following up on all telephone calls or requests from the media, and keeping media representatives informed of your activities—even if they seem to have forgotten about you! Only through group members' persistent efforts will your program receive the attention it deserves.

Powerful Message

Before dedicating a significant amount of your group's time and effort, make sure that the message you want to deliver is powerful and focused. The more detail that you can provide about your group's activities and goals, the better. The media, for example, will be much more interested in broadcasting information on a peer mediation group's efforts to reduce fighting in its high school if the group has a clear mission, specific activities, and success stories to report.

Step 4: Keep Media Contacts Lined Up

One of the most important elements of a strong working relationship with the media is an up-to-date media contact file. This can be a database on a computer, a paper list, or a set of index cards that allows your group to keep and update records. Whatever its form, the contact file should list media contacts for various subjects along with each contact's organization name, street address, telephone and fax numbers, and e-mail address.

Also keep a record of each media report on your program made by TV and radio stations, newspapers, newsletters, magazines, cable TV providers, and advertising firms. Organize your files. Collect information on how many people heard and/or saw each report. For example, keep track of how many phone calls your organization receives in response to an article or published report. You could develop a log or tracking sheet to be completed by all persons taking calls and tally them up periodically. Also keep a list of all calls your program received as a result of each news article, broadcast, advertisement, or other media communication. Survey people who heard your broadcasts or read articles about your program to determine what they learned from those media reports.

Reviewing records on a regular basis will provide clues about how your group can work more effectively with the media. The best way to track your results is with a clipping book or scrapbook. Log every one of your group's media reports—printed stories, broadcasts, advertisements, and publications—in this book. You may want to develop an intake sheet for doing so. This sheet should have space for you to enter the report's date, source (name of newspaper, newsletter, radio or TV station, or other media agency that ran the report), audience size, and response(s). If it was a printed communication, include a copy of the article or release as well. Remember to keep copies of all printed and media information—including negative articles—about your organization or event. This will help you focus on public perceptions, even if they are negative.

Professional "clipping services" can track and provide copies of all communications about your program that appear in the media. Youth can find out about clipping services available in their communities by checking with their schools, public libraries, or local newspapers. Although helpful, these services are expensive and probably will not be cost effective or necessary to keep track of the mostly local media coverage that your group will get. Instead, form a "media coverage" committee or subcommittee to be responsible for taping TV and radio segments, clipping articles about your program that appear in school, local, or national newspapers or in any other printed media (such as PTA or neighborhood newsletters), and describing any other media coverage that your program receives (on grocery store bulletin boards or local billboards, for example). A committee could also be formed to search national newspapers every so often for information about your group's community, town, school, or State.

Step 5: Develop Allies

In addition to relaying information about your program, the media may actively participate in or become strong advocates for your program. To gain the participation and support of media organizations in your community, your group needs to convince senior media personnel that your program does the following:

- Deals with a problem of concern to a large segment of the community.
- Is effective.
- Could be even more effective with greater media exposure.
- Has an interesting story to tell.
- Offers visual or print images that will attract readers.
- Will create a favorable public image for the station, newspaper, or company, if it chooses to cover, support, or participate in the program.

Developing allies in the media is a long-term process that requires personal commitment and continuous action and contact.

What does it take to Keep Working Successfully with the Media?

Whether seeking publicity for your group's activities or full partnerships with local media, you'll need to perform several activities on a regular basis:

- Write to media contacts whenever an important issue arises. Describe the issue, explain your program's impact on the issue, and outline how the media can help increase that impact.
- Set up appointments with public service managers, news directors, and editors of local media. Discuss your program and how it needs media support.
- Include media representatives on "very important person" (VIP) guest lists for any special events, workshops, or training seminars that your program hosts. Consider asking a radio or television broadcaster, newspaper columnist, or PTA president to act as host or deliver a speech or presentation at one of these events.
- Have media representatives sit on your program's board of directors.
- Encourage local news media to report on positive community crime prevention efforts—starting with your program.
- Give media contacts positive information on youth. Although youth may be involved in a small percentage of crime, they make many positive contributions

to the community (through programs like yours) and possess untapped energy, talent, and enthusiasm. Let the media know this!

What are some of the Challenges of Working with the Media?

Your single biggest challenge when working with the media will be showing that your message contains important and timely information for the entire community. You also need to make your group's story stand out from the dozens of others that come into newsrooms, TV and radio stations, advertising firms, and other media offices every day.

Another challenge is maintaining strong relationships with media contacts when personnel in media organizations and membership in your own group are constantly changing. Having new contact persons call to introduce themselves and outgoing contacts call to notify you of their departure and identify their successors is very helpful. By making sure you have a strong ongoing relationship with media contacts, you'll never be an unknown caller when a big event is being planned and you need coverage!

What are some of the Rewards of Working with the Media?

By developing and maintaining a strong relationship with the media, your group will enjoy the following rewards:

- People in your community—youth, adults, and children—will learn about your pro- gram and receive helpful crime prevention information.
- Media partnerships and support from local celebrities and officials will generate new resources, greater media exposure for your program, and ideas for rejuvenating your and radio stations, advertising firms, and ideas for rejuvenating your program.
- More people will learn about—and perhaps decide to volunteer for—your program.
- Volunteers will appreciate positive public recognition of their efforts.

Getting Messages Across

In addition to calling attention to your own projects, in some cases you also can help government agencies develop positive youth messages for the media. For the past 4 years, the Centers for Disease Control and Prevention (CDC) have staged a youth media contest to get youth involved in delivering its antitobacco message: "Tobacco— The Truth Unfiltered." Last year's contest entries were reviewed by a panel of celebrity judges (including cover model Christy Turlington) and media professionals. First-place winners had their entries promoted online and included in a national media campaign resource center.

The contest also demonstrates that you can interest the media in publicizing your message by presenting it in unusual ways. For example, several students won first place for their claymation video illustrating CDC's antitobacco theme. Other contest winners designed Web sites and posters, drew cartoons, wrote stories and essays, and produced radio and TV public service announcements. Be creative— the media and your audience will pay more attention if you are.

How can Work with the Media be Evaluated?

Evaluating your project can help you learn whether it has met its goals, but only if you decide up front what you want to evaluate and how you will go about doing so. The purpose of conducting an evaluation is "to answer practical questions of decision-makers and program implementors who want to know whether to continue a program, extend it to other sites, modify it, or close it down." When evaluating your media project, you will want to be able to show that it does one or all of the following:

- Allows you to reach people in a variety of places—such as their schools, their homes, their workplaces, and even in their cars.
- Helps you build relationships with representatives of the media in your school or community.
- Educates members of your community about crime prevention and informs them of the many positive activities of youth through articles, broadcasts, performances, or artwork.
- Reaches your target audience—whether they're children, adults, teenagers, or seniors—with an important crime prevention message.
- Builds partnerships with members of the media.

In evaluating your media project, also consider whether and how well it has met the following more general crime prevention goals:

- Reduces crime.
- Reduces fear of crime.
- Remains cost effective.

- Has a lasting impact.
- Attracts support and resources.
- Makes people feel safe and better about being in your school or community.

Be sure to include an evaluation step—such as keeping track of all phone calls or responses you receive on every article or broadcast—in your overall plan. Consider the positive and the negative feedback that you get, and ask yourself what you can do better to reach your goals, to involve more people in your project, and to spread your message to a wider audience. Then, adjust your activities to strengthen your project.

Learning to evaluate the things you do is a good skill, one you can apply to all aspects of your life. Good luck with your project and—Have fun!

Media, Conflict Prevention, and Peacebuilding: Mapping the Edges

Sheldon Himelfarb and Megan Chabalowski

Synopsis

There is growing recognition among policymakers and conflict management experts that the media should be a building block of any comprehensive peacebuilding strategy. Yet there are scant guidelines in this regard. Projects are still planned and implemented in a relatively ad-hoc manner, with minimal reference to lessons learned from previous initiatives.

On June 25-26, 2008, USIP's Media Conflict and Peacebuilding Center of Innovation and the Alliancefor Peacebuilding convened top media and conflict experts to review a comprehensive strategic framework to aid in the design of practical peacebuilding media. The framework was developed and presented by Vlado Bratic, Ian Larsen and Lisa Schirch in collaboration with USIP. While the framework still requires further development, the experts agreed on many of its propositions. This USI Peace Briefing contains their significant points of agreement but also raises points of debate or ambiguity, all of which are critical considerations when planning a media project.

Sheldon Himelfarb, associate vice president of the Media, Conflict and Peacebuilding Center of Innovation, moderated.

Media, Conflict Prevention, and Peacebuilding

Conflict prevention and peacebuilding programs use a number of approaches, from facilitating dialogue and negotiations between conflicted groups to using peacekeeping forces to separate armed factions. By incorporating media strategies, however, these programs can reach and potentially influence a far larger audience.

Recognizing the media's reach is but a first step in harnessing its power as a potential peacebuilder. Care must be taken to prepare media accordingly for the different roles it can play as information provider, watchdog, mobilizer and promoter, among others. Currently this is done in a haphazard manner, with policy makers and peacebuilding media practitioners often working independently of one another and without reference to previous experiences.

Strategic Framework for Peacebuilding Media

This framework is being developed to serve as a guide in planning and implementing peacebuilding media. A marriage of theory and practice, based on a thorough review of literature and peacebuilding media projects, it proposes two theses.

Thesis 1 states that a media project's impact is proportional to the number of media strategies it uses. Maximum media impact on conflict prevention and peacebuilding will occur when all five of the following strategies are employed:

1. Conflict-sensitive and peace journalism
2. Peace-promoting citizen media
3. Peace-promoting entertainment media
4. Advertising or social marketing for conflict prevention and peacebuilding
5. Media regulation to prevent incitement of violence

If the intent of peacebuilding and conflict prevention programs is to change attitudes and behaviors, a single media strategy is insufficient in an environment of pervasive violence. An integrated and diverse set of media practices, however, can carry maximum effect.

Thesis 2 proposes that a media project's impact corresponds with its integration into conflict prevention and peacebuilding efforts. Media will have maximum impact when it is fully integrated into the overall conflict management strategy, which will use media to assist in areas such as enabling refugee return, promoting human rights, addressing past abuses, etc. To accomplish this, all actors involved must collaborate on an overall strategy and share peacebuilding media practices and plans.

While there was some debate over the classifications of the strategies in Thesis 1, the experts concluded that the requirements of both theses must be met for a peacebuilding effort to have the greatest prospects for success. They further elaborated on the different forms that peacebuilding media strategies have taken to date, offering best practices, lessons learned and some areas for development.

Conflict-Sensitive and Peace Journalism

Basic journalism, teaching accurate, impartial and responsible reporting training, remains a core component of media development. Conflict-sensitive journalism goes beyond this by encouraging journalists to be aware of what effects their language and reporting can have on the conflict—as well as how they may become victims of the violence.

This experts group observed that conflict-sensitive journalism is often met with resistance from the news profession, as it is commonly conflated with peace journalism, a more agenda-driven reporting style. Peace journalism approaches activism, as it is intended to focus attention on peace efforts and the search for a nonviolent solution to conflict. In Colombia, for example, newspapers such as El Tiempo have had both war correspondents and peace correspondents. Participants observed that peace journalism can overlap with social marketing in that it works to "sell" peace.

Peace-Promoting Citizen Media

The experts agreed that citizen media largely falls into two sub-categories: community media and user-generated content emerging from new technologies.

Community media operates on a local level through traditional platforms such as television, radio and print. In general it serves as a conduit for community information. However, the specialists pointed to examples in Southeast Asia and Latin America where village radio stations have organized peaceful resistance against the surrounding violence.

User-generated new tech media begins with more independent, individualistic production of blogs, text messages, wikis, etc., but take their power from the social networking capabilities of these new technologies. Many examples were cited in which communities were mobilized quickly for both constructive and violent purposes on the basis of the new so-called Web 2.0 collaborative technologies.

The experts group observed that the power of citizen media lies in its grass-roots, bottom-up authenticity and spontaneity. Leveraging its potential therefore will come less from trying to "organize it" than from showing citizens, through training, how to use new tech media or how to counter hate media when it arises in community outlets.

Social Marketing—Entertainment, Advertising and use of other Typically "Commercial" Media Strategies to Promote Peace

This media leverages many distribution channels and formats, ranging from soap operas to public service announcements (PSAs), to street theater and concerts. Its dramatic, often fictional formats offer the advantage of being able to tackle contentious and divisive issues that might be too inflammatory to discuss in "real" life. For example, Nigeria's "The Station," produced by Search for Common Ground, is a television soap that follows the lives of a fictional television news team who examine current national issues along with the everyday drama of their lives.

PSAs, on the other hand, such as those produced to "sell" the Good Friday Peace agreement in Northern Ireland ("It's Your Decision") and the "Respect" campaign in Bosnia-Herzegovina in support of new property rights laws send more explicit messages and aim to have a more direct effect on the conflict.

Both formats, however, were considered "social marketing" by the experts group, although there was considerable discussion about whether indirect or direct peacebuilding messages are more effective. This led to a general consensus on the need to improve impact evaluation within and across peacebuilding media programs.

Media Regulation to Prevent Incitement of Violence

Media regulation, encompassing both codes of conduct and ownership issues, is the necessary "rule of law" component of every comprehensive media development project. While the previously discussed strategies create and encourage open media through production, regulation is a parallel effort to ensure that what is produced and aired is not inflammatory or contrary to the public's interest in peace. When done well, the peacebuilding benefits are substantial.

There was thorough consideration of Bosnia-Herzegovina as a regulation success story. Two years after the Office of the High Representative formed the Independent Media Commission, the country had 200 licensed television and radio broadcasters, a functioning market, virtually no hate speech, public broadcasters and local ownership over regulation. In contrast, the experts group reviewed the unsuccessful efforts made in Iraq to do something similar and the challenge of imposing regulation in an unstable environment.

Integration into Overall Conflict Prevention and Peacebuilding Strategy

The framework proposes that to maximize its effectiveness, a peacebuilding media program must be incorporated into other conflict management planning. An assessment of the broader media and conflict management environment was recommended at the outset of any media initiative to ensure optimal use of media dollars and avoid duplication of effort. A comprehensive assessment will also permit the program's developers to design appropriate evaluation criteria and protocols. It was observed that to date, most peace building media programs have had largely anecdotal evidence to back their claims of effectiveness. This has, in turn, made funders justifiably skeptical.

The field is maturing however, partly as a result of recently improved efforts at collaboration and information sharing. Just prior to the USIP meeting, Deutsche Welle Global Media Forum held its first annual worldwide gathering of media representatives and decision makers to discuss potential solutions to the world's greatest challenges. Other participants noted additional meetings, including, one specifically to consider impact evaluation in peacebuilding media initiatives.

Conclusion

The framework on media and peacebuilding considered by the experts group received strong endorsement and a number of recommendations, including:

1. Increased attention to participatory, user-generated citizen media. Although there was widespread agreement on the primacy of traditional media (TV, radio, print) in today's conflict zones, digital content and new technologies

have changed the media landscape so profoundly that the group recommended more expansive consideration within the framework.

2. Increased attention to impact evaluation. Participants observed the importance of such evaluation to drive forward the use of media in public health campaigns and recommended that the framework draw upon lessons learned in that field.

3. Increased consideration to "incentives" in recognition of market forces governing both distribution outlets and production. "If it bleeds it leads" journalism, reality tv, etc. are functions of these market forces. Any framework for developing more pro-social peacebuilding media must incorporate these realities.

USIP publication of the full framework in book form is expected in fall of 2009.

About the Authors

This USI Peace Briefing was written by Sheldon Himelfarb, associate vice president of the Media, Conflict and Peacebuilding Center of Innovation and Meghan Chabalowski, program assistant in the Center, at the United States Institute of Peace. The views expressed here are not necessarily those of USIP, which does not advocate specific policies.

About the Media, Conflict and Peacebuilding Center of Innovation

USIP's Media, Conflict and Peacebuilding Center of Innovation focuses on harnessing the power of the media for peacebuilding, and on developing new strategies for countering the abuse of media during conflict.

About the United States Institute of Peace

The United States Institute of Peace is an independent, nonpartisan, national institution established and funded by Congress. Our mission is to help prevent, manage, and resolve international conflicts by empowering others with knowledge, skills, and resources, as well as by our direct involvement in peacebuilding efforts around the world.

Assessing Information Needs and Communication Behaviors of National Forest Summer Visitors

James D. Absher

ABSTRACT

Information needs and satisfaction with various media are studied on the San Bernardino National Forest. Personal contact with rangers or staff is preferred, and about one-third to one-half of all visitors reported using various print media (brochures, maps, etc.). Least used were websites or mass media. Second, an adaptation of communication theory, uses and gratifications, is tested. Results suggest that the uses and gratifications scales are reliable and stable, and that visitors want orientation, reassurance and educational messages, in decreasing order of importance. Each of these topics was compared between day and overnight visitors.

Introduction

Participation in various outdoor recreation activities has significantly increased over the past decade. Increases have been particularly high in forestlands that are adjacent to urban areas. Of particular concern is the knowledge that visitors from these areas may have about natural resource management policies or proper use of forestlands for recreation. One approach is to study the communications between recreation area managers and current or potential visitors. Included would be an investigation into visitors' information needs and communication behaviors (Absher, 1998). Upon knowing visitors' information needs and communication behaviors, managers would be able to enact more effective and efficient ways to reach out to visitors, and better focus management efforts in terms of environmental education, minimal impact information, alerting visitors of policy changes, or simply assuring that visitors are able to achieve the highest quality experience.

Group Differences

Visitor communication in resource management has typically employed various print and non-print communication media such as interpretive bulletin boards, flyers, and brochures. Often the task has been to instill awareness, generate interest, and influence or modify behavior. Programs are only effective if the information positively influences recreationists' attitudes, and more importantly, creates an acceptable behavioral ethic during and after the visit to a recreational setting (Cole, 1999). For example, Oliver! Roggenbuck and Watson (1985) identified a fifty percent decrease in tree damage and litter in a campground as a result of creating awareness among campers via brochures about low-impact camping. Correspondingly, Cole, Hammond and McCool (1997) found that hikers exhibited a significant increase in knowledge after exposure to environmental messages encouraging low-impact practices.

However, the overall effectiveness of various print and non-print communication media is questionable, as the message is constrained due to the inability to reach all recreationists (Cole et al., 1997). Face to face communication can be much more effective, due to the credibility of the source of information (Knopf & Dustin, 1992; Vander Stoep & Roggenbuck, 1996), as in the case of a backcountry ranger informing a backpacker about the risks involved in the backcountry. Roggenbuck and Berrier (1982) found greater effectiveness with the combination of brochures and personal contacts among campers. Similarly, Olson, Bowan and Roth (1984) noted an increase in visitors' knowledge and attitudes via the use of brochures and direct personal communications, while the use of signs was much less effective among visitors. When given a choice, forest visitors seem to prefer face-to-face interaction to written or displayed information (James, Absher & Blazey, 1999).

However, visitor communication is typically concentrated on-site where the learning environment is informal and attention to the educational message is optional. It has been suggested that specific user groups with low awareness, knowledge or experience should be targeted with offsite communications (Confer, Mowen, Graefe & Absher, 2000). If information is received prior to site visitation or activity participation, there is the possibility that users will be more aware of appropriate behaviors and will choose to visit the 'right' place/setting (Vander Stoep & Roggenbuck, 1996). To achieve this objective, it is essential to understand the process of information search, as well as preferences for communication media among visitors (Brown, McCool & Manfredo, 1987).

Finally, information needs and communication behaviors often lack homogeneity across all users because they are dependent upon various factors such as level of experience, proximity to the destination, ethnic background, and activity participation. First time visitors are more likely than repeat visitors to seek information about a new setting. Hence, they might be more inclined to read the information provided by management, such as interpretive bulletin boards, flyers, and brochures. They might also be expected to seek basic and additional information about the setting (Rogers &. Ramthun, 1998). On the other hand, more experienced visitors or skilled recreationists may be more likely to pursue personal contacts to gather information about the setting, or may in fact feel comfortable in acting on incomplete or inaccurate information. For example, Williams and Huffman (1986) noted a difference in the process of information use by more and less experienced visitors; wherein specialized hikers demonstrated a greater propensity to seek additional information than nonspecialized hikers. Finally, ethnic or group composition variables may be a factor. Parker and Winter (1996) reported that Hispanics were less likely to approach a management agency for information, and more likely to obtain information about a recreation area via family or friends. Also, Hispanics have shown a greater proclivity to learn about the rules and regulations, while their preferred medium of communication was print media (Winter & Chavez, 1999). In summary, information needs and behaviors may vary by user group.

Communications Approach

Based on the above review, it is apparent that information services may be critical links enabling managers to communicate effectively with a broad range of visitors. Information needs and communication behaviors have been a relatively new subject of study within the outdoor recreation field, and research has primarily focused on the application of social psychological theories, notably persuasion theory and/or close variants of theories of reasoned action (Absher, 1998). Although the use of social psychological theories offers a valuable way to understand communication behaviors, research should incorporate other existing theories from various disciplines' to further extend our understanding of communication patterns. To be clear, the dismissal of currently used theories, notably socio psychological derivatives, is not advocated here. Rather a more integrated interdisciplinary approach is encouraged -one that may complement, advance or provide a more complete assessment (Absher, 1998).

A relatively untested approach to deciphering information and communication behaviors comes from the mass communication field. A popular theory known as "uses and gratifications" (U&G) has been employed over the last 50 years to study the public's perception of gratifications sought and obtained via engagement in mass communications across a variety of modalities such as television programs, phone usage and print media. It is important to note that gratifications sought and gratifications obtained are not synonymous. Gratifications sought (GS) are defined as 'needs, expectations, or motivations for media use,' while gratifications obtained (GO) reflect 'actual fulfillment' of the gratifications sought (Dobos, 1992, p. 30). The causal link between gratifications sought and gratifications obtained is important because, if sought after gratifications are not obtained during the process of media engagement, then the likelihood of further engagement is reduced, and future communication opportunities may be lost.

Basically, the U&O approach assumes that viewing audiences differ in the gratifications they seek and obtain while engaged in the mass media (Vincent & Basil, 1997). Also, this theory assumes that viewing audiences are not passive receivers but rather are actively involved in making a conscientious and motivated attempt to seek various gratifications (Anderson, 1987; McQuail, 1983). It is due to the various purposes or gratifications sought by the audiences that the outcome of the viewing experience fluctuates among individuals engaged in similar mass media outlets (Anderson, 1987).

That said, U&G might vary by setting. In other words, various media outlets may be sought for different gratifications. For example, newspapers were sought for sociopolitical knowledge and self-understanding was obtained by books, while broadcast media such as interpersonal channels, film, and television programs granted 'more affective gratifications' when compared with newspapers (Katz, Gurevitch & Haas, 1973 in Dobos, 1992, p. 31). Recently, Vincent and Basil (1997) indicated that newspaper reading resulted in better knowledge of current events when compared with newsmagazine reading among college students. It is evident that individuals resort to various media types to seek and fulfill various gratifications. It is unclear at this time which information needs are fulfilled in outdoor recreation settings.

Even though U&G has been extensively employed in media studies (mass communications), rarely has there been an attempt to incorporate this theory or other mass communication theories in the context of outdoor recreation, although the applicability is implicitly evident and strongly recommended (Absher, 1998). To date, a few exploratory studies have been conducted (Absher & Picard, 1998; Absher, 1999).

Uses and Gratifications Scales for Outdoor Recreation

The basic U&G principles were adapted and pilot-tested among Forest visitors to establish theoretical validity by Absher and Picard (1998). Based on this work this study focused on a four-dimension implementation of U&G scales: Orientation, Instrumental, Educational and Reassurance. Each dimension highlights one practical aspect of the outdoor recreation experience. The first dimension, Orientation, refers to seeking information about forest activities, events and various places within the forest. The second dimension, Instrumental, refers to visiting the Forest or Forest Service sites to gather logistic information about parking facilities, day-use permits and operating hours. The third dimension is Educational. As the name implies, it refers to seeking or visiting the forest to learn about various plants, wildlife, and preservation and conservation ideas and concerns. The fourth dimension, Reassurance, refers to the use of information to avoid getting lost, avoid potentially dangerous situations, and know where to get help if the need arises. A total of 24 uses and gratifications items were randomly arranged using a six-point, Likert scale format, ranging from strongly agree to strongly disagree. The dimensions demonstrated reliability alpha values ranging from .78 to .87. Analysis based on these scales indicated clear differences in the use of communication services across users groups (Absher, 1999).

Objectives

The work reviewed above provides a platform to build upon in terms of better understanding of visitor communications and further refinement of the U&G scales. Information services use needs to be systematically investigated. This involves various media as well as new measurement scales. Following from Absher and Picard (1998) and Absher (1999) the U&G scales need to be further tested to determine reliability among various user groups. Thus, the objectives of this paper are to:

1. Apply U&G theory to the assessment of information needs, preferences and uses among t\V0 major segments of National Forest summer visitors (overnight and day users), and

2. Assess the use of and satisfaction with various information sources (media) by these user groups.

Methods

Data were collected within the Angeles and San Bernardino National Forests, both located in Southern California. Both of these National Forests offer a diverse array of recreational opportunities including camping, hiking, swimming, boating, picnicking, sightseeing and fishing. A sampling plan was designed to target users on six days during the months 'of July, August and September 1997. The sampled sites included ten campgrounds and nine dayuse areas.

Interviewers attempted to sample all users at each site on the designated sampling periods. A single member of each group was requested to respond to the interview questions, which took about ten minutes to complete. A total of 633 subjects were approached, of which 566 users completed a questionnaire and 67 refused to be interviewed, yielding an 89 percent response rate. There were 379 respondents that were sampled at campgrounds and 217 in day-use areas. The three-page survey instrument was administered onsite, and a Spanish version was also available. The Spanish version was needed because California has a high Spanish speaking population and some of those users might feel more comfortable responding in their native tongue.

Respondents were asked about their frequency of visitation to National Forests within the last 12 months, and the primary activity undertaken during the course of their trip. A total of 16 items related to information needs and communication behaviors based on U&G theory as adapted by Absher and Picard (1998) were employed. As explained earlier, the U&G scales was conceptually designed with four dimensions that demonstrated to be reliable based on Cronbach's alpha values: Orientation, Instrumental, Educational and Reassurance. The original scales had 24 items, but 8 items were dropped due to redundancy or lack of statistical power, as recommended by Absher and Picard (1998). The remaining 16 items, four for each U&G subscale, were randomly ordered on the questionnaire with a six-point Likert type scale format, ranging from strongly agree to strongly disagree. These variables were subsequently reverse coded so that higher levels of agreement resulted in higher U&G scores.

Other sections of the questionnaire asked respondents to indicate the media sources they used in planning their trip and their satisfaction with the same media in terms of their usefulness. Basic sociodemographic and recreation use questions completed the questionnaire.

Results

Profile of Subjects

Among the 566 respondents, 65% reported they were White/Caucasian, 22% claimed to be Hispanic, and below 13% classified themselves into other ethnic groups (Black/African American, Native American or Alaska Native, Asian or Pacific Islander). About 39% reported incomes between $40,000 and $75,000, 28% indicated between $20,000 and $39,999, 13% reported below $20,000, and about 20% noted above $75,000. Visitors were predominantly from the Southern California region (97%), with about 3% from other states.

Within the past 12 months, 23 percent of the respondents indicated they visited the National Forest six or more times, while an equal number (23%) reported one visit. During their current visit, 23 percent reported a stay of 1 day or less (day users), while 77 percent were overnight visitors. This data is the result of an intentional stratification in the sample, and should not be used as a general estimate of the day use proportion in the forest. This variable was used to define the two analysis groups below.

Activities pursued at the forest varied with visitor ethnicity. About half of the day users (51%) were White, compared to nearly three-quarters of the overnight users (72%). Hispanics were twice as prevalent among day users (34%) than among overnight users (16%). About one-eighth of both campers (12%) and day users (15%) were members of other minority groups.

Information Needs and Communication behaviors

Table 1 shows that the most used information sources were family/friends (60% or the respondents), followed by maps (55%), brochures and flyers (54%), and rangers/staff (53%). Next came three moderately used media: trail/road signs (49%), bulletin boards (42%) and guidebooks (37%). Only the World Wide Web (Internet) and radio/TV/newspapers/magazines registered low usage (13% each).

Independent of how often the various media were actually used, respondents were asked to rate their satisfaction with the sources they did use. Technologically newer and conventional mass media, such as the World Wide Web (Internet) and radio/TV/magazines/newspapers, registered low levels of satisfaction as well as relatively low use levels. Information from rangers or other Forest Service employees, and from family and friends, received the highest levels of satisfaction. These are, of course, the two personal media on the list. Maps, brochures & flyers, bulletin boards, guidebooks, and signs along roads or trails (all print media) seem to fall in the middle in terms of satisfaction.

Table 1. Communication Media Use and Usefulness (Satisfaction) by Group

Variable	Day User	Overnight User	All	Significance Test
1. Media used[2]				
Brochures/flyers	53.8%	53.7%	53.7%	.535[2]
Rangers/ FS employees	44.5	55.5	52.9	.023
Bulletin boards/notices at sites	42.0	42.0	42.0	.539
Signs along roads/trails	52.1	47.6	48.6	.224
Maps	47.1	57.8	55.3	.026
Websites	7.6	14.2	12.7	.034
Radio/TV/newspaper/magazines	15.1	12.7	13.3	.296
Guidebooks	32.8	32.2	36.9	.169
Family/friends	57.1	60.6	59.8	.287
2. Medium usefulness (satisfaction) [3]				
Brochures/flyers	3.34	3.34	3.33	.964[1]
Rangers/ FS employees	3.69	3.69	3.62	.459
Bulletin boards/notices at sites	3.54	3.38	3.41	.131
Signs along roads/trails	3.51	3.26	3.31	.024
Maps	3.55	3.39	3.42	.192
Websites	3.00	2.94	2.95	.732
Radio/TV/newspaper/magazines	3.23	2.90	2.99	.028
Guidebooks	3.49	3.37	3.39	.296
Family/friends	3.50	3.59	3.56	.427

[1] This section is based on a t-test between groups.
[2] This section reports the percentage that used the medium listed, and significance test is based on Chi-square test (Fisher's exact) of groups by use percentage.
[3] Scale is 1= "Not at all satisfied" to 5= "Extremely satisfied."

In order to better understand these results, they were compared between the day and overnight groups. The significance tests in Table 1 show that there were few differences. Overnight visitors reported using three media sources more often than their day use counterparts: rangers/employees, maps, and websites. And they rated their satisfaction (usefulness) with signs along roads/trails and radio/TV/ newspaper/magazines lower.

Uses and Gratifications Scales

The items within each U&G dimension were subjected to a Cronbach's alpha reliability analysis to identify their internal consistency (see Table 2). The first dimension, Orientation, had a standardized alpha of .78; the second dimension, Instrumental, registered .78; the third dimension, Educational, had .87, while the fourth dimension, Reassurance, was .83. These reliability values are considered good to very good, and are consistent with the earlier works of Absher and Picard (1998) and Absher (1999), with no one scale differing by more than .05 from the pilot test. This suggests that the U&G scales are stable and reliable at least for this user population.

As far as the actual needs these scales measure, the Instrumental scale was the lowest rated at 2.78 out of 5. Then came Educational (2.86), Reassurance (3.07) and finally Orientation (3.30), the highest rated of the four. This suggests that orientation concerns are the predominant need followed by reassurance and educational functions. To check this further, the day and overnight users were compared with a t-test of the mean scores (Table 2). The differences for each scale were relatively small, ranging from .06 to .13 scale points. None of the group comparisons were statistically significant, which suggests that the information needs are the same for each group. Apparently it makes no difference whether they are day users or longer-term visitors in terms of the kinds of information visitors are seeking.

Summary and Conclusions

In summary the results show that visitors reported personal interaction (family/friends or rangers/staff) when communicating about outdoor recreation more than other forms of communication. Printed media (bulletin boards, guidebooks, maps, brochures, and signs) were in the middle range of use, and mass media outlets (Internet, radio, TV, newspaper, magazines) were used relatively infrequently.

There were some differences between those who stayed overnight and day users, with overnight users always reporting more use of those media that were significantly different (rangers/employees, maps, and websites). One management implication from these results is that personal services are highly valued. Whether they are provided by a staffed office, roving patrols, or non-agency employees such as volunteers or partners (e.g., chambers of commerce), the users rate these information sources highly.

The print media are also being accessed by many visitors (roughly a third to a half of all visitors). Managers will need to more carefully assess the impact of these media to assure effectiveness in message delivery. The websites and mass media are not being used much and in some cases are low rated in terms of usefulness. The application of these technologies/media would need to be improved if they are to be more successful for a broad range of visitors.

Table 2. Uses and Gratifications Scales, Alpha Reliability and Group Comparisons

U&G Subscales[1]	Cronbach's Alpha:		Mean Scores and Group Comparison:				
	Standardized Item Alpha	Previous Alpha[2]	Overall Mean	(Std. Dev.)	Overnight Users' Mean	Day Users' Mean	t-test Signif.
Orientation Scale	.83	.78	2.70	(1.46)	2.71	2.65	.92
Instrumental Scale	.74	.78	3.22	(1.18)	3.23	3.17	.89
Educational Scale	.85	.87	3.14	(1.22)	3.18	3.06	.15
Reassurance Scale	.88	.83	2.93	(1.26)	2.97	2.84	.33

[1] Questions used a six–point Likert Scale format, reverse coded, so that 6= Strongly Agree and 1= Strongly Disagree.
[2] Compared to pilot study results (Absher, 1998).

The U&G scales were shown to be reliable and consistent for these forest visitors. Orientation concerns were the top rated need, followed by reassurance and educational functions. Moreover, there were no significant differences in these needs between the two groups studied. Managers may want to review the mix of messages they, and perhaps their partners, provide through various media to ensure that these functions are met in ways that are accessible to both day and overnight users.

Finally, this study provides only a brief account of U&G scale performance. The original U&G development work intended to produce scales that could be used broadly in outdoor recreation, and the results from this application of the scales is encouraging. Nonetheless, they should be more fully tested across a variety of outdoor recreation settings and activity types to gauge their suitability and impact in general use.

References

Absher, J. D. (1998). Parables and paradigms: An introduction to using communication theories in outdoor recreation research. In H. Vogelsong (Ed.), Proceedings of the 1997 Northeastern Recreation Research Symposium (Gen. Tech Rep. NE-241, pp. 36–39). Radnor, PA: US Department of Agriculture, Forest Service, Northeastern Forest Experiment Station.

Absher, J. D. (1999). The utility of a uses and gratifications approach to assess the information needs of forest visitors: An activity-based market segmentation test. In H. Vogelsong (Bd.), Proceedings of the 1998 Northeastern Recreation Research Symposium (Gen. Tech Rep. NE-255, pp. 93–96). Radnor, PA: US Department of Agriculture, Forest Service, Northeastern Forest Experiment Station.

Absher, J. D., & Picard, R. (1998, May). Applying a communication theory to National Forest recreation use. 7th

Paper presented to the International Symposium on Society and Resource Management, Columbia, MO.

Anderson, J. A. (1987). Communication research: Issues and methods. New York: McGraw-HiII.Brown.

Brown, P. r, McCool, S. F., & Manfredo, M. l (1987). Evolving concepts and tools for recreation user management in wilderness: A state of knowledge review. In Proceedings in National Wilderness Research Conference: Issues, state of knowledge, future directions (Gen. Tech. Rep. INT-212, pp. 320–346). USDA, Forest Service.

Cole, D. N., Hammond, T. P., & McCool, S. F. (1997). Information quantity and communication effectiveness: Low-impact messages on wilderness trailside bulletin boards. Leisure Sciences, 19.59–72.

Cole, D. N. (1999). Low-impact recreational practices for wilderness and backcountry. http://www.itrc.umt.edu

Confer, L, Mowen, A., Graefe, A., & Absher, J. (2000). Magazines as wilderness information sources: Assessing users' general wilderness knowledge and specific leave no trace knowledge. In D. Cole, S. McCool, W. Borrie, & J. O'Loughlin (Comps.), Proceedings of the Wilderness Science in a Time c:>f Change Conference (RMRS-P-15VOL-4, pp. 193-(97). Ogden, UT: USDA, Forest Service, Rocky Mountain Research Station.

Dobos, J. (1992). Gratification models of satisfaction and choice of communication channels in organizations. Communication Research, 19(1), 29–52.

James, K., Absher, t.; & Blazey, M. (1999). Assessing information needs motivations and use of information services at Grassy Hollow Visitor Center (RWU-4902 Tech. Rep.). Riverside, CA: USDA Forest Service, Pacific Southwest Research Station.

Katz, E., Gurevitch, M., & Haas, H. (1973). On the use of the mass media for important things. American Sociological Review. 38. 164–181.

Knopf, R. C., & Dustin, D. L. (1992). A multidisciplinary model for managing vandalism and depreciative behavior in recreation settings. In M. Manfredo (Ed.), Influencing human behavior: Theory and applications in recreation. tourism and natural resource management (pp. 209–261). Champaign, IL: Sagamore.

McQuail, D. (1983). Mass communication theory: An introduction. London: Sage.

Murdock, S. H., Backman, K., Hoque, N., & Ellis, D. (1991). The implications of change in population size and composition on future participation in outdoor recreational activities. Journal of Leisure Research. 23(3), 238–259.

Oliver, S. S., Roggenbuck, 1. W., & Watson, A. E. (1992). Education to reduce impacts in forest campgrounds. Journal of Forestry, 83.234–236.

Olson, E. c, Bowan, M. L., & Roth, R. E. (1984). Interpretation and nonformal environmental education in natural resources management. Journal of Environmental Education. 15(4), 6–10.

Parker, J., & Winter, P. L. (1996). Angeles National Forest wilderness visitors' characteristics and values. Unpublished draft manuscript.

Rogers, J., & Ramthun, R. (1998). A study of information search by visitors to the Blue Ridge Parkway. In H. Vogelsong (Ed.), Proceedings of the 10th Northeastern Recreation Research Symposium (Gen. Tech Rep. NE-255, pp. 86–92). Radnor, PA: US Department of Agriculture, Forest Service, Northeastern Forest Experiment Station.

Roggenbuck, 1. W., & Berrier, D. L. (1982). A comparison of the effectiveness of two communication strategies in dispersing wilderness campers. Journal of Leisure Research, 14(1), 77–89.

Rubin, A. M. (1981). An examination of television viewing motivations. Communication Research. 9. 141–165.

Vander Stoep, G. A., & Roggenbuck, J. W. (1996). Is your park being "loved to death?": Using communications and other indirect techniques to battle the park "love bug." In D. Lime (Ed.), Congestion and crowding in the National Park system (pp. 85–132). St. Paul: Minnesota Agricultural Experiment Station.

Vincent, R. C., & Basil, M. D. (1997). College students' news gratifications, media use, and current events knowledge. Journal of Broadcasting & Electronic Media. ±.L. 380–392.

Williams, D. R., & Huffman, M. G. (1986). Recreation specialization as a factor in backcountry trail choice. In R. Lucas (Ed.), Proceedings in National Wilderness Research Conference: Issues. state of knowledge. future directions (GTR-INT-212, pp. 339–344). Ogden, UT: USDA, Forest Service, Rocky Mountain Research Station.

Winter, P. L., & Chavez, D. J. (1999). Recreation in urbanproximate natural areas. In H. K. Cordell (Ed.), Outdoor recreation in American life: A national assessment of demand and supply trends (pp. 268–279). Champaign, IL: Sagamore.

Parables and Paradigms: An Introduction to Using Communication Theories in Outdoor Recreation Research

James Absher

ABSTRACT

Studies that employ communication theories are rare in recreation resource management. One reason may be unfamiliarity with communication theories and their potential to provide useful results. A two-dimensional metatheoretical plane is proposed, selected recreation and communication theories are located in it, and functional comparisons are made among eight disparate theories. Communication theories have much to offer scientists and managers, and both are encouraged to use them.

Introduction and Background

Communication theories have much to offer those who are concerned with outdoor recreation management and research. Managers' experiences with (mis)communication, whether they are considered frustrations or successes, are commonplace. Nonetheless few research approaches to systematically investigate these experiences have been reported in either the leisure studies or recreation resource management literature. Why don't outdoor recreation researchers use communication theories more often? Clearly it is, in part, due to a lack of familiarity with communication theories. Yet communication theories have much in common with familiar and more often used social psychological theories. To bridge this gap a paradigmatic perspective that gives the reader a unifying view of the research process is presented, followed by examples of theories from the recreation and communication literature.

To begin, the research process itself needs to be viewed as if it were short narrative (story). These "stories" of the initial phases of a particular study when presented in a short, summary form can be analyzed as a text (data) from which the behavior (choices) of the controlling character (scientist) can be obtained. Such research narratives serve as more than an objective statement of the work done: they are like parables, providing a paradigmatic insight about the norms and conditions that define a particular research enterprise.

For instance, a recent communication focused article reported a study of low impact messages on wilderness trailside bulletin boards (Cole, Hammond & McCool, 1997). The study was concerned with communication effectiveness. The authors chose a persuasive communication theoretic approach to an information processing problem and used a quasi-experimental design method. The paradigmatic choices made by the authors are clear: their approach is individualistic and rationalist. Similar "parables" could easily be constructed from other studies with a communication or information flow objective. If analyzed as a set they would empirically define the approach (paradigm) currently taken by scientists working at the interface between communication and recreation resource management.

The existing body of recreation resource management studies is ample evidence that there is a recognized need to better understand the ways in which recreationists learn, and decide, about when, where and how to do various activities. This logically includes the application of mass media effects, social network, information processing, and other useful communication theories. Nonetheless, as in the example above, most of the work currently being done in this literature conforms to paradigms rooted in a few social psychological theories, especially persuasion theory or other close variants of theories of reasoned action (e.g., Manfredo, 1992).

This is not an undesirable state of affairs, but there are many other potentially useful theories, especially among the relatively untapped work of mass communication theorists. To many recreation researchers these other theories may seem strange or not applicable. Knowing more about their strengths or weaknesses, and how or when to employ them, is a logical first step. This paper will not try to promote one theory over another. Instead the goal will be to reduce the uncertainty about communication theoretic approaches in order to make some of them more immediately useful to future research.

The Paradigm Plane

Metatheoretical Concerns: A Comparative Framework

All science makes some philosophical assumptions: this is a problem of approach, or paradigm. There are unwritten rules or exemplars that quietly, and some might say insidiously, guide recreation researchers to choose one or another approach to a management "issue." For this paper, two distinct metatheoretical aspects are presented to reveal the underlying theory choices: these are normative utility and epistemological frame.

Utility is axiological: it is self-evident that a theory must be useful in explaining or understanding actual behavior(s) at some level. Sometimes a theory may encompass a close modeling of specific behavioral characteristics, or a strong and immediate link back to the "real world." At other times, research is focused at a more abstract level, or is general in scope, or even intentionally removed from the application of results. Thus theories exist in a range of types from those whose utility is relatively abstract, general or nomothetic (law-like) to theories whose utility is quite applied or aimed at site-level contexts. Consequently the theory "at risk in any given study can be distinguished as to its immediacy or closeness to a particular recreational setting or decision context. This immediacy or utility delimits the study's generalizability. In practical terms, theories tailored in one setting may not be appropriate in others, and nomothetic theories may require additional effort to apply them to specific settings. It is a necessary tradeoff. In choosing a theory to apply to a problem, a researcher has acceded to a normative imperative to pick an approach and, ipso facto, it will have a utility level. Of course many times this may be done uncritically; i.e., merely assuming the approach previously taken by others is "good enough."

Second, the epistemological frame of a theory can yield useful distinctions as well. When a researcher follows a paradigm (e.g., picks a theory) the meaningful concepts of that theory also delimit discourse. This is another metatheoretical concern. By necessity each theory makes assumptions about how people come to know things and the categories of knowledge they employ. This is the purview of epistemology. In the context of devising a study, these assumptions reside in the tacit agreement scientists make on behavioral issues through the choice of a given theory or in the type of analysis needed. They are not always explicit nor obvious, and these distinctions too are often ignored.

In short, each theory contains epistemological assumptions about the nature of a subject's action, thought, and reality. Although this area is extremely complex, the approach here is to make it manageable by crudely modeling this domain through a tripartite typification of theories that distinguishes idiosyncratic, sociological, and highly individualistic types of explanations. The differences among these categories mirror important differences in approach to recreational behavior(s) that the researcher subsumes in the theory (either because they are felt to have been established by other scientific work or because it is a pure and arguably logical assumption).

At one end is the idiosyncratic approach: few, if any, assumptions are made to group respondents and the subject is often investigated with a strong emic (roughly, from the subject's own viewpoint) stance. The uniqueness of individuals and setting dynamics, e.g., culture or power relationships, play a strong role. Typical theories of this sort in communication research are those that focus on symbolic content or latent values.

On the other hand, a theory might make substantial assumptions that allows the grouping of individuals or eases variable measurement. Some theories that focus on, say, choice behavior may wish to assume a rational thought process or that setting differences do not substantially affect the behavior in question. Finally, a third group of theories may investigate a person's actions in support of, or in relation to, a social role or status. Again some assumptions will be made about the actor's view of the world and the focus is largely on sociological behaviors. In order, constructivist theories, rational exchange theories, and symbolic interactionist theories may serve as familiar examples of these three types of epistemological assumptions.

Therefore, in this paper the epistemological dimension is grouped into three "camps," which reflect (1) strongly rationalist and individualistic theories, (2) a middle ground in which relations, roles, and group processes are the focus, and (3) a broadly open intellectual tradition that makes few assumptions about the thoughts and commonalities of the subjects and focuses on symbolic, meaning and valuation processes in various contexts.

Taken together the utilitarian and epistemological dimensions of paradigm type define a plane of choice that will co-locate the many useful and distinct communication theories (see figure I). The next step is to place familiar or potentially useful theories in this space. For clarity, two theories commonly applied to recreation behaviors are presented. These would be placed along the left edge of the plane (rational column). Following that, selected communication theories are presented that could be, or currently are, used in studies of outdoor recreation settings.

Recreation-Related Theories

Persuasion theory is typical of theories that occupy the upper left portion of the paradigm plane. It is relatively abstract, and meant to apply to a broad range of settings and people, and is therefore a general theory. Moreover it is clearly rationalist in its approach to the behavior studied. People are hypothesized to have measurable responses to inputs, which are in the form of information, usually by either central or peripheral routes. The assumptions of broad scale utility and reasoned behavior make it both general and rational.

At the lower left corner of the plane one might find recreational crowding theories. The actor is usually seen as a rational processor of stimuli, and the clear level of application is meant to be activity, if not site, specific. Numerous studies have been done along this line of inquiry to the point where summary papers listing dozens of individual studies are now in print with an eye toward generalizing more broadly to the behaviors in question. These studies are not fully representative of all recreation or visitor studies and are not presented as a characterization of the entire field, but they are examples that illustrate two long standing research traditions in resource recreation research.

Communication Theories

One objective of this paper is to provide an overview of communication theories with reference to the paradigmatic plane presented above. The two rational mass communication theories, one general and one specific, occupy much the same position as the two recreation theories previously presented (see figure 1). These are reviewed first.

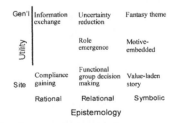

Figure 1. Paradigm plane with selected communication theories

Rational Theories

Information Exchange Theory is a general theory meant to apply to most, if not all, communication settings. In this theory, messages are considered objectively describable and exist independent of the receiver. The receiver in turn is affected by these messages (persuaded, informed, etc.) in a linear process of response. Berelson and Lazarfeld (1948) defined its essence nearly 50 years ago as "objective, systematic and quantitative description of the manifest content of communication."

A more applied or setting dependent version of this perspective is Compliance Gaining Theory, where specific behavioral outcomes are desired from the communication events that are being measured. In this theory, the actor is rational and the communication events are still largely objective facts. That is, they do not depend largely upon specific individuals or social requirements, and the specific behavior of interest, such as rule compliance, is explicitly included in the theory (Krippendorf, 1993). A recreation example might be a prohibited behavior such as having a campfire in certain areas. A researcher would measure which "rules" campers know about, where they obtained site use information, and whether they saw signs, notices, or written prohibitions.

Relational Theories

The second column of figure 1 locates communication theories that differ from the first by relaxing the strongly individualistic assumptions of the rational approach. Instead the actor is set in a role-bound context where relational features interact with the communication elements to give rise to meanings, interpretations, and ultimately behaviors. All relational theories assume an epistemological need for social structure, but emphasize different aspects of the communication process. Some are more client-centered than others. Each in its own way contributes to a particular place in the paradigmatic plane.

A general relational theory is Uncertainty Reduction Theory (Berger and Calabrese, 1975). It too focuses on the relational aspects of communication as a means to define and uphold societal structures or symbols. Many of the key social facts for this theory are roles or authorities. For example URT might be useful to understand how communication can reduce uncertainty and lead to efficiency as district rangers do their job in communicating with the public.

A fairly general theory in this vein is Role Emergence Theory (Bormann, 1990). The objective is to understand decisionmaking in small groups by classieing the utterances of actors according to the role they have in a group process, such as a jury deliberation, and how these are used to signifi. status, provide leadership, etc. Both utility and assumptions about the actors are in the middle range of the paradigm plane. By restricting the concern for a particular task group, such as a quality assurance committee, a more specific theory such as Hirokawa's (1985) Functional Theory of Group Decision Making may be a good choice. This approach would be especially useful when the focus is on communications in groups trained to decide relatively specific issues and the goal is to understand how better decisions might be engendered. The paradigmatic focus is still relational but the utility level is more specific and would not be generalized to other small groups that don't share decision making roles and characteristics. For the prohibited campfires example a scientist might investigate how or why a given campfire regulation achieves compliance or non-compliance within certain user groups by investigating who says what to whom, who are the group decisionmakers, etc.

Symbolic Theories

Finally there are numerous communication theories that seem to have more in common with the humanities than social science. They make no claim to provide behavioral predictions and favor situated understanding and explanation as the primary goal. This sort of intellectual tradition is typical among social scientists and educators from constructivist, feminist, and post modern approaches to science. In communication there are general theories that provide a means to assess the meaning of communication events to particular groups especially on their own terms (emic) or as embedded regularities not previously recognized. A well-known one is Fantasy Theme Analysis (Bormann, 1982) wherein communication is analyzed to pull out the themes and symbols that are operative in that setting. For instance, consider the slogan "Only you can prevent forest fires." Who promotes this idea and how is it received and transmitted through society? What is the symbolic reality that Smokey Bear embodies for a given group, and how different might it be for a mountain community surrounded by National Forest lands than one in an urbanized area? According to FTA, people who share a way of communicating about an issue are termed a rhetorical community, and their symbolic use of language and media can be studied theoretically to arrive at an understanding of the entire community.

A more focused or middle level utility theory might be Motive-Embedded Analysis. It is essentially a particularized form of dramaturgical analysis where the symbols used in conversations, writings, ads, or speeches are analyzed to uncover the motives that underlie them (Bullis & Tompkins, 1989). Although this study focused on communication among forest rangers, MEA might have particular usefulness to resource managers who are faced with conflicting demands from stakeholder groups in a planning context or discussions with a particularly important customer group. The theory allows a trained analyst to attribute motives to a person or group based on a study of behaviors, anecdotes, and discourse.

Finally, figure 1 presents a theory that relies heavily on symbolic analysis but is more specific in its utility: Value-Laden Story, which is a form of Narrative Paradigm Theory. The researcher preselects a particular class of events (e.g., health care workers servicing HIV patients). The core idea is to "unpack" the values, both instrumental and terminal, found in the narratives (stories) of individuals in a particular circumstance. For instance, by evaluating closely the value-laden components of subjects' stories, a strong sense of the differences in goals and values between HIV patients and their doctors was accomplished (Vanderford, Smith, & Harris, 1992). Similar approaches would be useful in selected recreation resource decision making contexts. For instance in the campfire issue from above a researcher might interview managers and selected user groups to uncover substantive differences in their values, needs, and preferences. Both groups are treated emicly; i.e., the researcher's task is to understand the issue from each group's own perspective and make comparisons or conclusions afterward. Their subjective values and evaluative statements are the data that emerges from interviews and drives the analysis.

Summary and Conclusions

Returning to the broader picture, thoughtful application of communication theories will assist the larger enterprise of multimethod social science (e.g., triangulation) applied to resource recreation management. No argument is made that communication theories are meant to supplant existing recreation behavior theories. Increased use of communication theories is far from antithetical to current practice in the leisure paradigm. In many instances it is complementary and occupies the same metatheoretical place as existing outdoor recreation research. This paper has only scratched the surface and planted a few selected seeds. Scientists are encouraged to attend to the concepts and models of the broad field of communication so that these theories can be applied beyond the arenas of product marketing and mass media studies and, thereby, be brought fruithlly into the outdoors.

References

Berelson, B. & Lazarfeld, P. F. (1948). The Analysis of Communication Content. Chicago & New York: University of Chicago & Columbia University.

Berger, C. R. & Calabrese, R. J. (1975). Some explorations in initial interaction. Human Communication Research, 1, 99–112.

Bormann, E.G. (1982). A fantasy theme analysis of the television coverage of the hostage release and the Reagan inaugural. Quarterly Journal of Speech, 68, 133–144.

Bormann, E.G. (1990). Small Group Communication: Theory And Practice (3rd ed.). New York: Harper Collins.

Bullis, C. A., & Tompkins, P. K. (1989). The forest ranger revisited: a study of control practices and identification. Communication Monographs, 56, 287–306.

Cole, D. N., Hammond, T. P., & McCool, S. F. (1997). Information quantity and communication effectiveness: low impact messages on wilderness trailside bulletin boards. Leisure Sciences, 19, 59–72.

Hirokawa, R. Y. (1985). Discussion procedures and decision-making performance: a test of the functional perspective. Human Communication Research, 12, 203–224.

Krippendorf, K. (1993). The past of communication's hoped-for future. Journal of Communication, 43, 3, 34–44.

Manfredo, M. (Ed.). (1992). Influencing Human Behavior: Theory and Applications in Recreation, Tourism, and Natural Resources Management. Champaign, IL: Sagamore.

Vanderford, M. L., Smith, D. H., & Harris, W. S. (1992). Value identification in narrative discourse: Evaluation of an HIV education demonstration project. Journal of Applied Communication Research, 20, 123–160.

Wildland Fire and Fuel Management: Principles for Effective Communication

Eric Toman and Bruce Shindler

Introduction

Federal agencies have many options for communicating with the public (e.g., brochures, newspapers, Web sites, public meetings, demonstration sites), but often have limited resources for completing the outreach job. Ultimately, agency professionals have to make difficult choices about the most effective use of personnel and financial resources. The purpose of this paper is to highlight successful communication strategies and illustrate a set of four guiding principles for building successful fire and fuels management outreach programs in forest communities.

Public support for fire and fuels management is greatly enhanced through effective public communication and outreach programs. Many management units are well along in their own communication programs and are finding success through multiple methods and support of outreach personnel (Toman et al. 2006). The communication principles presented in this chapter, developed from research examining wildfire outreach efforts, suggest how programs can be focused to encourage citizens to share the responsibility for fuels management. We believe a long-term commitment to outreach and education will yield positive outcomes for managers and citizen stakeholders. Not all outcomes will be achieved immediately, nor will each one be achieved everywhere. But as this paper demonstrates, a set of guiding principles can be used to organize outreach activities for effective communication. When implemented, outcomes of outreach and education will include the following:

Internal

- Management units will have an internal planning process for public outreach.
- Personnel will reach agreement on how to proceed and avoid surprises later on.
- Public information materials and programs will be refined; financial resources can be directed at the most productive and useful methods.
- The best personnel for leading the outreach effort will emerge, and resources for doing the job will be identified.
- The agency will appear better organized and ready to respond to citizens' concerns.
- Units will focus on methods that achieve local solutions and be less concerned with national or regional agendas.

External

- A more supportive, more action-oriented constituency will emerge within the community.
- Other citizen groups (homeowner associations, watershed councils) will help carry the fuels reduction message and move the agency off the perpetual hot seat.
- Community capacity will be built for responding to fire and fuels reduction problems.
- Citizens will help identify trouble spots that need active management.
- Community residents will take greater responsibility for defensible space and fuels reduction activities on their own property.
- Citizens will demonstrate greater support for agency fuels reduction programs on adjacent public lands.

Principles for Effective Communication

Four principles of effective communication have emerged from recent studies designed to measure citizen responses to fire outreach (research described in the Research Context section). These principles are further supported by findings from related projects, several of which are discussed in this volume.

These organizing principles are:

- Effective communication is a product of effective planning.

- Both unidirectional (one-way) and interactive approaches to communication have a role in public outreach. The strengths of each should be used to build a program.

- Communication activities that focus on local conditions and concerns can decrease the uncertainty that citizens associate with fire management and build their capacity to participate in solutions.

- A comprehensive communication strategy will emphasize meaningful interaction among participants and build trust along the way.

Principle 1: Effective Communication is a Product of Effective Planning

Fuel managers would never implement a prescribed burn without a comprehensive plan detailing treatment objectives and appropriate conditions. Yet, it is not uncommon for outreach activities to be implemented with nothing more than a vague goal of "educating the public." Not surprisingly, such a simplistic approach is unlikely to succeed. Effective planning depends on the ability of resource professionals to determine communication objectives and organize an appropriate approach to outreach before inviting the public into the process (Jacobson 1999). Two researchers, Delli Priscolli and Homenuck (1990), refer to this as "up-front thinking" and argue that thoughtfully planning outreach activities can help avoid costly problems such as confrontations, delays, appeals, and lawsuits.

First and foremost, agency personnel should identify what they want to achieve by communicating with the public. For example, objectives may be classified as (1) building awareness or (2) influencing attitude or behavior change (Atkin 2001, Rogers 2003). Is the primary purpose to call attention to basic wildfire prevention (Smokey Bear-type messages) or to encourage property owners to take action in creating defensible space? Perhaps the primary purpose is to enlist public support for agency fuels reduction activities. Each is a worthy objective, and each requires a different outreach approach.

Planning for outreach should consider specific audiences—their information needs, the role they will play, their previous interactions with agency personnel, and the local conditions they are familiar with. Key questions to help organize this approach are presented in table 1. Depending on the communication objectives, the audience may vary from homeowners in a particular neighborhood to residents of an entire community or region. Agency personnel will need to understand stakeholders' awareness of fuel problems as well as their attitudes about severity levels and potential management actions (Jacobson 1999). In some cases, this information may already be available, but in others it may be necessary to assess community characteristics through formal methods (stakeholder surveys or interviews) or informal means ("coffee-shop" meetings or discussions with community leaders).

Table 1. Planning the communication approach

Organizing questions[1]
1. Determine objectives
What do we hope to accomplish with this outreach program?
What should the public know, or be able to do, as a result of this communication process?
What does the public need to know to participate effectively?
What do we need from the public?
2. Assess the target audience(s) and contextual influences
Who is "the public" for this issue?
Are there specific groups or stakeholders for this problem or issue?
What are their initial attitudes or understanding of the issue?
How might the history of agency-citizen relationships affect reactions to the issue?
What past management actions might contribute to citizen reactions to the issue?
What is the public's role in this process and how will it be communicated?
What other contextual circumstances should be considered?
3. Evaluate internal resources
How will decisions be made and who will make them?
What resources can we dedicate to this process?
Who are the appropriate individuals to be in the lead on outreach activities?
What internal constraints will influence the types or scope of activities that can be implemented?

[1] Adapted from Priscolli & Homenuck (1990), Shindler et al. (1999), Jacobson (1999).

Outreach planning also includes considering internal resources and constraints, particularly identifying staff with the necessary skills to lead communication activities. Shindler et al. (2002) argued that "most effective public processes historically have involved one or two agency members with genuine interpersonal skills" (p. 46).

Outreach programs will be more effective when such individuals are given a lead role and supported in their efforts by their management unit.

Photo credit: Ryan Gordon

Photo 1. Interactive communication, such as here where community members discuss fuel management options with a District Ranger, can help reduce uncertainty and increase trust in resource agencies.

Once these questions have been addressed internally by relevant personnel, outreach activities can be developed and implemented. Ultimately, these planning efforts will result in communications that focus more on contextual conditions within the community while also meeting objectives of the management unit. Working through this planning process also forces personnel to wrestle with difficult questions before being confronted by citizens. This provides an opportunity to generate a consensus among staff about appropriate actions, get everyone "on the same page" about the need for communicating with the public, identify the best individuals in the unit for working on the front lines of the outreach effort, and organize the necessary resources to carry out the job.

Principle 2: Both Unidirectional (One-Way) and Interactive Approaches to Communication have a Role in Public Outreach. The Strengths of each should be used to Build a Program

Public agencies often feel it is their responsibility to develop information and deliver it to the public. But the facts do not speak for themselves; they must be interpreted and appreciated. Generally programs that just provide information are not very successful in improving, understanding, or changing behavior (Jamieson 1994). Individuals progress through various stages in a decision process. They first develop basic awareness of the issue or topic (such as defensible space or agency-implemented fuels treatments), then form opinions about its appropriateness, and, finally, decide whether or not to support or adopt the new behavior. Research suggests individuals rely upon particular communication channels during these different decision stages (Rogers 2003). Mass, unidirectional outreach methods (e.g., public service announcements, brochures) are particularly useful in the first stage when individuals seek basic information about new practices; interactive communication approaches (e.g., personal contacts, guided field trips) are more likely to increase citizen support or encourage behavior change.

The primary advantage of mass communication is the ability to reach a large number of people relatively easily. However, as Atkin writes, messages with the "broadest reach can deliver only a superficial amount of information" (p. 56). At best, these message formats are useful for instilling a central idea or for communicating a general theme (e.g., forest health conditions, need for defensible space around homes, or role of fire in forest systems). These formats are not for delivering details; people will not be able to recall specifics from PSAs, brochures, or signs at kiosks. Accordingly, mass or unidirectional messages can be effective at generating recognition of an issue, sensitizing participants to later messages, and encouraging people to seek additional information (Atkin 2001, Rogers 2003). In limited cases, mass communication methods can influence attitudes among already supportive audiences or among individuals who understand little about an issue (Toman and Shindler 2005). In sum, outreach activities that rely only on unidirectional means appear to have a limited influence on public attitudes or behavior change (e.g., Rogers 2003, Toman et al. 2006).

Research has found that people generally turn to interpersonal communication methods when deciding whether to adopt new ideas or change behavior (Rogers 2003). At this stage, individuals want more specific information about likely outcomes of a practice—or alternatively, of doing nothing—either to them or to places they know and care about (such as the impacts of thinning or prescribed fire around a homesite or favorite recreation area). More specifically, they want to know how serious and certain the outcomes are and how soon they will occur in the context of these places (Shindler et al. 2002).

Public preference for more interactive forms of information exchange is particularly high for activities such as fuels treatments that may hold a degree of risk or uncertainty for citizens (Jamieson 1994). The ability to engage in discussion, visit a site where treatments have been implemented, or actually view a demonstration of fuels reduction practices can reduce the uncertainty about treatment outcomes. The give-and-take of interactive exchanges allows citizens to become more comfortable with the available options and decide how they feel about managers' ability to carry out fuels reduction.

Recent studies have evaluated interactive forms of outreach including small workshops, field trips, demonstration sites, and interpretive programs. McCaffrey (2004) evaluated a multi-faceted wildfire information program that used both unidirectional (brochures, mass media) and interactive methods (personal contact, group presentations, neighborhood meetings) and determined that personal contact contributed substantially to communication success. Indeed, educational materials, including unidirectional items, were more effective if delivered via personal contact. Similarly, in two recent comparisons of wildfire outreach programs we conducted, interactive methods were preferred over unidirectional approaches and were more effective at influencing public attitudes (Toman and Shindler 2005, Toman et al. 2006).

Ultimately, both unidirectional and interactive methods play an important role in a comprehensive communication strategy. At any given point, citizens are likely to be at different stages of the communication process and, thus, have different information needs. For example, residents in a wildland-urban interface community are likely to range from some who have not heard of defensible space practices to others interested in seeing a demonstration of treatment outcomes and to still others who want to confirm the value of treatments following implementation. A comprehensive strategy will target each of these audiences with activities and information designed to meet their specific needs. Unidirectional and interactive approaches can play complementary roles in these efforts. Mass messages are relatively inexpensive and can be used to build awareness as well as to motivate participants to seek more information. Interactive opportunities, although more time-consuming and requiring a certain skill set, can reduce the uncertainty associated with new activities and increase trust in resource agencies.

Principle 3: Communication Activities that Focus on Local Conditions and Concerns can Decrease the Uncertainty that Citizens Associate with Fire Management and Build their Capacity to Participate in Solutions

At the local level, citizen decisions about adopting defensible space or supporting fuels treatments on nearby Federal lands often boil down to the risk and uncertainty people associate with perceived outcomes (Shindler and Toman 2003, Winter et al. 2002). Of particular importance are concerns about the perceived compatibility of treatments with other values specific to the location (such as aesthetics, recreation use, and privacy), perceptions of the local planning process used by the agency (scientifically sound, fair, and inclusive), as well as citizen trust in personnel to do what they say they will do (Nelson et al. 2003, Shindler and Toman 2003, Winter and Fried 2000). Evaluations of these factors are place-dependent and can vary over time and across locations. Accordingly, activities acceptable in one situation may be unacceptable elsewhere (Brunson and Shindler 2004). Gaining acceptance among local residents for specific treatments will require more than general interpretive messages. The implementation of specific projects will require effective communication tailored to ecological and social issues at the local, and perhaps the neighborhood, level (Brunson and Shindler 2004).

Communication activities that target local conditions and public concerns about the rationale behind specific practices, potential outcomes, and implementation scenarios are more likely to resonate with participants. Although addressing local needs can be accomplished in varying degrees with many forms of outreach, programs that allow for interactive exchanges, such as guided field trips to project sites and conversations with agency personnel, are better suited to relating information to the local context. One limitation of many unidirectional methods (e.g., brochures, newspaper sections, television messages, and newsletters) is that they rely on fixed messages, whereas interactive formats include citizens in the discussion and can be adapted to the concerns and interests of the parties involved. Such an interactive approach provides greater flexibility to address participant needs and tailor activities to the local context.

Strong evidence for keeping a local focus comes from citizen reactions to an agency-led field tour to see the aftermath of a 90,000-acre fire on the Deschutes National Forest (Shindler et al. 2005). Following the tour, a majority of participants had a greater understanding of and support for proposed management activities. In particular, responses indicated the ability to see fire impacts firsthand and the opportunity to discuss proposed restoration activities helped participants understand the rationale behind and likely outcomes of treatments. By offering an opportunity for meaningful interaction in a place that is familiar and important to participants, these tours were able to address their concerns and improve their ability to participate in crafting solutions.

Principle 4: A Comprehensive Communication Strategy will Emphasize Meaningful Interaction among Participants and Build Trust Along the Way

Fire managers and outreach personnel must recognize that citizens do not come with a readymade ability to engage in constructive, deliberative discussions of fuels management. The use of prescribed fire may seem risky, and thinning (often viewed as harvesting) may be something citizens initially oppose. In any case, the topic may just recently have become relevant to them and will likely involve a degree of emotion that other issues do not. Thus, agency managers will need to consider how they can help residents and communities engage in meaningful discussions (Jacobson et al. 2001, Jamieson 1994).

Initially, public judgments of conditions are likely to be based on visual references from personal exposure to forests and interpreted through previous experiences. As citizens begin to receive additional technical information about the landscape, the nature of the communications is likely to be just as important. Accordingly, a comprehensive communication strategy will focus not only on the types and content of the information disseminated, but also on the process of how it is communicated. Specifying conditions and engaging citizens in discussion about the nature of the options is just as essential as providing objective, unbiased information. Thus, personnel must be forthcoming about the difficult decisions, including the uncertainty of outcomes associated with the use of fire and thinning treatments.

While outreach programs typically focus on improving awareness, equally important objectives are often overlooked, including relationship- and trust-building. Indeed, for some projects, changes in the level of trust among stakeholders—because of a well-planned and articulated outreach program—may be the only measurable benefits that accrue (Shindler and Neburka 1997). The value of relationship-building can have long-term impacts on management success and should not be underestimated (Lawrence et al. 1997). For example, following the Deschutes bus tours described earlier, nearly all participants expressed increased appreciation for and confidence in agency personnel. This confidence translated into support for proposed management activities as participants were vocally supportive of a proposed 13,000-acre thinning project on adjacent forest land.

Ultimately, public trust is central to an agency's ability to act (Kramer 1999) and significantly influences citizen support for fire management (Winter et al. 2002, Shindler and Toman 2003). Trust is more likely to develop in the context of personal relationships than through mass information (Jamieson 1994). The give-and-take of interactive exchanges is much more favorable to developing these relationships than programs that rely on an impersonal, one-way flow of information.

Research Context

Prior Research

Two important findings from research on the social aspects of fire management are central to the ideas we have outlined. First, numerous studies over the past three decades have found that citizens with higher fire-related knowledge are more supportive of fuel management activities such as prescribed fire and thinning programs (e.g., Stankey 1976, Shindler and Toman 2003). However, such associations are not evident for all natural resource issues. For example, attitudes toward clearcutting are unlikely to change simply on the basis of new information (Bliss 2000). Additionally, overall public understanding and acceptance of fuels treatments is on the rise. Early studies found that citizens generally overestimated the negative impacts of fire; not surprisingly, a majority preferred complete fire suppression (Stankey 1976). But as the media have begun to cover fires more extensively and fuels reduction programs are underway in local communities, more citizens recognize the role of fire in the landscape (Loomis et al. 2001, Shindler and Brunson 2003).

Second, research has demonstrated that fire-related outreach can positively influence citizen understanding and attitudes toward fire management. In related studies, briefly summarized in table 2, several authors evaluated responses following exposure to various communication activities (e.g., brochures, slide shows, workshops). As described, communication strategies can be classified as unidirectional or interactive based on the type of outreach experience they provide. Unidirectional methods consist of a one-way flow of information from agency personnel to the public, while interactive activities allow for two-way communication. For example, brochures, news releases, and displays at kiosks represent unidirectional approaches, while interpretive programs, guided visits to demonstration sites, neighborhood meetings, and agency workshops are typically interactive. Table 2 shows that both unidirectional and interactive methods have

Table 2. Outcomes of outreach activities and methods

	Increased understanding	More supportive attitudes
Brochures		
Taylor and Daniel 1984	X	
Loomis *et al.* 2001	X	X
Slide presentation		
Nielsen and Buchanan 1986	X	X
Interpreter guided walk		
Nielsen and Buchanan 1986	X	X
Field visit to affected sites		
Self-guided: Toman *et al.* 2004[1]		X
Agency-led: Shindler *et al.* 2005[1]		X
Interactive, hands-on workshop		
Parkinson *et al.* 2003	X	X
Communication campaigns		
Unidirectional methods only:		
Posters, brochures, news releases (Marynowski and Jacobson 1990)	X	
Unidirectional and Interactive methods:		
Newspapers, personal contact, group presentations, neighborhood meetings (McCaffrey 2004)[2]	X	X
Interpretive centers, brochures, interpreter-guided walk (Toman and Shindler 2005)	X	X

[1] Understanding not measured.
[2] Educational materials were more effective if delivered via personal contact.

increased understanding and, in many cases, resulted in more supportive attitudes. Ultimately, each method can achieve management objectives and will play an important role in a comprehensive communication strategy. As described in principle 2, both strategies can be used in a complementary fashion to build a successful outreach program.

Methods

The principles presented here are based on citizen responses to a range of agency outreach and communication activities. Overall, more than 1,300 respondents across nine study locations participated in this research. The research was conducted in two main phases. First, mail surveys were sent to residents in four fire-prone regions in Arizona, Colorado, Oregon, and Utah. The surveys targeted the credibility and overall usefulness of 11 commonly used outreach methods, including six unidirectional (Smokey Bear, TV public service announcements, brochures, newspaper inserts, newsletters, and Web pages) and five interactive approaches (interpretive centers, conversations with agency personnel, elementary school programs, guided field trips, and public meetings).

The second phase of research evaluated participant responses to specific outreach activities in five locations. Participants in Sequoia and King's Canyon National Park in central California assessed a range of unidirectional (e.g., park newsletter, brochures, static displays at interpretive centers) and interactive (e.g., conversations with agency personnel, guided interpretive walks, evening naturalist programs) methods. Those at the World Forestry Center in Portland, Oregon, evaluated the exhibit "Fire: Forces of Nature," which consisted of traditional, unidirectional formats including photographs and text descriptions, examples of fire suppression equipment, and videos. The High Desert Museum in Bend, Oregon, included an interpretive trail through a recent prescribed burn. The self-guided trail included interpretive signs highlighting natural forest conditions, post-fire revegetation, ladder fuels, slash piles, and a historic fire line. Next, respondents in Coeur d'Alene, Idaho, evaluated a public service announcement campaign consisting of daily advertisements in the local newspaper, the Coeur d'Alene Press. Lastly, we also drew upon responses from participants in an agency-guided field trip following a 90,000-acre fire on the Deschutes National Forest.

References

Atkin, C. 2001. Theory and principles of media health campaigns. In: Rice, R.; Atkin, C., eds. Public communication campaigns. 3d ed. Thousand Oaks, CA: Sage Publications, Inc.: 49–68.

Bliss, J. 2000. Public perceptions of clearcutting. Journal of Forestry. 98(12): 4–9.

Brunson, M.; Shindler, B. 2004. Geographic variation in the social acceptability of wildland fuels management in the western U.S. Society and Natural Resources. 17: 661–678.

Delli Priscolli, J.; Homenuck, P. 1990. Consulting the publics. In: Lang, R., ed. Integrated approaches to resource planning and management. Banff, AB: The Banff Centre School of Management: 67–80.

Jacobson, S.K. 1999. Communication skills for conservation professionals. Washington, DC: Island Press. 351 p.

Jacobson, S.K.; Monroe, M.; Marynowski, S. 2001. Fire at the wildland urban interface: the influence of experience and mass media on public knowledge, attitudes, and behavioral intentions. Wildlife Society Bulletin. 29: 929–937.

Jamieson, D. 1994. Problems and prospects for a Forest Service program in the human dimensions of global change. In: Geyer, K.; Shindler, B., eds. Breaking the mold: global change, social responsibility, and natural resource management. Corvallis, OR: Oregon State University: 23–28.

Kramer, R.M. 1999. Trust and distrust in organizations: emerging perspectives, enduring questions. Annual Reviews in Psychology. 50: 569–598.

Lawrence, R.; Daniels, S.; Stankey, G.H. 1997. Procedural justice and public involvement in natural resource decision making. Society and Natural Resources. 10(6): 577–589.

Loomis, J.B.; Bair, L.S.; Gonzalez-Caban, A. 2001. Prescribed fire and public support: knowledge gained, attitudes changed in Florida. Journal of Forestry. 99(11): 18–22.

Marynowski, S.B.; Jacobson, S.K. 1999. Ecosystem management education for public lands. Wildlife Society Bulletin. 27: 134–145.

McCaffrey, S.M. 2004. Fighting fire with education: What is the best way to reach out to homeowners? Journal of Forestry. 102(5): 12–19.

Nelson, K.C.; Monroe, M.C.; Johnson, J.F.; Bowers, A.W. 2003. Public perceptions of defensible space and landscape values in Minnesota and Florida. In: Jakes, Pamela J., comp. Homeowners, communities, and wildfire: science findings from the National Fire Plan. Proceedings of the 9th International symposium on society and management; 2002 June 2-5; Bloomington, IN. Gen. Tech. Rep. NC-231. St. Paul, MN: U.S. Department of Agriculture, Forest Service, North Central Research Station: 55–62.

Nielsen, C.; Buchanan, T. 1986. A comparison of the effectiveness of two interpretive programs regarding fire ecology and fie management. Journal of Interpretation. II(1): 1–10.

Parkinson, T.; Force, J.E.; Smith, J.K. 2003. Hands-on learning: its effectiveness in teaching the public about wildland fire. Journal of Forestry. 101(7): 21–26.

Rogers, E.M. 2003. Diffusion of innovations, 5th ed. New York, NY: The Free Press. 512 p.

Shindler, B.; Aldred-Cheek, K.; Stankey, G.H. 1999. Monitoring and evaluating citizen-agency interactions: a framework developed for adaptive management. Gen. Tech. Rep. PNW-452. Portland, OR: U.S. Department of Agriculture, Forest Service, Pacific Northwest Research Station.

Shindler, B.; Brunson, M. 2003. Fire conditions on public forests and rangelands: a nationwide survey of citizens. Research Report for Joint Fire Science Program. Corvallis, OR: Oregon State University. 20 p.

Shindler, B.; Brunson, M.; Stankey, G.H. 2002. Social acceptability of forest conditions and management practices: a problem analysis. Gen. Tech. Rep. PNW-537. Portland, OR: U.S. Department of Agriculture, Forest Service, Pacific Northwest Research Station. 68 p.

Shindler, B.; Neburka, J. 1997. Public participation in forest planning: eight attributes of success. Journal of Forestry. 91(7): 17–19.

Shindler, B.; Toman, E. 2003. Fuel reduction strategies in forest communities: a longitudinal analysis. Journal of Forestry. 101(6): 8–15.

Shindler, B.; Toman, E.; Olsen, C.; Kakoyannis, C. 2005. Communicating in postfire environments: lessons from agency-citizen tours of a wildland fire. Res. Rep. Corvallis, OR: Department of Forest Resources, Oregon State University.

Shelby, B.; Speaker, R.W. 1990. Public attitudes and perceptions about prescribed burning. In: Walstad, J.D.; et al., eds. Natural and prescribed fire in Pacific Northwest forests. Corvallis, OR: Oregon State University Press: 253–259.

Stankey, G.H. 1976. Wilderness fire policy: an investigation of visitor knowledge and beliefs. Res. Pap. INT-180. Ogden, UT: U.S. Department of Agriculture, Forest Service, Intermountain Forest and Range Experiment Station. 17 p.

Taylor, J.; Daniel, T. 1984. Prescribed fire: public education and perception. Journal of Forestry. 82(6): 361–365.

Toman, E.; Shindler, B. 2005. Communicating about fire: Influences on knowledge and attitude change in two case studies. Res. Rep. Corvallis, OR: Department of Forest Resources, Oregon State University.

Toman, E.; Shindler, B.; Brunson, M. 2006. Fire and fuel communication strategies: citizen evaluations of agency outreach programs. Society and Natural Resources. 19: 321–336.

Toman, E.; Shindler, B.; Reed, M. 2004. Prescribed fire: the influence of site visits on citizen attitudes. Journal of Environmental Education. 35(3): 13–17.

Winter, G.; Fried, J.S. 2000. Homeowner perspectives on fire hazard, responsibility, and management strategies at the wildland-urban interface. Society and Natural Resources. 13: 33–49.

Winter, G.J.; Vogt, C.; Fried, J.S. 2002. Fuel treatments at the wildland-urban interface: common concerns in diverse regions. Journal of Forestry. 100(1): 15–21.

Benefits of an Educational Program for Journalists on Media Coverage of HIV/AIDS in Developing Countries

Jorge L. Martinez-Cajas, Cédric F. Invernizzi,
Michel Ntemgwa, Susan M. Schader and Mark A. Wainberg

ABSTRACT

Objective

a) To assess the suitability of the curriculum content and didactical quality of information delivered to educate journalists in the J2J program in HIV/AIDS (process evaluation) and b) to explore the effects of such programs on journalists' reporting of HIV/AIDS related information (outcome evaluation).

Design

Descriptive study.

Methods

For the process evaluation, each J2J program curriculum was evaluated for accuracy and pertinence by individuals with high familiarity with HIV/AIDS research. For the outcome evaluation, a survey of J2J attendees and evaluations of the program lectures by attendees were performed in chronological order to determine their perception on usefulness of the program.

Results

Overall, the J2J curriculum is successful in providing journalists with a clear understanding of the current HIV/AIDS medical research objectives and issues with most journalists reporting an increased ability to better investigate and disseminate accurate information on this subject. Furthermore, the journalists surveyed reported positive community responses directly as a result of the J2J training.

Conclusion

The J2J program helps to increase global awareness of pertinent HIV/AIDS concepts. Through this professional development strategy, journalists from around the world may help to amplify efforts to prevent new HIV infections and quench the dissemination of inaccurate information and folklore.

Introduction

The detrimental impact of the acquired immunodeficiency syndrome (AIDS) on global health has continued since the first reported cases of human immunodeficiency virus (HIV) infection in the early 1980s. Thus, facilitating worldwide awareness of HIV/AIDS is of paramount importance in public health campaigns aimed at prevention of new infections.

The dissemination of HIV information is a task largely undertaken by community health care workers, advocacy groups, and journalists. Of these professions, journalists probably are the most able to efficiently disseminate pertinent information on a global scale [1,2] and must do so in languages that are understood by the general public. By contrast, misinformation about HIV/AIDS might result in an increase in HIV transmission.

Thus, effective communication between HIV/AIDS research groups and journalists from around the world is essential if we are to improve the understanding of HIV/AIDS worldwide. This was the premise that led to establishment of a Journalist-to-Journalist (J2J) HIV/AIDS training program as a component of the International AIDS Conference in 2002.

The program was developed as a satellite meeting by the National Press Foundation (NPF) in advance of the main conference, the purpose of which was, "preparing selected journalists to cover the International AIDS Conferences, and then to continue to cover the subject at a higher level than previously imagined." It is important to note that the journalists accepted into the program did not have specialized scientific training.

The program was first launched at the Barcelona International AIDS Conference in 2002, and has been held three other times since then in Bangkok in 2004, Toronto in 2006, and Sydney in 2007. Fellows are invited to participate based on their journalistic competence and experience after submitting a successful application to attend. Preference is given to journalists from developing countries since such areas are considered to be most at risk for new HIV infections and because journalists from developing countries are often least able to afford the costs involved in participating in such a conference.

The invited individuals had to be journalists or communicators in any field, had to have previously written or broadcast about HIV/AIDS and have to had the support of their supervisors to attend. They also needed had to supply a printed or video version of a piece that they had done in the field of HIV/AIDS. After these criteria had been met, a second evaluation involved ability to speak English, the type of medium used the candidate and the country of origin so that as many countries or regions as possible would be represented. Financial assistance for travel, lodging, registration, and meals for the duration of the J2J program and conference was provided by the program that is funded by a grant to the NFP by the Bill and Melinda Gates Foundation.

Thirty nine of 74 journalists who were invited attended the Barcelona J2J program, but this number dropped to only 9 of 75 for the Bangkok conference primarily because poor communications from the conference organizers to members of the journalistic community. In contrast, 95 of 105 invited journalists attended the Toronto conference and 42 of 44 invited journalists attended the Sydney program.

Researchers in each of the basic, social and clinical sciences strongly agree with the crucial role that journalists can play by accurately informing the public on issues that relate to the global HIV/AIDS epidemic [3-5]. Prevention of HIV infection, accessible health care for HIV positive individuals, and public policy are all issues that may be highlighted through journalism. Furthermore, journalists are often able to translate the objectives of HIV/AIDS advocacy and research groups into language that is more likely to be understood by the communities to which these messages are targeted. In fact, programs on HIV prevention, stigma, the health care needs of those infected by HIV/AIDS, and advocating for government intervention can all be directly affected by what journalists choose to report.

Purpose of this Evaluation

The authors of this report (two Ph.D.s, one M.D., and two Ph.D. candidates), all very familiar with the HIV/AIDS scientific literature, were asked to evaluate the J2J program in order to:

a. assess the relevance of the curriculum content and didactic quality of information delivered to journalists (process evaluation) and,

b. explore the effects of such programs on reporting of HIV/AIDS related information (outcome evaluation).

Our secondary objectives were to:

c. assess journalists' perceptions as to how this training program affected their coverage of HIV/AIDS, and

d. determine whether the program had resulted in improved provision of information to communities about truths and misconceptions about HIV/AIDS.

Methods used for Assessment

Our team was provided by the J2J program organizers with the following material for evaluation of the program:

a. E-mail addresses of all participant journalist fellows who possessed such an address.

b. A large sample of news stories on HIV/AIDS written by journalists who attended the training sessions and conferences.

c. Evaluation reports of the Bangkok and Barcelona programs previously prepared by the National Press Foundation.

d. Evaluations by journalists Sydney program.

e. Data accessible online from a number of slide presentations delivered in each of the following J2J training programs (Barcelona 2002, Bangkok 2004, Toronto 2006, Sydney 2007). Presentations from Sydney also included voice recordings of scientific presentations.

Careful study of the J2J curriculum (included as part of each conference program) was completed by at least two evaluators. Each evaluator issued a descriptive statement on the completeness of the program by answering the following questions:

Is the content of the J2J curriculum suitable and complete?

What key subjects were lacking?

What subjects might be excluded?

After each individual evaluation, a group discussion resulted in agreement on the completeness of the curricula. In the same fashion, a sample of 24 slide presentations (available online) were evaluated for relevance, complexity, organization and quality of slide presentation. Each slide presentation was scored using the following scale: 1 = poor, 2 = fair, 3 = good, 4 = excellent.

In addition, journalists' evaluations of the Sydney conference J2J program (n = 42), which had used the same scoring scale, was taken into consideration.

To establish the benefits of the program, two types of analyses were performed. First, a random sample of 39 news reports (of 84 available in English or with an accompanying English translation) completed by journalists who participated in any of the J2J programs was examined for relevance and accuracy (using the scoring scale described above). These 39 news reports represent a sample of 46% of the total of reports available in English. Each report was reviewed by at least two members of our team. In cases of non-agreement, which were very rare, the senior author of this paper made a definitive assignment of grade.

A short survey in the form of a questionnaire (Additional file 1) was also distributed to all participating journalists to assess the overall perceived benefits (if any) of the J2J program. Journalists' responses were compiled, reviewed and analyzed.

Results

1. Evaluations of Curricula

For the Barcelona and Bangkok conferences, comments from attending journalists were available in reports prepared by the NPF [6,7]. The Barcelona, Bangkok and Toronto conferences were each multidisciplinary and the J2J programs at those conferences were intended to enable journalists to acquire necessary knowledge of a meeting with a broad scientific, social and cultural agenda. In contrast, the Sydney conference focused on biomedical research, improved treatment, and prevention strategies, as well as on obstacles toward attainment of these goals. The content of each J2J program is presented in Table 1.

Table 1. Curriculum of each J2J program at the International AIDS Conferences

Conferences with interdisciplinary focus			Conference with biomedical focus
BARCELONA	**BANGKOK**	**TORONTO**	**SYDNEY**
Basic and clinical science	**Basic and clinical science**	**Basic and clinical science**	**Basic and clinical science**
Basic Science of HIV/AIDS What HIV/AIDS Does in the Body Treatments, Current & Future	What HIV Does in the Body Treatments, Current & Future	HIV/AIDS & Vaccine Research	Living With HIV/AIDS All You Need to Know About Microbicides PLENARY PREVIEW: T-cell loss, immune activation and potential therapeutic interventions PLENARY PREVIEW: Understanding the Task: ARV Rollout and research issues in the developing world
Medical and therapeutic issues in HIV	**Medical and therapeutic issues in HIV**	**Medical and therapeutic issues in HIV**	**Medical and therapeutic issues in HIV**
Prevention	Tracking HIV/AIDS: Numbers that Count: The Demographic and Health Surveys (DHS) project provides quality data on the What, Why, Where and When of HIV/AIDS	Epidemiology 101	PLENARY PREVIEW: Pediatric Therapeutic Issues
Access to Treatments	Preventing HIV/AIDS Integration Of Prevention Into Treatment Programs And Other Issues Posed By Treatment Access	Developing HIV Prevention Options for Women: Microbicides Female Condoms Paediatric AIDS HIV/AIDS and nutrition in rural areas HIV/AIDS in Latin America and the Caribbean, Asia and Africa: The differences between the epidemics, the different responses, and the different issues in various regions HIV/AIDS & TB	
Journalism and HIV/AIDS	**Journalism and HIV/AIDS**	**Journalism and HIV/AIDS**	**Journalism and HIV/AIDS**
Journalists' Discussion Groups + session Journalists' Discussion Groups + session leaders	Beyond He Said/She Said: Giving Depth to HIV Stories Field Trip: Presentation: AIDS in Thailand	Discussions on Covering HIV/AIDS Special Presentation Ontario Room The Blood of Yingzhou District	Plenary Preview: Male Circumcision *Journalist to Journalist Discussion:* AIDS Denialism What it is, how to recognize it, how to dispute it, with a focus on a recent Australian legal case
Practical Tips & Story Ideas for Covering the XIVth International AIDS Conference Tracking the Money	Journalists' Discussion: Privacy, Reporting & HIV/AIDS Trends, Trends & Q&A	Congratulations and a Charge to Journalists Tips for covering the Toronto conference	*Journalist to Journalist Discussion:* The Multiple Layers of AIDS Coverage Tips for Covering the Sydney Conference *Overview of different tracks from the conference: what they mean, what they'll cover, how to choose what to attend*
News & Numbers	Training the Trainer Health Beyond HIV/AIDS & Why the Media Should Care	HIV/AIDS in Context Looking Beyond Toronto to Mexico City in 2008 Trends and Q&A	
Social and economical sciences	**Social and economical sciences**	**Social and economical sciences**	**Social and economical sciences**
Economic & Medical Consequences of the Epidemic Myths & Misperceptions	Macroeconomics & AIDS AIDS Orphans & Vulnerable Children AIDS in Context	The Stigma Faced by People Living With HIV/AIDS Human Rights & HIV/AIDS	A New Initiative on MSM Sex Workers: Part of the Solution, Not Part of the Problem

Curriculum Completeness

We observed a progression in the quality of the curriculum throughout the J2J series from the initial program attempt in Barcelona. The J2J program content was adjusted based on feedback from journalists after each J2J event. This was done both with respect to content and the topics for lectures at the J2J satellite meeting. A succinct assessment of the content of each J2J program follows:

Barcelona 2002 J2J Program

This program was graded as fairly complete by our team of evaluators. The agenda allowed ample time for discussion and interactive sharing of ideas between experts and attendees. It included three lectures that introduced scientific and biomedical concepts and terminology frequently used in HIV/AIDS research. The Barcelona program also included discussions of economic and cultural issues surrounding HIV/AIDS. However, it was pointed out that the program would have been strengthened if a visit to local HIV care facilities or with community-based HIV/AIDS health groups had been arranged. It was also felt that socioeconomic issues surrounding the pandemic needed more attention.

Our evaluation also revealed that the Barcelona J2J program did not contain adequate information on how decisions are reached regarding the efficacy of drug interventions. This was in spite of the fact that the intention was to enable journalists to recognize basic principles of good scientific methods, especially in therapeutics and efforts to prevent transmission of HIV.

Journalists need to have basic tools to be able to identify overtly false science, which can be a common and widespread cause of public misinformation. Also lacking was an introduction to epidemiologic terminology frequently used to address public health issues.

Bangkok 2004 J2J Program

Compared to the Barcelona J2J curriculum, the reviewers perceived the Bangkok J2J program as more complete. Of note, the reviewers found that a session on issues of people living with HIV (PLWHIVs) adequately allocated time for journalists to become informed of the diverse needs of PLWHIVs, including the issue of HIV-related stigma. Journalists who attended this series of seminars acknowledged the opportunity to speak to HIV/AIDS activists.

Topics that were determined to be insufficiently represented at this J2J satellite included:

1. An introduction to principles of scientific research.

2. Development of tools that enable journalists to ask the right questions about epidemiologic research.

3. Discussion of how the needs of PLWHIVs might be met by local government and non-government organizations.

Also lacking was a specialized seminar on how to access HIV/AIDS data on prevalence, trends, projections, public programs, as well as obstacles toward implementing HIV/AIDS health programs in various countries.

It was pointed out that assessments of local health agencies, government and non-governmental organizations (NGOs) would have been beneficial.

Some of the Bangkok J2J delegates felt that the biomedical research lectures presented at the J2J Satellite were burdened with excessive detail. There were also requests for implementation of country-specific J2J professional development curricula.

Toronto 2006 J2J Program

The overall J2J satellite offered a rich epidemiological and cultural experience. On the other hand, the Toronto J2J curriculum was felt to be lacking in seminars about clinical research methodology and on how to decipher scientific jargon commonly used among HIV/AIDS scientists. Presentations on HIV prevention were appreciated by the delegates as were lectures on behavioral and medical interventions.

Sydney 2007 J2J Program

The Sydney IAS 2007 conference focused primarily on biomedical research and the J2J program prepared for this through a comprehensive curriculum that spanned several days before the conference. The J2J organizers also offered comprehensive discussions on particular issues that were anticipated to be especially important. An introduction to scientific jargon was presented in the context of a session on vaccines and microbicides. A more general introduction to scientific jargon might also have proved useful. The reviewers felt that an informative session describing how certain scientific results are chosen for presentation at international conferences should have been included and also a session on how decisions are made by individual scientists to present their work.

In all J2J programs a paucity of participants from the private sector was evident. This is despite the fact that the drug companies are well represented at every IAS conference. It therefore seemed strange that this sector was not better represented in the J2J program.

A post-conference follow-up meeting was absent from the program. Such a meeting would serve to reinforce understanding of key issues/topics and enable journalists to clarify what they have or have not understood.

2. Journalists' Evaluations of J2J Sessions

At the Sydney conference, we gained access to journalists' evaluations of each presentation in the context of the J2J program. On average, journalists gave grades of excellent or good to fourteen of the sixteen presentations delivered. Thirteen of the sixteen lecturers (76%) were evaluated by attendees as good or excellent. The average grade for all lecturers was 3.08 which was comparable to previous averages from Barcelona and Bangkok, i.e. 3.1 and 3.19, respectively (maximum score is 4.0). Overall evaluations by journalists were good or excellent for each topic covered. Only three of thirteen presentations failed to score in the excellent range.

3. Assessments of Presentations by the Evaluation Committee

Our committee evaluated 24 J2J presentations available online on the basis of relevance, complexity, organization, slide quality and background information. Only two presentations had an average score less than 3. The area in which presentations were frequently weak was in slide quality (five of twenty-four had poor quality and ten had fair quality). The content of all presentations, except two, was considered to be highly relevant.

A comparison of the evaluations by journalists of the Sydney J2J sessions with our own evaluations of the same sessions revealed concordant excellent grades for five of seven lectures, while the other two were only discordant between good vs. excellent grades. This is consistent with the observation that the presentations were of high caliber in regard to the objective of educating journalists.

4. Evaluations of News Reports

Thirty-nine news reports from those that were written in English or had an accompanying English translation were randomly chosen for review by two evaluators. In almost all cases, the reports were from journalists working on developing countries (Figure 1).

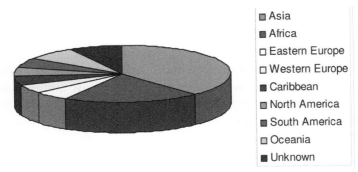

Legend:
- Asia
- Africa
- Eastern Europe
- Western Europe
- Caribbean
- North America
- South America
- Oceania
- Unknown

Figure 1. The reports from journalists who participated in the J2J program and filed HIV/AIDS primarily represented areas of the world where HIV/AIDS is, or will likely be, of great impact.

Those in the categories of excellent and good were grouped together and the extent of agreement between the evaluations was determined. Discordant evaluations were adjudicated by an additional reviewer, if necessary. Reports in English were deliberately overrepresented in the sample analyzed, as the reviewers were mainly English-speaking. In almost all cases, the reports were from journalists working in developing countries (see Figure 1).

In regard to quality of the reports (relevance and accuracy), thirty-three of the 39 (84%) reports from all of the J2J sessions evaluated were found to be good or excellent. The topics discussed in these journalists' reports are summarized in Table 2.

Table 2. Topics discussed in journalists reports

Topics	Number of reports
Global epidemiology and public health priorities of HIV/AIDS	8
Conference coverage	6
Innovative methods to increase public awareness about HIV/AIDS in developing countries	2
Coverage of government responses	1
Restricted ART access in developing country settings	5
Information on low use of MTCT prevention, pediatric ARV limitations, and the growing problems of orphans due to HIV/AIDS worldwide	3
Culturally-related responses to prevention strategies, importance of youth, women, and NGOs in fighting HIV/AIDS	2
Coverage of J2J the program and its benefits	2
Coverage of people with HIV/AIDS, stigma-related issues and family effects of MTCT of HIV/AIDS	2
Discussion on social aspects of HIV transmission in heavily-affected areas, risk reduction strategies in high-risk populations, enhancing prevention strategies, non-typical higher risk populations.	5
Information about microbicide trials and ARV treatment in case of rape.	1
Financial support for HIV/AIDS-affected people in developing countries	1

Some reports covered more than one topic

5. Online Survey

We emailed a request to complete an online survey to 160 journalists. Seventeen e-mail messages did not reach recipients. Forty-two journalists completed the survey.

The respondents were almost unanimous in judging that the J2J program was very useful and 79% of them have increased their reporting of HIV/AIDS since the conference (Figure 2).

In addition, the knowledge gained has continued to help journalists in their subsequent coverage of HIV/AIDS. No journalist had a negative attitude toward either the J2J program or community groups working in the HIV/AIDS field. The great majority of journalists perceived that their coverage of the IAS conferences was greeted more enthusiastically by the communities that they serve than would have been the case if not for the J2J program.

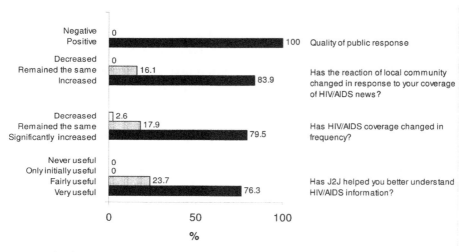

Figure 2. This figure presents the responses given by J2J attendees to questions about their perception on usefulness of the J2J program. The data was obtained through an online survey.

Print and Radio Journalists

The majority of the J2J journalist fellows wrote newspaper articles or reports to be posted on the worldwide web. The median number of print articles and radio presentations by journalists has been 3 and 4, respectively, per month in the time since the conference. Radio and newspaper coverage are the most likely means for dissemination of information in the developing world, since only minimal infrastructure is required.

Television

Television was used less frequently as a medium by journalists in the developing world, although 6 of the J2J journalists aired HIV/AIDS related programs on TV.

The broadcasting frequency of each report varied. One was aired once, whilst another aired four times in one week. One journalist reported that his/her program was broadcast monthly.

6. Examples of Experiences of Journalists

Two sources of descriptive evaluations of the program were available. A database from the J2J Sydney program and an additional survey carried out by our team. Of note, the vast majority of comments from the journalist evaluation database was favorable and acknowledged appropriate organization, pertinence of the program, and usefulness of the presentations.

The following comments provide a reasonable idea of some journalists' impressions of the J2J program:

"Honestly, without the J2J training, I would have spent half of my time at the IAS conference referring to either a science dictionary or googling up certain complicated scientific phrases."

"The AIDS Denialist session was fantastic: it's good to be reminded of tactics for handling the denialists, which are a real headache here in South Africa."

"In addition to its comprehensiveness, the programme represented a huge effort to reach out to and include journalists from the developing world."

"To me it was the best effort. But I would suggest if every one of us can share his/her stories done afterwards because it would help every one of us."

"It is good to have a hands-on training on science reporting for the AIDS pathogenesis, treatment and prevention conference."

"I think what was on offer at this years training program was perfect. If you can inspire someone to act and feel different about how they view HIV/AIDS in just a week then you have succeeded. Please know your program is inspirational."

"I feel the program offered a thorough overview of the HIV/AIDS pandemic and gave me a unique opportunity to share observations and ideas with colleagues from around the world."

There were few comments on program failures.

"Next time, NPF could improve its trainings by advising or asking presenters to avoid scientific jargon., That is, putting their presentation in simpler words that could be understood by ordinary people including journalists. And they should be brief and to the point."

"I would suggest that next time the training should be 5 days long and we should have more field visits to have a face on what we would be doing. Thanks for taking us to Kirketon Xentre. We really learnt a lot and we have since adopted their approach here in."

Discussion

Strengths of the Program

The program appears to have fully met its main purpose of enabling journalists to effectively transmit medical, epidemiological and scientific information to the general public in lay language.

This, in turn, may to help to raise the interest and awareness of the general public in developing countries about resources that can effectively be mobilized to both reduce transmission of HIV and to treat those living with HIV/AIDS. This is important since the vast majority of journalists trained by the J2J program come from and work in developing countries in which HIV/AIDS is a major public health threat.

Weaknesses of the Program and Opportunities for Improvement

Although the program does an excellent job at enhancing journalistic skills to translate scientific information into lay language, there appears to be a shortage of information as to what journalists should be doing at a local level. Should they be querying their own local communities with respect to local practices and the role of local health promotion authorities? This subject is complex, and, in some countries, it should be recognized that journalists may sometimes feel intimidated by the types of questions they might wish to ask.

Second, several scientific presentations within the J2J program did not attempt to use non-scientific terminology and/or the presenters did not take the time to try to explain their findings to journalists in lay language. Emphasis needs to be placed on the transmission of scientific concepts over a range of HIV/AIDS disciplines.

Third, a weak representation of the private sector was evident in all the J2J programs. Clearly, journalists would like to have the opportunity to ask questions to representatives of the pharmaceutical industry (including generic industry spokespersons). This is a key area for consideration, since the public is poorly informed in general about the roles played by drug companies in scientific research and may be easily seduced by 'conspiracy theories' that attribute false motives to companies. Responsible reporting on relationships between the private and public sectors, including academia, may help to quench misconceptions.

Finally, presentations of exemplary work by leading world-class HIV/AIDS journalists might also enhance the J2J curriculum. Less experienced journalists might be paired with more experienced 'mentor' journalists from their own countries, as well as from developed countries, for in depth discussions. Former fellows might also be able to share experiences with new fellows and help the latter to improve their communications skills. There could then be a 'trickle-down effect' if journalists were to conduct smaller, albeit less ambitious J2J-like programs, in their own countries.

Implications for Global Public Health

The need for education of communities about HIV is evident. Several reports have documented insufficient knowledge in populations at risk of acquiring HIV infection [8-10]. In this regard, the mass media could have a positive impact on improving the public's knowledge of HIV. For instance, media are able to affect audience behavior in a way that might favor prevention (e.g. discussion of HIV/AIDS with a partner, awareness that consistent condom use reduces HIV risk, asking about condom use at last intercourse, or increasing voluntary HIV testing) [4,11-13].

The World Health Organization has stated that impact may vary, depending on the place and campaign, but that comprehensive mass media programs are valuable in helping to change HIV/AIDS-related behavior, at least among young people in developing countries [1]. Therefore, education of journalists, who are often partners in such efforts worldwide, is consistent with the types of activities that advance public health.

The J2J program has an opportunity to engage in outreach to help direct and/or support international education campaigns through the networks that have now been established. A continuous and synchronized effort to promote education of communities through written publications and/or radio programs might be established using the broad human resource represented by the J2J program. The creation of material based on the J2J presentations and local replication of similar programs could be encouraged, and could also be carried out in languages other than English. Ongoing feedback from such efforts could then be used to improve the overall effort, which could be implemented and locally tailored to regional needs for use in subsequent initiatives.

Limitations of the Study

The response rate for the survey was only 26%, evidently raising the issue of bias. On the other hand, favorable grades were given to the j2j program by attendees who evaluated the program at previous conferences and these were consistent with the later grading found through the survey.

Despite the heterogeneous educational background of the journalists attending the J2J program, we observed a high quality of accuracy and pertinence in the reports written by attendees. Altogether, these observations suggest a beneficial effect of the program on the communication skills of the journalists in the HIV/AIDS field. Nevertheless, a sample of reports by the journalists before the J2J session would have been ideal for comparison with those available after the session. Unfortunately, such information was not available to us.

For future evaluations, and in order to accurately determine the effect of J2J on journalists' skills, it might be advisable to obtain and evaluate a baseline set of reports from the invited journalists before the session.

Although we cannot definitively conclude that J2J improved skills in reporting of HIV/AIDS in general, the perception from attendees at the end of the each J2J program and those who responded to our survey were all positive suggesting that the goals of the program were realized.

Usually, lack of response to a survey represents low motivation to spend time answering questions and not necessarily a negative perception of the issue involved. In addition, emails to contact journalists in developing countries might not be the best strategy for future surveys since internet access may be limited or unstable for a proportion of potential respondents.

Conclusion

The J2J program of the National Press Foundation has accomplished its main goal of gathering journalists from around the world to be trained in how to better report HIV/AIDS news.

Journalists have consistently indicated that the program is highly useful and that it enables them to cover and inform the public in a variety of areas: experiences of people living with HIV/AIDS, impact on society, the reasons for stigma, how to work toward destigmatization of HIV, hopes and limitations of current therapy including issues of drug access in developing countries, prospects for novel therapeutic and prevention initiatives, and the successes and failures of research and/or public health measures.

Vital information in each of these areas needs to reach the general public, who will ultimately decide what it is important to pay attention to and in which areas to establish priorities.

Journalist reports are an effective means of providing information on HIV awareness to vulnerable populations, hopefully helping to lower rates of infection and educating those who are infected by HIV to seek adequate help. Public awareness can help to guide public opinion and influence government policy in a positive way and to counter stigma, which is often a result of misperceptions about HIV/AIDS. Journalists play important roles in each of these areas and the J2J program has been key in educating journalists worldwide to do their jobs better.

Competing Interests

MAW was an invited speaker at the J2J Conference in Sydney.

Authors' Contributions

JLMC led in the study design, data analysis and manuscript preparation. CFI participated in the study design, data analysis and manuscript preparation. MN and SMS participated in review and evaluation of news reports and of the J2J program's curriculum. MAW participated in study design, evaluation of news reports, and manuscript preparation.

Acknowledgements

We thank Mr Robert Mayers of the National Press Foundation for many useful discussions and for providing key sets of data that were used in our analyses. We thank Beatriz E Alvarado, PhD for assisting with data analysis and survey implementation. JLMC was the recipient of a fellowship from the Canadian HIV Trials Network and both Michel Ntemgwa and Susan M Schader received fellowhip support from the Canadian Institutes of Health Research which also provides support to the laboratory of Dr MAW.

References

1. Bertrand JT, Anhang R: The effectiveness of mass media in changing HIV/AIDS-related behaviour among young people in developing countries. World Health Organ Tech Rep Ser 2006, 938:205-241. Discussion 317–241.

2. Bertrand JT, O'Reilly K, Denison J, Anhang R, Sweat M: Systematic review of the effectiveness of mass communication programs to change HIV/AIDS-

related behaviors in developing countries. Health Educ Res 2006, 21:567–597.

3. Agha S: The impact of a mass media campaign on personal risk perception, perceived self-efficacy and on other behavioural predictors. AIDS Care 2003, 15:749–762.

4. Karlyn AS: The impact of a targeted radio campaign to prevent STIs and HIV/AIDS in Mozambique. AIDS Educ Prev 2001, 13:438–451.

5. Underwood C, Hachonda H, Serlemitsos E, Bharath-Kumar U: Reducing the risk of HIV transmission among adolescents in Zambia: psychosocial and behavioral correlates of viewing a risk-reduction media campaign. J Adolesc Health 2006, 38:55.

6. National-Press-Foundation: Final Report: The Bangkok J2J Program. Journalist to Journalist The Global Media Responds to HIV/AIDS. Washington DC

7. National-Press-Foundation: Final Report: The J2J Program at AIDS 2002 Barcelona. XIV International AIDS Conference. Journalist to Journalist The Global Media Responds to HIV/AIDS. Washington, DC

8. Hossain MB, Kabir A, Ferdous H: Knowledge of HIV and AIDS among tertiary students in Bangladesh. Int Q Community Health Educ 2006, 26:271–285.

9. Manji A, Pena R, Dubrow R: Sex, condoms, gender roles, and HIV transmission knowledge among adolescents in Leon, Nicaragua: implications for HIV prevention. AIDS Care 2007, 19:989–995.

10. Shrotri A, Shankar AV, Sutar S, Joshi A, Suryawanshi N, Pisal H, Bharucha KE, Phadke MA, Bollinger RC, Sastry J: Awareness of HIV/AIDS and household environment of pregnant women in Pune, India. Int J STD AIDS 2003, 14:835–839.

11. Farr AC, Witte K, Jarato K, Menard T: The effectiveness of media use in health education: evaluation of an HIV/AIDS radio [corrected] campaign in Ethiopia. J Health Commun 2005, 10:225–235.

12. Keating J, Meekers D, Adewuyi A: Assessing effects of a media campaign on HIV/AIDS awareness and prevention in Nigeria: results from the VISION Project. BMC Public Health 2006, 6:123.

13. Olshefsky AM, Zive MM, Scolari R, Zuniga M: Promoting HIV risk awareness and testing in Latinos living on the U.S.-Mexico border: the Tu No Me Conoces social marketing campaign. AIDS Educ Prev 2007, 19:422–435.

Issues in Evaluating Mass Media-Based Health Communication Campaigns

Vicki Freimuth, Ph.D., Galen Cole, Ph.D., M.P.H.
and Susan Kirby, Ph.D.

Introduction

Most premature deaths in developed countries can be linked to action or the lack of action by individuals and/or communities (1). As a result, public health practitioners have developed interventions to promote healthful attitudes and actions and to suppress those which place life and health in jeopardy. Health communication, which we define as the study and use of strategies to inform and influence individual and community decisions that enhance health, plays an increasingly central role in these interventions.

Communication may be a dominant player or may have a supporting role in an intervention. Some roles may include communication strategies such as public relations, where the objective is to get the health issue on the public agenda;

entertainment education, where desired behaviors are modeled in an entertainment program; and media advocacy which entails using the media as an advocacy tool to achieve policy level change. All of these strategies may include a range of communication activities that can occur at the individual, small group or mass media level. This paper addresses only those communication activities that use mass media outlets and, more specifically, the issues surrounding the evaluation of the development, implementation, and effects of mass media health communication campaigns. These evaluation issues will be discussed under the commonly known headings of formative, process and summative evaluation.

Health Communication Campaigns

Rogers and Storey (2) maintain that health communication campaigns have four defining characteristics. These campaigns strive to (1) generate specific outcomes or effects (2) in a relatively large number of individuals (3) usually within a specified period of time and (4) through an organized set of communication activities. Health communication campaigns that rely on mass media outlets frequently consist of a series of television and radio public service announcements (PSAs) or paid commercials with collateral print materials such as posters, booklets, and brochures.

Most health communicators would agree that there are a common set of variables considered in the development of a mass media health communication campaign and a common set of outcomes that one can reasonably expect as a result of a communication experience. Communication development or independent variables can be categorized into four broad areas: 1) psychosocial attributes of the receiver, 2) the source or spokesperson, 3) settings, channels, activities, and materials used to disseminate the message, and 4) the message itself, including content, tone, type of appeal, audio characteristics, and visual attributes . Taken together, any combination of these four independent variables constitutes what we refer to as the Communication Strategy (3, 4, 5, 6, 7, 8, 9, 10). The outcomes or dependent variables of a mass health communication effort may be categorized into six broad areas which include: 1) exposure, 2) attention, 3) comprehension, 4) yielding, 5) attitude change, and 6) behavior (4, 5, 11, 12). We acknowledge at the outset that these outcomes are not exhaustive, nor do we mean to imply that the progression of these outcomes are linear in nature. We do, however, believe that these terms will provide a common language pertinent to this discussion.

Formative Research and Evaluation Issues

The research carried out prior to the implementation of a mass media-based health communication campaign is often referred to as formative research or formative evaluation. This preimplementation research assists in understanding and developing effective communication strategies and tactics aimed at mitigating or eliminating problems (6, 9, 13, 14, 15).

Our purpose in this section is to discuss issues related to the formative research and formative evaluations carried out during the developmental stages of mass communication strategies and tactics. These issues pertain to 1) the data required to understand and profile the receiver characteristics of audiences that are the target of mass health communication, and 2) the evaluation or pre-testing of communication strategies and tactics prior to their implementation.

Data Issues

The strategic development of a mass-mediated health communication campaign requires descriptive and analytic epidemiologic data to understand the nature and extent of the health problem as a basis for determining 1) whether mass communication is an appropriate intervention, 2) which audience(s) are the most appropriate targets of a mass communication intervention, and 3) what the overall goal of the communication should be. In addition to relying on traditional epidemiologic data, health communicators also need data required to segment and characterize potential audiences on independent variables that have the most bearing on how one communicates with them (6, 9, 13, 14). As stated above, this includes data on the 1) psychosocial attributes of the receiver, 2) source or spokesperson, 3) settings, channel-specific communication activities, and materials that are used to support communication activities, and 4) the message itself, including content, tone, type of appeal, audio characteristics, and visual attributes. These data allow the communicator to disaggregate the population of interest into homogeneous subgroups or audience segments. Health-related audience segments are usually defined by being alike in one of two ways; a) regarding predictors of the behavior (similar levels of self-efficacy, social norms, or knowledge) or b) regarding communication strategy factors (e.g., they are motivated by a fear based message, or they prefer a lay person to communication the message).

Although there are numerous sources of health-related data as well as many sources of data on consumers used for marketing purposes, to our knowledge the only national data generated in the U.S. which combines health behavior predictor data with data on communication variables is called Healthstyles8 (14) and has been collected since 1995 by Porter Novelli, a social marketing firm located in Washington D.C. The lack of data puts communication planners in a position of having to 1) collect primary data, 2) merge or retrofit epidemiologic and marketing data, or 3) plan interventions without a clear understanding of communication-relevant differences that may exist in the populations they are targeting. Obviously, if adequate time and resources are available, the first option is preferred. However, when working on a short timeline with a limited budget it would be helpful to have multi-variate datasets (16, 17, 18, 19, 20, 21, 22, 23, 24) available that provide information on salient health-related and communication variables. In view of this, we recommend that researchers take steps to systematically link or create databases that provide the etiologic data required to understand health behavior incidence and prevalence [e.g., Behavioral Risk Factor Surveillance Study (25)], data that helps us understand what is driving health problems that can be addressed by mass communication interventions, and the communication data that can help planners understand how to effectively tailor mass communication strategies to the receiver characteristics of homogenous segments of the population.

Pretesting Communication Strategies and Tactics

Once an audience is segmented into groups who share similar characteristics that are important to the communication process, specific communication strategies and tactics can be crafted for each segment of the population. The crafting of a communication strategy that is tailored to the health information and communication needs of a particular audience segment is facilitated by providing those responsible for developing the strategy with a creative brief which consists of a profile of the health-relevant knowledge, attitudes, actions and communication-related characteristics of each target audience. Although, at this point in the communication planning process, existing research may provide much guidance on each variable in the communication strategy, research on how to put those variables together most effectively for a particular audience segment is rare. Hence, health communication planners rely on a type of formative evaluation referred to as pre-testing.

In short, pre-testing is a process for systematically determining which combination of options represented by each communication variable (i.e., the communication strategy) tend to be most effective in achieving the communication objectives. This type of formative research shares characteristics of both process and summative research in that it can be designed to examine both the simulated delivery and the effects of a communication strategy and its tactics. At the same time, pre-testing is different from process or summative evaluation research in that it is carried out before final production and execution of a communication strategy to determine whether each element in the mix helps achieve the communication objectives of the project and meets the information needs of the intended audience (27, 28). A point which will be made under the summative evaluation section of this paper is relevant here. That is, because it is so difficult to directly attribute changes in individuals to a mass communication intervention, a high priority should be placed on pre-testing a strategy before it is executed to ensure that it is feasible, it produces intended cognitive effects in a sample of individuals who are representative of each target audience, and it does no harm.

While it is consider an indispensable formative evaluation method, there are some issues surrounding how pre-testing is carried out. Namely, rigor of the research methods employed and comparison data for decision-making. This is particularly true with focus group interviews which have steadily increased in the non-profit and health community (29). A simple search of Medline7 indicated a 266 percent growth over eight years in reported focus group studies from 45 (1988-1991) to 165 (19921995). Although all research methods have inherent advantages and disadvantages, the problems posed by the potentially inappropriate use of focus groups are worthy of a brief discussion.

Focus groups are based on conducting a series of small group discussions with members of intended audience segment. A series of groups is recommended because the unit of analysis is the group itself, not each member of the group. Because of various constraints, program planners often conduct too few groups for each segment of interest. This tendency can result in conducting one focus group session for each segment type (e.g., one group each of black females, white females, and Asian females), which is not adequate for drawing research conclusions and is far too few to find any between-group differences (29). Another problem in using focus group research is the temptation to quantify participants' answers (e.g., by asking for a hand count on agreement) which leads others to believe that the data may adhere to the rules for quantitative data integrity, such as independent observations or central limit theorem. Focus group authors have long cautioned practitioners not to quantify results (29, 30, 31) because it misleads readers and destroys the true value of qualitative research, which is to gain a richer and deeper understanding of a topic, not a more precise or accurate measurement. Health communication planners need to be able to judiciously use focus groups to their best advantage while maintaining a high level of confidence in the findings. Focus groups, not to be confused with group interviewing, should be not be used for message pretesting, except to explore answers to quantitative measures.

There are several other qualitative research methods that can be used along with quantitative methods to gather information in connection with pre-testing messages. These include methods such as case studies, one-on-one interviews, and record abstraction (32, 33, 34). In most instances, we prefer one-on-one interviews or central intercept interviews, as they are often called in communication research, to test messages. We prefer this method of message testing because: 1) it's easier to connect with harder-toreach respondents in locations convenient and comfortable for them; 2) we can access an increased number of respondents within the intended population if an appropriate location is selected; 3) it's a cost-effective means of gathering data in a relatively short time; 4) we can get a larger sample size than focus groups, and 4) these one-on-one interviews tend to eliminate group bias that is possible in focus groups.

Lastly, once formative researchers have some pretest data in hand, little comparison data are available to help decide if the pretested materials performed well enough to create change in a real world setting. Aside from the Health Message Testing Service (35), few health communication programs have conducted quantitative message pretesting, published their findings, or related pretesting data to outcome evaluation data. Without knowledge of pretesting data and actual communication outcomes, health communication planners cannot forecast how well a communication strategy will help reach communication objectives. The advertising world, which refers to message pretesting as copytesting, may have some useful models that can be adopted to help overcome this lack of data.

Most advertising agencies employ some method of copytesting (36) and have established marketing surveillance systems for the purpose of consistently collecting, analyzing, and cataloging the data generated by the copytesting process. The rigor and systematic collection of these data is demonstrated by the 1982 Positioning Advertising Copytesting (PACT) agreement (37). The document outlining the PACT agreement, prepared by 21 of the leading advertising agencies in 1982 (37), articulates nine principles of copytesting which target multiple measures, representative samples, reliability, and validity. Since the PACT agreement was published in 1982 (37), a plethora of research firms have been established to help deliver on these nine principles (BehaviorScan, the Starch Report, AHF Marketing Research, ASI Marketing Research, Gallup and Robinson, McCollum/Spielman, and Mapes and Ross (38).These firms research, track, and collect copytesting data for primary purchasing and reselling to retail organizations. These data help identify the most effective and efficient communication strategy for the marketing communication dollar.

While it is true that outcomes like consumer recall and purchase data are easily assessed and collected in the retail marketing world, cognitive and behavioral outcomes of health communication activities are not as easily assessed or collected. Thus, health communication campaigns that rely on mass media outlets are usually challenged with making formative decisions based on relatively little data and, even in the best situations, making decisions without up-to-date information or comparison data. However, as was noted above, for health communication planners to bring the best messages to the prevention marketplace to attack the root causes of the health problems of our times, they will need timely comparison data systems, not unlike those established by the private sector, to identify and improve weak and inadequate programs before implementation.

Process Evaluation Issues

Generally speaking, process evaluation is used to answer questions about whether a program is delivered as planned (28). In the present context, process evaluation addresses questions concerning how well and under what conditions a mass media health communication campaign was implemented, and the size of the audience that is exposed to the message. A number of issues should be understood and addressed when planning and conducting a process evaluation of mass media campaigns. These include: 1) the utility of process evaluation, 2) theoretical considerations and cause/effect attributions, and 3) changing an intervention during the course of an evaluation.

The Utility of Process Evaluation

The clamor for data on the intended effects of campaigns by stakeholders has led many evaluators to become preoccupied with program impacts and outcomes (26, 39, 40). This focus on the effects of interventions has led many evaluators to rely heavily on controlled experimental methods. An enticing feature of these methods is that an understanding of how a campaign works is not necessary to estimate its net effects through random experimental methods (41). Hence, evaluators can satisfy the demand for effects without carefully considering, through the auspices of process evaluation, the program mechanisms that produce these effects.

The negative result of evaluating outcomes without knowledge of implementation is that stakeholders receive very little information upon which to act (26). That is, even though an experimentally based evaluation may demonstrate that an intervention produces intended effects, if the implementation processes of a campaign are not accounted for through a formal process evaluation, there is very little basis for taking action to improve a program because stakeholders lack information about what produced the observed outcomes (26). For example, if an evaluation of a PSA campaign to increase moderate physical activity among adults in a particular community does not include surveillance to determine what proportion of the target audience is exposed to the PSA, it is impossible to attribute observed effects to the intervention. Weiss (42) makes this point wherein she says: Does it make any difference...whether the program is using rote drill, psychoanalysis, or black magic? There are evaluators who are sympathetic to such an approach. They see the program as a black box, the contents of which do not concern them; they are charged with discovering effects. But, if the evaluator has no idea of what the program really is, s/he may fail to ask the right questions (26). The point is, without process evaluation, one cannot differentiate between a bad campaign and one that is poorly implemented. This is particularly true if one is trying to improve campaign effects through modifying, enhancing and, if necessary, eliminating campaign processes. In sum, the best evaluation considers both processes and effects.

Theoretical Considerations and Cause/Effect Attributions

Although many recognize the importance of both process and summative evaluation, these assessments are sometimes conducted independently as if there is no connection between the two. This results in a post hoc cut-and-paste job where, after the data are collected on both process and outcome markers, the evaluators attempt to link effects with specific processes. To prevent this, we advocate that health communication evaluators clearly delineate, a priori, linkages between program processes and intended outcomes. The importance of this is explained by Patton (26), Weiss (40), and Chen (41) who all state that evaluators should define a campaigns theory of action before initiating evaluation. That is, before beginning the evaluation, each important intervention process (independent variable) should be explicitly linked with each desired outcome (dependent variable). This approach is often referred to as theory-based evaluation (41).

In theory-based evaluation, the standard for comparison is the program's theory, or sub-theories, if the evaluation is aimed at examining sub-components of the program. Therefore, the first phase in theory-based evaluation is theory construction. This requires an understanding of what program theories are and how best to develop them.

If the program theory is examined as a whole, only one program theory is necessary. However, if one wants to know about different sub-components—domains of the program theory, as Chen (41) refers to them—such as its development, delivery, cost, or effects domain, a separate sub-theory must be constructed for each program domain to be evaluated. Chen (41) notes that program theory domains can be considered independently (basic types) or in some combination (composite types). In short, the evaluator must construct a separate theory for each basic and/or composite domain selected for a theory-based evaluation, with each theory serving as a standard of comparison.

The idea of comparing what theoretically should happen to what actually happens, in terms of the performance of the program, and/or comparing a problem theory against the reality of the problem as discovered by a theory-based evaluation is a rather simple notion. What is not so straightforward is how to construct a problem theory or an expected program theory of action (i.e., the standard of comparison) that accurately reflects how a program is supposed to perform and the nature of the problem(s) it is designed to overcome. Fortunately, a number of different strategies have been developed to assist with this process (40, 43, 44).

These strategies help users systematically construct program development, implementation, and cause/effect theories and sub-theories that serve as standards of comparison against which evaluation data can be compared to identify the extent of discrepancy or congruence that exists between how the campaign activities are supposed to bring about intended effects and what actually happens (44).

Changing an Intervention During the Evaluation

Evaluation is an iterative process designed to provide relevant and timely feedback to stakeholders to make decisions aimed at improving the program. The implicit assumption is that if this feedback dictates the need to change the program to improve it, the program should be changed, particularly with social marketing programs where the aim is to respond rapidly to feedback. However, changing a program is at odds with the scientific dictum to standardize or keep the intervention constant throughout the course of an evaluation.

To overcome these conflicting purposes we suggest that evaluators and program implementers agree, from the outset, to an appropriate schedule specifying when feedback will be reported and, if appropriate, changes in the program will be made. Threats to the validity of the findings can be minimized by ensuring that: 1) changes in the campaign processes are documented, 2) process evaluation tracking protocols are modified to account for these changes; and 3) measurements are taken on key outcome variables both before and after important changes are made in the implementation process. This will ensure the constancy needed to pick up effects that may result from changes in the campaign processes while allowing planners to respond to timely and relevant feedback that can be used to improve the program.

Summative Evaluation Issues

Summative evaluation of a mass-mediated health communication program assesses whether the intended audience was reached and the impact and outcome objectives of the program were achieved to the satisfaction of the stakeholders. In this section we will discuss issues around both of these types of summative assessment.

Issues Pertaining to the Summative Assessment of Reach

In order for a message to have a desired influence, receivers must first attend to it (5). Hence, an early effect of communication that must be observed in a summative evaluation is whether the intended audience paid attention to the desired message. As stated previously, even if a program is implemented as planned, and desired effects result, these effects can not be attributed to the intervention unless there is evidence that the campaign actually reached the intended audience.

A necessary first step in determining whether the intended audience was reached by mass communication messages is to determine whether a message airs and the number of times it airs. If one can afford paid advertising, this process is greatly simplified because the time, place, and frequency of airing can be controlled. However, for a number of reasons—with cost being a leading factor— paid advertising is seldom used by public sector health communicators in the United States.

When paid advertising is not an option in a mass media campaign, health communicators often rely on PSAs which are aired at no cost to the producer. Unfortunately, airing of PSAs in the U.S. is at the discretion of Public Service Directors at the various television and radio stations, making the tracking of airings difficult. Attempts to overcome these difficulties have included relying on services that monitor commercials and PSAs. For example, Nielson Media Sigma Service (NMSS) operates an electronic tracking service that detects the airing of PSAs in over 1,100 broadcast stations (including 40 Spanish language stations) in all 211 designated market areas plus 28 national cable networks. This service ascertains the number of times a PSA plays, the market(s) where it played, the station call letters, air date, and air time. This monitoring goes on 24 hours a day, seven days a week.

To get some idea concerning the extended reach of broadcast and print media that may have been triggered by our mass media campaigns, we consistently track both broadcast and print media. The services used to track broadcast media is called Video Monitoring Services, Inc. (VMS). The print news tracking service we use is Lexis-Nexis.

VMS monitors news and public affairs programming in 46 of the top media markets. This includes 300 local television stations and 50 network and cable channels such as CNN, CNBC and MS-NBC. VMS also monitors selected news radio programming generated by 60 radio stations in 15 of the top media markets.

Lexis-Nexis continually updates and maintains a Regional News library which consists of a combination of news sources grouped together by geographical area. It contains more than 125 fulltext U.S. regional news sources together with selected documents from Business Dateline, ABI/INFORM, and abstracts from Miami Herald and Philadelphia Inquirer. The UPI State & Regional wire service is also included.

Together, NMSS, VMS and Lexis-Nexis services allow us to estimate the overall reach of both broadcast and print media. Although these data satisfy the need to determine whether, when, and where a PSA is aired, along with the extended reach of collateral media that may have been triggered by the campaign, these services and the data they generate do not account for who attended to, comprehended, and yielded to the key messages of a campaign. Further audience research must be carried out to make this determination.

In the U.S., to determine who was watching or whether those who were watching were attending to the central messages broadcast on television as a part of a national health communication campaign one can rely on services like the Nielson Station Index (NSI) which generates information regarding the TV viewing behavior of individuals (>100,000) living in randomly selected households in each of the U.S. TV markets. NSI characterizes viewers demographically by their age and gender. Data are collected using diaries for each TV in a participating home. Participants record the programs they watch and for how long, the station the program was aired on, and the date and time the program was aired. Data collected with diaries are further verified and adjusted based on TV set meters that electronically capture household viewing events in a sample of TV markets.

To further characterize the audiences who may have viewed a particular message, NSI data can be merged with geo-psychographic data aggregated into neighborhood clusters that represent demographic and/or psychographic profiles of individuals living in different neighborhoods in various locations across the U.S. Merging these data with NSI data allows for the indirect approximation of the psychographic characteristics of those who view a message in question. For example, through their PRIZM cluster analysis system the Claritas Corporation— perhaps the most prominent vendor of geo-psychographic data clusters—provides information on households categorized to one of 62 neighborhood audience segments based on six criterion factors: social rank, household composition, residential mobility, ethnicity, urbanization, and types of housing. Also available in the database is information on media habits, small and large purchase patterns, political beliefs, geographic location, and demographics. The point here is that the process of merging a variety of data sets allows for an indirect approximation of who is watching what and when they are watching.

What is still missing, however, is whether these audiences attended to the messages. Some approaches to determining whether a particular audience attended to and comprehended messages are to: 1) conduct a general population survey to determine audience awareness of a campaign; 2) add specific relevant questions to an Omnibus survey; 3) rely on data collected in national probability sample surveys; and/or 4) add tags to a televised message which are designed to motivate viewers to call a particular number for more information with the assumption that a burst of calls just after the airing of a the message with such a tag almost certainly indicates the audience attended to the messages. Questions directed at those who call in can help further determine whether those who attended to the message actually understood it. All of these summative evaluation approaches have been used at the CDC in attempts to monitor the reach of our HIV/AIDS health communication efforts carried out by what was the National AIDS Information and Education Program (45).

As with tracking electronic media, one must be highly creative in determining who is exposed to messages in newspapers or magazines and even more so with collateral materials such as brochures, flyers, posters, and billboards. This often becomes labor intensive and expensive.

Issues Around Assessing Intended Effects

Flay and Cook (46) have identified three models which have been used to conduct summative evaluations of health communication program effects. These are the advertising model, the impact-monitoring model, and the experimental model. The advertising model is used most frequently and consists of a baseline survey before the program is implemented followed by another survey at the end of the program. The evaluation of the Cancer Prevention Awareness Campaign (47) is a representative example of this approach. A national probability survey was conducted before the launch of the campaign and again a year later, after a multi-channel cancer prevention campaign was implemented. Materials included booklets, radio and TV PSAs, and special events. The evaluation compared knowledge of risk factors and concern about cancer before and after the campaign. This evaluation model is simple and often criticized because the lack of a control group prohibits establishing a direct cause and effect relationship between the campaign and its outcomes.

The impact-monitoring model uses routinely collected data from a management information system to monitor outcomes and impacts of a health communication campaign. For example, as part of their evaluation of the national AIDS campaign, CDC examined knowledge, attitude, and behavior measures from its annual National Health Interview Surveys. This method is easy and cost-effective, but it usually measures only behavioral outcomes and often fails to provide information which can explain successes and failures.

The experimental model contrasts two or more equivalent groups, one of which is a no-treatment control group. An anti-smoking campaign, designed to recruit women cigarette smokers with young children to call for information on quitting, used this evaluation model (48). The campaign included a mix of professionally produced broadcast and print media which encouraged mothers who were smokers to call the National Cancer Institute's Cancer Information Service (CIS) for information on quitting. Careful placement of media messages was possible because paid advertising was used. Fourteen media markets in New York, Pennsylvania, and Delaware were size-matched and one of each pair was randomly assigned to the experimental group who received the campaign and the other to the control group. Response to the campaign was gauged by monitoring calls to the area CIS offices from smokers residing in these experimental and control media markets. This model is usually considered the most rigorous, but has been challenged as inappropriate for evaluating what is essentially a messy social process (49).

The choice of an appropriate model of evaluation depends on an understanding of the way health communication campaigns work. Hornick (49) presented a compelling argument against the controlled randomized experimental design. He contrasted the limited effects attributed to such well-known community-based health promotion efforts as Stanford's Three and Five City Studies, the Minnesota and Pawtucket Heart Health Programs, and the Community Intervention Trial for Smoking Cessation (COMMIT) with the impressive evidence of behavioral change from the National High Blood Pressure Education and Control Program (NHBPEP), the original televised smoking counter-advertising campaign between 1967 and 1970, the public communication around the AIDS epidemic in the U.S., and the current California antismoking campaign. He attributed this surprising contrast in effectiveness to the constraints imposed by the research design itself. It is quite misleading to think that no background communication on a health issue is occurring in control communities; treatment communities may only have slightly more exposure to messages about these issues. Stanford, for example, claimed that it provided 25 hours of exposure on average to heart disease messages over five years in its treatment communities. This estimate suggests that most people only received one hour of messages per year on each of the five behaviors promoted. Hornick (49) contrasted this limited exposure to the more intense scale of the NHBPEP which represents the complex social diffusion process—deliberate communication messages, the conversations that ensue, the coverage by other media sources, the demands put on institutions which then respond, health institutions which offer different advice and treatments, the commercial institutions which make new products and advertise different benefits, and on the political institutions which change public policy to be supportive of the health behaviors. He argued that communication is a social process, not a pill, and should be evaluated as such.

Hornick's reasoning also reinforces the difficulty in disentangling communication effects from those of other intervention components or disentangling the effects of several communication activities. If we assume that a complex social change process has occurred, we have to either develop more sophisticated tools for measuring this diffusion process and disentangling its separate components or be content with assessing overall effects without attribution to individual components of the intervention. It may be reasonable to expect practitioners to do only the latter in routine evaluations of campaigns but to ask health communication researchers to design studies to capture this complex social diffusion process and discover how individual communication components contribute to it.

Above all, we must resist the effort to design rigorous, controlled experimental studies that strive to compare the effects of individual communication products such as pamphlets, PSAs, and posters with the goal of answering which product is the most effective to use across all situations. That kind of evaluation is inconsistent with the research and practice literature that recommends multiple messages and channels and cautions that finding the right channels to reach the right audiences with the right messages delivered by the right sources at the right times is best answered with formative research conducted early in the campaign development.

Even after an appropriate evaluation design is selected, summative evaluations of health communication campaigns face some serious methodological issues. The most common problems are described in the following sections.

Measurement Problems

Frequently, health communication components of interventions have several objectives. One of the most critical measurement problems involves determining which effects to measure. Earlier we described these potential effects, i.e., the individual has to attend to the message, comprehend it, relate it to other information he has, yield to it, and translate his new beliefs into behaviors that are then tested repeatedly. Does the evaluator measure comprehension, attitude change, or behavior change? One might argue that the further along this chain you measure, the more important the effects. On the other hand, the potential effects of the messages decrease as one measures further along this chain, as does ability to control extraneous variables. For example, is it realistic to assume that the direct cause of a smoker quitting is an anti-smoking PSA? Undoubtedly, the causal chain is more complicated than that. In addition, many behavioral changes advocated in health messages are impossible to observe directly. For example, how can hypertensives' use of medication or a woman's breast self-examination be observed? In such cases, self-reported behavior is measured. Such measurement is subject to error because of the tendency to over-report socially desirable behavior. Some evaluations are able to validate self-report measures with behavioral or physiological data. For example, smoking cessation studies often validate a percentage of their self-report measures with saliva continine testing and proxy data from people who are willing to observe the smoking behavior of an individual who participates in the cessation program.

Most summative evaluations of health communication programs attempt to measure exposure to the messages by questioning respondents about their recall of the messages. Unaided recall generally produces an artificially low estimate of audience exposure. Most evaluators use some form of aided recall; that is, they provide the respondent with some information about the message and then ask if the respondent remembers hearing or seeing it. With the use of aided recall, however, there will be some over reporting of exposure. Over-reporting occurs when respondents acquiesce or try to be helpful by giving what they think is the desired answer. In an attempt to avoid over-reporting, verbatim descriptions of the messages often are requested. Only respondents whose descriptions can be clearly tied to the message in question are identified as having been exposed. This approach requires rigorous coding procedures to classify the respondents.

A measurement compromise we suggest is the use of unaided questions followed by a series of aided questions, such as, ARecently, ads showing fatal car accidents in which seat belts were not worn have been broadcast. Have you seen any of these ads? Estimates of the magnitude of error due to over-reporting can be calculated based on measure of (spurious) reported awareness among respondents not exposed to the ads (i.e., in a control condition) or on reported awareness to bogus messages.

Sampling Problems

As we described in an earlier section of the paper, most mass media health communication campaigns are targeted to a specific segment of the audience but the evaluation frequently is not limited to that segment. When sampling for a post campaign evaluation, how does one find women who have not had a mammogram, individuals who build campfires in the forest, hypertensives who do not take their medication regularly, or drivers who do not wear seat belts? At best, there are some demographic data available, but these are far from perfectly descriptive of the target group. This difficulty in identifying the target group is compounded by the frequently low exposure to many of these messages. It is not uncommon for recall of a health message to be as low as 10 percent. Consequently, every random sample of 1,000 may only yield 100 persons who remember seeing the message. Imagine how these numbers decrease if we are looking for women who have not had a mammogram who recall seeing messages recommending mammograms. Most surveys used to measure the effectiveness of health messages need to screen respondents carefully, a time-consuming and costly process.

Summary and Discussion

Because of communications varied roles in public health interventions, there are a number of issues involved in evaluating health communication campaigns. This paper has highlighted these issues and provided a number of ways to resolve them within the context of formative, process, and summative evaluation.

Formative evaluation of health communication campaigns involves conducting research to assist in developing the most effective communication strategy and then testing that mix to forecast how effective it will be in reaching communication objectives. This entails breaking the audience into smaller homogeneous segments and then characterizing, or profiling, those segments in order to more closely tailor campaign messages and implementation. Profiling audience segments can best be accomplished with the benefit of datasets that include both etiologic data on the distribution and determinants of health problems that may be mitigated by mass communication, and information on variables that allow planners to understand how to best communicate with each audience targeted by the communication strategy (50).

Formative evaluation carried out prior to the implementation of a communication strategy is key to ensuring that the strategy is feasible, produces intended effects in each target audience, and does no harm. While it is consider an indispensable formative evaluation method, there are some issues surrounding how pre-testing is carried out. Namely, which research methods should be employed and how they are used in the pre-testing process. In this vein, we recommend that formative evaluators judiciously select quantitative and qualitative methods that are best suited to pre-testing and that these methods are employed in a technically acceptable manner.

Once a mass media health communication campaign is underway, process evaluation begins to assess how the program is rolling out and working. Without knowing how the campaign worked, we cannot determine whether the program brought about desired effects or if other factors influenced those effects. This knowledge is also critical in determining what aspects of a mass media campaign should be changed or eliminated, if any, to improve the campaign. We recommend applying the principals of theory-based evaluation to construct models that explicitly state how the program will bring about intended effects in order to have a basis for comparing how the program actually worked. Furthermore, we recommend that health communication researchers design studies to capture the complex social diffusion process that occurs in and around a mass media campaign in an effort to systematically discover how individual communication components contribute to the campaign process as a basis for explaining and replicating them when they work.

Process evaluation can be used to determine a program's effectiveness while it is ongoing. This allows for changes to be made to a program midstream in order to increase the likelihood of desired outcomes. Implementers and evaluators of the program should agree from the outset on a schedule for reporting feedback and making informed changes in the campaign to assure its maximum relevance, efficiency and effectiveness.

Summative evaluation of a mass media health communication campaign aims to determine whether the intended audience was reached and the objectives of the program were achieved. This type of evaluation, however, is complicated by several factors.

First, while we can monitor whether messages were disseminated, it is more difficult to assess whether the intended audience was exposed to the messages and attended to them. In the case of PSAs in a national media campaign, for example, a broadcast play verification company can help determine if the intended audience was exposed to the campaign's messages. But to find out if the audience attended to those messages, it is often necessary to conduct surveys, rely on data collected in national probability sample surveys, or use tags on PSAs that are designed to motivate viewers to call a particular number for more information. The latter method assumes that a burst of calls just after a PSA's airing will indicate the audience saw and paid attention to the PSA.

To determine whether the campaign messages had the intended effect(s), we can employ one of three models: advertizing, impact-modeling, and experimental. The advertizing model, consisting of a baseline survey before the campaign's implementation and another after its conclusion, is most frequently used, but it is also draws criticism because it lacks a control group. The impact-monitoring model uses routinely collected data from a management information system to monitor behavioral outcomes and impacts of the campaign. This method, while easy and cost-effective, fails to provide information that explains success or failure. The experimental model contrasts two or more equivalent groups, one of which is a no-treatment control group. We argue that this method is imperfect because it assumes that no background communication is going on in control communities, a belief that is unrealistic.

Even after a summative evaluation design is selected, a number of concerns arise. When using surveys, over-reporting can result, especially when dealing with socially desirable behaviors. For example, will drivers who say they saw PSAs on safety belts admit that they do not use them? There is also difficulty in identifying the target audience after the campaign. Exposure may be low, many people may have forgotten seeing a message, and people may not admit to seeing a message if they have not adopted the behavior encouraged in the message.

We have identified and discussed issues that are important to consider in the conduct of formative, process, and summative evaluations of mass media health communication campaigns. These issues and our recommendations pertaining how they might be resolved should provide a basis for further improvements in conceptualizing, planning, implementing, and reporting feedback on evaluations aimed at improving mass media health communication campaigns to promote health-enhancing behaviors.

Acknowledgements

Carole Craft and Linda Cockrill for editing the paper

References

1. McGinnis, J.M., & Foege, W.H. Actual causes of death in the United States. Journal of the American medical association, 270:18, 2207–2212 (1993).

2. Rogers, E. M. & Storey, J. D. Communication campaigns. In: Berger, C. & Chaffee, S., eds. Handbook of communication science. Sage Publications, Newbury Park, California, United States, 1987.

3. Flora, J. A., & Maibach, E. W. Cognitive responses to AIDS information: The effects of issue involvement and message appeal. Communication research, 759–774, (1990, December).

4. Flay, B.R., DiTecco, D., & Schlegel, R.P. Mass media in health promotion: An analysis using extended information-processing model. Health education quarterly 7(2):127–147 (1980).

5. McGuire, W. J. (1989). Theoretical foundations of campaigns. In: Rice, R. E., & Atkin, C.K., eds. Public communications campaigns (2nd ed., pp. 43–65). Sage Publications, Newbury Park, California, United States, 1989.

6. Sutton, S. M., Balch, G., & Lefebvre, C. Strategic Questions For Consumer-Based Health Communications. In: 5 a day for better health: NCI media campaign strategy (pp. 1-12). Washington D.C.: National Cancer Institute, 1993.

7. Gorn, G.J. The effects of music in advertising on choice behavior: A classical conditioning approach. Journal of marketing, 46: 94–101 (1982).

8. Messaris, P. Visual persuasion, Sage Publications, Thousand Oaks, California, United States, 1997.

9. Donohew, L., Lorch, E., & Palmgreen, P. Sensation seeking and targeting of televised anti-drug PSAs. In: Donohew, L., Sypher, H., & Bukoski, W. eds.

Persuasive communication and drug abuse prevention, Lawrence Earlbaum Associates, Hillsdale, New Jersey, United States, 1991, pp. 209–226.

10. Prochaska, J.O., Norcross, J.C., & DiClemente, C.C. Changing for good, Avon Books, Inc., New York, New York, United States, 1994, pp. 287–289.

11. Backer, T.E., Roger, E.M., and Sopory, P. (1992). Generalizations about health communication campaigns. In: Designing health communication campaigns: What works? Sage Publications, Newbury Park, California, United States, 1992, pp. 30–32.

12. Petty, R. E., Cacioppo, J. T., & Schumann, D. Central and peripheral routes to advertising effectiveness: The moderating role of involvement. Journal of consumer research, 1983, September, pp. 135–146.

13. Atkin, C. & Freimuth, V. (1989). Formative Evaluation Research in Campaign Design. In: Rice, R. & Atkin, C., eds. Public communication campaigns, 2nd ed., Sage Publications, Newbury Park, California, United States, 1989, pp. 131–150.

14. Maibach, E.W., Maxfield, A.M., Ladin, K., & Slater, M.D. Translating health psychology into effective health communication: The American healthstyles audience segmentation project. Journal of health psychology, 1(3): 261–277, (1996).

15. Slater, M.D. Theory and method in health audience segmentation. Journal of health communication, 1: 267–283, (1996).

16. Slater, M.D. Choosing audience segmentation strategies and methods for health communication. In: Maibach, E. & Parrott, R. L., eds. Designing health messages: Approaches from communication theory and public health practice, Sage Publications, Thousand Oaks, California, United States, 1995, pp. 169–185.

17. Slater, M. & Flora, J.A. Health Lifestyles: Audience segmentation analysis for public health interventions. Health education quarterly, 18(2): 221–233, (1991).

18. Patterson, R.E., Hanes, P.S., & Popkin, B.M. Health lifestyle patterns of U.S. adults. Preventive medicine, 23: 453–460, (1994).

19. Maibach, E. Psychobehavioral segmentation: Identifying audiences and tailoring cancer prevention programs. Presentation to the Harvard Center for Cancer Prevention, Harvard School of Public Health, December 4, 1996.

20. Maibach E.W. & Cotton, D. Moving people to behavior change: A staged social cognitive approach to message design. In: Maibach, E.W. & Parrott, R. L., eds. Designing health messages: Approaches from communication theory and

public health practice, Sage Publications, Thousand Oaks, California, United States, 1995, pp. 169–185.

21. Velicer, W.F., Hughes, S.L., Fava J.L., Prochaska, J.O., & DiClemente, C.C. An empirical typology of subjects within stage of change. Addictive behaviors, 20(3): 299–320, (1995).

22. Williams, J.E. & Flora, J.A. Health behavior segmentation and campaign planning to reduce cardiovascular disease risk among Hispanics. Health education quarterly, 22(1): 36–48, (1995).

23. Morris, L.A., Tabak, E.R. & Lins, N.J. A segmentation analysis of prescription drug intervention-seeking motives among the elderly. Journal of public relations and marketing, 11: 115–125, (1992).

24. Albrecht, T.L. & Bryant, C. Advances in segmentation modeling for health communication and social marketing campaigns. Journal of health communication, 1: 65–80, (1996).

25. Behavioral Risk Factor Surveillance Survey. State- and sex-specific prevalence of selected characteristics--behavioral risk factor surveillance system, 1994 and 1995. Morbidity and mortality weekly report. 46:(SS-3), August 1, 1997.

26. Patton, M.P. Utilization-focused evaluation. Sage Publications, Thousand Oaks, California, United States, 1986.

27. Freimuth, V. Developing public service advertisement for nonprofit contexts. In: Belk, R.W., ed. Advances in nonprofit marketing, JAI Press, Inc., Greenwich, Connecticut, United States, 1985, pp. 55–94.

28. Cole, G., Pogostin, C., Westover, B., Rios, N., & Collier, C. Addressing problems in evaluating health-relevant programs through a systematic planning and evaluation model. Risk: Issues in health, safety and environment , 6(1), 37–57, (1995).

29. Krueger, R.A. Focus groups: A practical guide for applied research, second edition. Sage Publications, Thousand Oaks, California, United States, 1994.

30. Stewart D.W., & Shamdasani, P.N. Focus groups: theory and practice. In: Applied social science research methods series, Volume 20. Sage Publications, Newbury Park, California, United States, 1990.

31. Templeton, J.F. The focus group (revised edition). Irwin Professional Publishing, Burr Ridge, Illinois, United States, 1994.

32. Crabtree, B. F. & Miller, W. L. Doing qualitative research: Research methods for primary care, Volume 3 (pp 3–28). Sage Publications Inc., Newbury Park, California, United States, 1992.

33. U.S. Department of Health and Human Services. Making health communication programs work. NIH Publication Number 92–1493, April, 1992.

34. Patton, M. Q. How to use qualitative methods in evaluation. Sage Publications. Newbury Park, California, United States, 1987.

35. U.S. Department of Health and Human Services. Pretesting in health communications: methods, examples, and resources for improving health messages and materials. NIH Publication Number 84-1493. January, 1984.

36. Shimp, T.A. Promotion management and Marketing Communications, 2nd ed. The Dryden Press, Chicago, Illinois, United States, 1990, pp. 428–432.

37. PACT Document. Journal of Advertizing. 11(4): 4–29, 1982.

38. Stewart, D. W. Furse, D. H., & Kozak, R. P. A Guide to Commercial Copytesting Services. In: Leigh, J. H. & Martin, C. R. Jr., eds. Current issues and research in advertising (Ann Arbor, MI: Division of Research, Graduate School of Business, University of Michigan. 1983, pp.1–44.

39. Gardner, D.E. Five evaluation frameworks. Journal of higher education, 48(5): 571–593, (1977).

40. Weiss, C.H. Nothing as practical as good theory: exploring theory-based evaluation for comprehensive community initiatives for children and families. In: Connell, J. P., Kubisch, A. C., Schorr, L. B. & Weiss, C. H., eds. New Approaches to evaluating community initiatives: Concepts, methods, and contexts. The Aspen Institute, Queenstown, Maryland, United States, 1995, pp. 65–92.

41. Chen, H. Theory-driven evaluations. Sage Publications, Thousand Oaks, California, United States, 1990.

42. Weiss, C.H. Evaluation research: Methods of assessing program effectiveness. Prentice-Hall, Englewood Cliffs, United States, 1972.

43. Shern, D.L., Trochum, W.M.K., & LaComb, C.A. The use of concept mapping for assessing fidelity of model transfer: an example from psychiatric rehabilitation. Evaluation and program planning, 18(2): 143–153, 1995.

44. Cole, G. E. Advancing the development and application of theory-based evaluation in the practice of public health. American Journal of Evaluation, 20(3): 453–470, 1999.

45. Nowak, G.J., & Siska M.J. Using research to inform campaign development and message design: Examples from the America Responds to AIDS Campaign. In: Maibach, E. W., & Parrott, R. L., eds. Designing health messages: approaches from communication theory and public health practice. Sage Publications, Thousand Oaks, California, United States, 1995, pp. 169–185.

46. Flay B.R., & Cook, T.D. Three models for summative evaluation of prevention campaigns with a mass media component. In Rice, R. and Atkin, C. (Eds.), Public communication campaigns, 2nd ed. Sage Publications, Newbury Park, California, United States, 1989, pp. 175–196.

47. U.S. Department of Health and Human Services. Technical report on cancer prevention awareness survey wave II. Bethesda, MD: National Institutes of Health, 1986.

48. Cummings, K. M., Sciandra, R., Davis, S., & Rimer, B. Results of an anti-smoking campaign utilizing the Cancer Information Service. Monographs - National Cancer Institute, 14: 113–118, 1993.

49. Hornick, R. Public health communication: Making sense of contradictory evidence. Presentation at the Annenburg public policy center public health communication meeting, Washington, D.C., 1997.

50. Chervin, D.D., Nowak, G.N., & Cole, G.E. Using audience research in designing public health initiatives at the federal level. Social Marketing Quarterly. 5(3): 34–39, September 1999.

The Impact of Mass Media Campaigns on Intentions to Use the Female Condom in Tanzania

Sohail Agha and Ronan Van Rossem

ABSTRACT

Objective

To determine whether a mass media campaign to promote the use of the female condom had an impact on intentions to use the female condom among men and women of reproductive age in Tanzania.

Methods

We used data on 2712 sexually experienced men and women in Tanzania from an exit survey conducted at outlets that sell the female condom. Respondents were asked about their exposure to mass media campaigns, peer education, and a medical provider's explanation of the female condom. They were also asked about their intention to use female condoms in the future. Path analysis was used to determine the impact of mass media, peer education, and a provider's explanation on intentions to use the female condom.

Results

A relatively small proportion of respondents were reached by a peer educator or by a provider: about 6% were exposed to peer education and 6% were given an explanation by a provider on use of the female condom. In contrast, about 38% of respondents were exposed to mass media campaigns promoting the female condom. For both men and women, mass media significantly increased the likelihood that a man or a woman would discuss use of the female condom with a partner. In turn, discussion of the female condom with a partner strongly influenced the intention to use the female condom in the future. Although the reach of peer educators and providers was relatively low, the impact of these components of the intervention on an individual's intentions to use the female condom was stronger than the impact of mass media.

Conclusions

Mass media campaigns are likely to increase an individual's motivation to use condoms because they encourage the discussion of condom use with a partner. While mass media campaigns do not have as strong an impact on a particular individual's motivation to use condoms as do peer educators or providers, mass media campaigns have a substantial impact at the population level because of their considerably greater reach.

Introduction

In order to change sexual behavior for AIDS prevention, social marketing programs balance the use of mass media with the use of interpersonal communications. Experimental studies have shown that interpersonal communication approaches, such as peer education and provider promotion of contraceptive methods, can have a significant impact on contraceptive use. However, evidence of the magnitude and quality of impact that mass media campaigns have on promoting change in behavior is less readily available. In part, this is because of the difficulty of designing experimental studies to measure the impact of mass media campaigns (Sherry, 1997; Kim et al., 2001).

In the absence of experimental studies, it is still possible to estimate the impact of mass media campaigns on condom use by using path analysis. Path analysis is a regression-based approach that uses cross sectional data but permits the ordering of a set of variables in a manner consistent with causal interpretation (Duncan,

1966). In this study, we use path analysis to assess whether a mass media campaign to promote use of the female condom had an impact on intentions to use the female condom among men and women of reproductive age in Tanzania. Previous research has shown that the intention to use a contraceptive method is a powerful predictor of future use of a method (Curtis et al., 1993).

Background

Based on experience in developed countries, a substantial body of communications literature has shown that exposure to mass media campaigns is not necessary and sufficient to produce changes in behavior. In fact, usually, mass media messages reinforce attitudes and produce small changes in beliefs: it is less common for mass media to convert a person from one opinion to another. The effect of mass media on behavior is indirect and operates through various factors. For example, how people communicate with each other about the mass media messages that they are exposed to may determine their response (Klapper, 1969).

In developing countries, many analyses of cross sectional surveys have shown strong associations between exposure to mass media and contraceptive use (Westoff and Rodríguez, 1995; Kincaid et al., 1996, Kim and Marangwanda, 1997; Kane et al., 1998; Jato et al., 1999). Because self-selection may explain the association between exposure to mass communication messages and contraceptive use (i.e. those who are already convinced about the usefulness of contraception may be more likely to remember contraceptive use messages), cross-sectional associations cannot be interpreted as evidence of an impact of mass media campaigns (Sherry, 1997). Instead, the identification of plausible mechanisms through which mass media has its impact is likely to be important in developing an understanding of how and to what extent does mass media impact on behavior or its antecedents.

Diffusion theorists postulate that mass media affects contraceptive use by stimulating the discussion of contraceptive use between partners (Rogers et al., 1999). Studies show that informal personal appeals have a very strong effect (Klapper, 1969). Through sharing information and mutual feedback, people give meaning to information, understand each other's views, and influence each other (Bandura, 1986). Thus, the discussion of contraceptive use between partners leads to the development of better understanding of reproductive health goals. Indeed perceived partner disapproval is an important deterrent to contraceptive adoption (Ezeh, 1993). When individuals' goals coincide or when agreement can be negotiated concerning the need for contraceptive use, couples are likely to implement contraceptive use. Several studies have shown that discussion of contraceptive use with a partner is highly predictive of future contraceptive adoption (Jato et al., 1999; Rogers et al., 1999). A recent studies shows that mass media campaigns can stimulate discussions of reproductive health issues (Kim et al., 2001), while another shows that the indirect effects of interventions on behavioral antecedents have a powerful impact on contraceptive behavior (Kincaid, 2000).

In this study, we assess whether mass media (radio and newspaper) promotion of the female condom motivated Tanzanian men and women to use the female condom. We evaluate whether mass media stimulates the discussion of female condom use and, in turn, discussion influences the intention to use the female condom. Aside from the mass media, the female condom intervention had two additional components: peer education and explanation by medical providers on how to use the female condom. Research shows that interventions that use mass media and interpersonal communication are particularly likely to have an impact on behavior (Agha, 2000; Ashford et al., 2000). Interpersonal influence is thought to have a greater impact than mass communication, although it is not a necessary factor in producing change (Klapper, 1969). We assess the impact of these two interpersonal communication components on the intention to use the female condom.

The Female Condom Intervention

Population Services International (PSI) introduced the female condom in Dar es Salaam towards the end of 1998. The Government of the Netherlands donated the female condoms to PSI. Resources for marketing the product were provided jointly by USAID and the Government of the Netherlands. PSI had experience in marketing the female condom through its programs in Zimbabwe and Zambia (Meekers, 1999; Agha, 2001a; Agha, 2001b) and lessons learnt in these two countries were used to develop the female condom marketing strategy for Tanzania. In addition, an acceptability study was implemented among 125 professional men and women in Dar es Salaam (Forrest, 1997; PSI Tanzania Quarterly Report, January to March 1998). Most participants in the acceptability study showed interest in using the female condom.

One of the fundamental issues related to the adoption of condoms in sub-Saharan Africa is the difficulty that women have in negotiating the use of condoms (Schoepf, 1988; Ulin, 1992; Mwale and Burnard, 1992). Because condoms carry the stigma of sexually transmitted infections (STIs), proposing condom use raises the issue that one does not trust one's partner or that one is infected. To prevent stigmatization of the female condom, PSI marketed the female condom as a contraceptive method that had the added benefit of STI protection. Research in Kenya has shown that male partners are more accepting of the female condom when it is introduced as a family planning method, even though women may actually use it for disease prevention (cited in Jones, 1999).

Messages that had been developed for the female condom intervention in Zimbabwe were pre-tested through focus groups with target audiences in Tanzania to ensure they were suitable for the Tanzanian social context. Consistent with messages in Zimbabwe and Zambia, the emphasis in the advertising and promotion was to provide women the language and tools to discuss and negotiate use of the female condom. Because the intervention was intended to promote the discussion of the female condom among partners, communications messages were targeted towards both men and women. The product was marketed as a method for couples who wanted to protect themselves against pregnancy and HIV. It was branded as "care," with the caption "For couples who care."

Mass media campaigns to promote the female condom were implemented during 1999. Radio campaigns promoting use of the female condom were implemented in April/May and in October/November 1999 (PSI Tanzania Quarterly Report, January-March 1999; PSI Tanzania Quarterly Report, July-September 1999). Newspapers were another important source of information about the female condom.

Focus groups were conducted to assess the effectiveness of the marketing strategy after approximately 8 months of the launch of care. These focus groups indicated that the strategy of emphasizing family planning and AIDS prevention messages had been effective: study participants associated use of the female condom with marital relationships but reported that the most important reason for their own use of the female condom was HIV prevention (Jones, 1999).

Interpersonal communication components were an integral part of the female condom intervention. Previous experience in sub-Saharan Africa had shown that peer counseling improves women's ability to negotiate the use of the female condom (Kabira et al., 1997) and communications between couples increased the acceptability of the female condom (Jones, 1999). Potential users were given a detailed explanation of the female anatomy by community-based peer educators and health care workers, such as nurses, doctors, and pharmacists, who were trained to counsel potential users.

Pharmacies were a logical primary distribution point for the female condom because the project intended to reach middle and upper income professional men and women. It was also sold through NGOs and community based agents and was priced at US$0.44 for a pack of two condoms. In contrast, PSI was marketing the Salama male condom to low-income individuals (3 Salama condoms could be purchased for US$0.06) (Agha and Meekers, 2000).

Data and Methods

Objectives of the Survey

The objectives of the 1999 Tanzania Female Condom Consumer Profile Survey (TFCCPS-99) were to determine a) the level of exposure that men and women of reproductive age had to the female condom mass-marketing intervention and b) the level of female condom use and c) the intention to use the female condom in the future.

What is a Consumer Profile Survey?

The TFCCPS-99 is an outlet-based exit survey in which respondents visiting pharmacies and NGOs are interviewed. Because people who visit commercial outlets are more likely to be wealthier than the general population, exit surveys tend to capture a higher socio-economic status population (Meekers and Ogada, 2001). Exit surveys can be a useful tool to measure the knowledge and use of products when they are first introduced because diffusion of new technologies usually starts with higher socio-economic status (SES) individuals.

Based on sales of the female condom, we estimated that the level of use of the female condom in the general population of reproductive age in Tanzania was below 1%. Therefore, instead of conducting a large and expensive household survey, we decided to conduct an exit survey. The methodology used in Tanzania was adapted from a similar survey conducted in Zambia (Agha, 2001b).

Sampling

The survey was restricted to outlets where the female condom was being sold: pharmacies and NGOs in Dar es Salaam. A multi-stage random sampling method was used to draw a representative sample of outlets. The first stage involved creating the master-sampling list of outlets that sold the care female condom and drawing a random sample that included 50% of all female condom outlets. The second stage involved randomly selecting eligible clients, men and women aged 15-49, at each selected outlet.

Out of the 67 outlets in the master list (58 pharmacies, and 9 NGOs), stratified random sampling was used to select 33 outlets (29 pharmacies and 4 NGOs). The probability that a pharmacy was selected was 0.5; for an NGO it was 0.44.

At each of the 33 outlets selected, women and men 15-49 who exited from the outlets were randomly selected for interviews. The number of clients entering the outlet during a particular day and the number of refusals were recorded for weighting purposes.

Questionnaire Development

Based on questionnaires used in Zimbabwe and Zambia (Meekers, 1999; Agha, 2001a), a quantitative questionnaire was developed for the TFCCPS-99. This questionnaire was adapted to the Tanzanian context. It was designed to gather information on socio-demographic characteristics of respondents, as well as information on knowledge, discussion, ever use, and intention to use the female condom. This questionnaire was translated into Kiswahili and pre-tested prior to survey implementation.

Data Collection, Entry and Cleaning

Twenty-six interviewers (13 female, 13 male) were recruited and participated in a five day training during December 1999. The training included an explanation of the survey objectives and methodology. Although the interviewers were experienced, refresher training was given on interviewing techniques. The questionnaire was discussed in detail and interviewers became familiar with it by conducting role-plays. The final day of training was used to administer practice interviews in the field. One interviewer dropped out on the first day of data collection because she fell ill and the remaining 25 interviewers (12 female, 13 male) collected the data. The data was collected the last week of December 1999 through January 2000. During data entry and cleaning, sixteen records were eliminated because of missing data, leaving 3,013 respondents.

Interviewers were deployed at outlets in pairs. This was done to collect information on client flows: one interviewer would interview a client while the other would count reproductive age men and women who entered the outlet. There were two shifts per day at each outlet. The first pair of interviewers (one female, one male) arrived at a provider outlet at 8:30 am and stayed till 1:00 p.m. The second pair arrived at the outlet at 1:00 p.m. and stayed there till 6:00 p.m. Because of the different working hours of NGOs, only one shift was conducted at NGO outlets (from 8:30 am to 2:30 p.m).

Weights

The data were weighted to take into account the different probabilities of selection of outlet types, of individuals at each outlet and the refusal rate at each outlet.

The probability of selection of individuals at each outlet and the refusal rate was obtained from client flow information. During the 13 days of fieldwork at 29 pharmacies and four NGO clinics, 11,175 adult men and women (15 years or older) visited these outlets. The frequencies reported here are based on weighted numbers but the number of cases shown is based on the unweighted numbers.

The Path Model and Variables

We use a simple model to assess the impact of mass media promotion on intentions to use the female condom in the future. Path analysis permits the assessment of both direct and indirect effects of exogenous variables on dependent variables. This is particularly useful in the case of assessing the impact of mass media on motivation because a) developed country literature indicates that mass media has an indirect effect on motivation and b) diffusion theory postulates that the impact of mass media on motivation operates through encouraging discussion between partners.

Exogenous variables include age (in completed years), number of years of formal schooling (in completed years) and partnership status (single vs. other). Components of the social marketing intervention including peer education, a medical provider's explanation of how to use the female condom, and exposure to radio or newspaper campaigns were treated as exogenous variables. Two jointly dependent (or endogenous) variables were included in the model: 1) discussion of the female condom with a partner and 2) the intention to use the female condom in the future.

This model is shown in Figure 1. Socio-demographic characteristics of respondents (age, marital status and education) serve as controls in the path model. We are primarily interested in the impact of peer educators, provider promotion and the mass media campaign on intentions to use the female condom. In particular, we are interested in exploring whether the effect of mass media is through promoting discussion of the female condom between partners or through another, unidentified, mechanism. We also want to assess the impact of peer education and provider promotion on the intention to use the female condom.

Statistical Analysis

To analyze the model depicted in Figure 1 we relied on structural equation modeling techniques. For the actual analysis the LISREL package was used (Jöreskog and Sörbom, 1996b). A two-group analysis was run using separate covariance matrices for men and women, which allowed us to test for differences in the causal pathways for men and women. The final models shown in Figures 2 and 3

were achieved in a three step process. In the first step a baseline model was estimated. In this model we assumed: 1) the presence of the structural model shown
in Figure 1 in which all exogenous variables (age, marital status, education, peer
education, provider explanation, and mass media messages) affect all endogenous
variables (discussion of FC with partner, and intention to use FC), and discussion of FC with partner also has an effect on the intention to use FC; and 2) that
the causal models for men and women are identical. The latter assumption was
achieved by implementing equality constraints on B and Γ matrices, i.e., by forcing the unstandardized regression coefficients in the male and female subsamples
to be equal. The fit for the baseline model was marginally acceptable with a x^2
of 45.9 with 13 df (p = 0.000) and a root mean square error of approximation
(RMSEA) of 0.043.

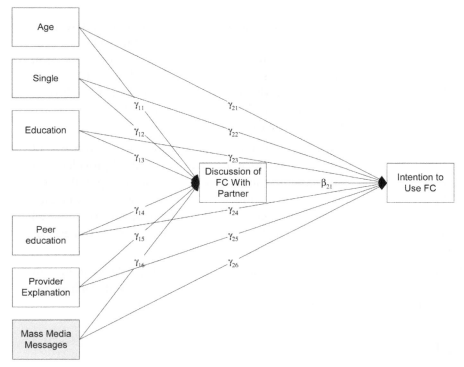

Figure 1

In the second step, modification indices (MI) were used to decide which
equality constraints should be lifted. As the MI follow a x^2-distribution with 1
df (Jöreskog and Sörbom, 1993, 1996 and 1996b), a MI of 3.814 or greater,
corresponding to a α of 5%, was considered indicative of an ill-fitting equality

constraint. This model had a x^2 of 6.93 with 9 df (p = 0.644) and an RMSEA of 0.0. This indicates a very good fit of the model and a significant improvement over the baseline model (x^2 (4) = 39.0, p = 0.000). In the third and final step the model was made more efficient by fixing non-significant regression coefficients to zero. The fit of this final model was a x^2 of 17.9 with 15 df (p = 0.267) and an RMSEA of 0.012. The fit of this final model was not significantly worse than that of the step 2 model (x^2 (6) = 11.0, p = 0.089). This final model is presented in Figures 2 and 3. All coefficients shown in these figures are significant at α = 5%. The correlations among the exogenous variables and residual effects are not shown in the figures. Coefficients estimated under an equality constraint are marked with 'α'.

Sample Description

About 10% of respondents (301 respondents out of 3,013) were not sexually experienced. Since sexually experienced persons were targeted for the female condom intervention, these 301 sexually inexperienced persons are not included in any of the subsequent analysis. All subsequent analysis is based on 2712 respondents (1186 women and 1526 men). The mean age of respondents was 29 years and the mean number of years of formal schooling completed was 13.4 years. About 42% of respondents were single (not shown).

Peer educators discussed the use of the female condom with about 6% of respondents (8% of women and 5% of men, p<0.01) and medical providers also reached about 6% of respondents (9% of women and 5% of men, p<0.01). Radio and newspaper promotion reached a much larger percentage of respondents. About 38% of respondents (41% of men and 34% of women, p<0.01) reported having received information about the female condom through radio or newspapers (not shown).

Approximately, 8% of respondents had discussed use of female condom with a partner, 11% intended to use the female condom in the future and 3% had ever used the female condom (no difference by gender, not shown).

Results

The models estimated and shown in Figures 2 and 3 predict a respondent's likelihood of discussing the female condom with their partner and the respondent's intention to use the female condom. The explained variance in the discussion of the female condom with one's partner is around 10% for both men and women. With regard to the explained variance in the intention to use the female condom, the model explains almost twice as much of the variance for the male sample (R^2 = 0.220) as for the female sample (R^2 = 0.117).

Impact of the Program on a Woman's Intentions

Figure 2 is the final model showing the pathways through which programmatic and socio-demographic variables influence a woman's intention to use the female condom. All paths shown in the model are statistically significant at p<0.05.

After controlling for all variables in the model, mass media does not directly impact a woman's intention to use the female condom, as is indicated by the absence of an arrow from the "mass media" variable to the "intention to use FC" variable in Figure 2. Mass media does have a statistically significant impact on intentions (total effect (TE) = 0.009, p < .010, standardized total effect (STE) = 0.014), but its effect operates through increasing discussion of the female condom between a woman and her partner. In turn, discussion of the female condom is a powerful predictor of a woman's intention to use the female condom. These findings are consistent with communications research which shows that mass media has an indirect impact on behavior.

Peer education has a relatively strong direct influence on a woman's intention to use the female condom, but does not affect her discussing the female condom with her partner. In contrast, the provider's explanation has a small direct effect on the intention to use the female condom and a substantial indirect effect (IE) (0.070 or 58% of TE, p < 0.001, standardized IE (SIE) = 0.067) by encouraging partner discussion of the female condom. The impact of peer education and provider's explanation on intentions to use the female condom confirm the importance of interventions that use interpersonal communication to promote use of the female condom.

Impact of Socio-Demographic Variables on a Woman's Intentions

Our analysis did not show any effect of age on a woman's intention to use the female condom. We expected a negative effect of age on intention to use the female condom because older women tend to be more interested in preventing pregnancy rather than STDs and because other reliable methods are available for family planning. It may also be that other demographic variables, such as marital status and education, explain the relationship between age and the intention to use the female condom. Consistent with this argument, single women are more likely to intend to use the female condom. A woman's level of education did not have a direct effect on her intention to use the female condom, but it did have a weak indirect effect on it by increasing the likelihood of discussing the female condom with a partner (TE = 0.002, p < 0.001, STE = 0.029). Overall, these findings are consistent with previous analyses of intentions to use the female condom (Agha, 2001a).

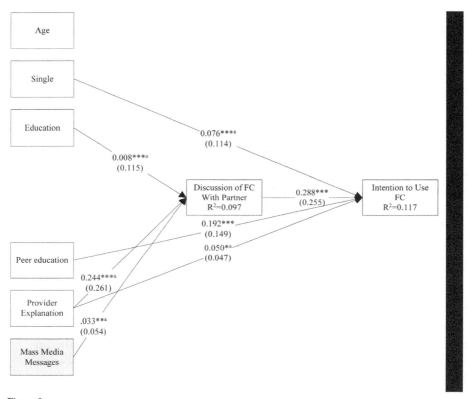

Figure 2

Impact of the Program on a Man's Intentions

Figure 3 shows the pathways through which socio-demographic and programmatic variables influence a man's intention to use the female condom. As before, all paths shown in the model are statistically significant at p<0.05.

A first observation here is that the effect of discussing the female condom with one's partner on one's intention to use the female condom among men is significantly greater than among women (0.444 vs. 0.288, respectively). Thus, the indirect effects of program and socio-demographic variables on one's intention to use the female condom are larger among men than among women.

As with women, after controlling for other variables, there is no direct influence of mass media on a man's intention to use the female condom. However, a man exposed to mass media messages about the female condom is significantly more likely to discuss use of the female condom with a partner—and discussion with a partner is predictive of a man's intention to use the female condom. These findings are consistent with findings regarding the impact of mass media on a woman's intentions. No significant gender differences were observed in the effect of mass media exposure on the respondent's discussion of the female condom with a partner. Although the total effect of mass media exposure on intention to use the female condom among men (TE = 0.014, p < 0.010, STE = 0.022) is somewhat larger than among women, the difference is not significant.

Consistent with the findings for women, peer education has a powerful direct influence on male intentions to use the female condom. Among men the direct effect is even larger than among women. Peer education also encourages a man to discuss use of the female condom with his partner. The total effect of peer education on his intention to use the female condom was 0.362 (p < 0.001, STE = 0.249), of which 22% was indirect (IE = 0.079, p < 0.001, SIE = 0.055). No gender differences were observed in the effect of a provider's explanation on either one's discussion of the female condom with one's partner or one's intention to use it.

Impact of Socio-Demographic Variables on a Man's Intentions

In contrast to women, older men are more likely to intend to use the female condom. The effect of marital status on one's intention to use the female condom was the same for men and women. Single men also had a higher intention to use the female condom than married men. As was the case among women, marital status did not affect a man's likelihood of discussing the female condom with his partner. Finally, a man's education increases the likelihood of his discussion of the female condom with a partner, while there is no direct relationship between his education and motivation to use the female condom. Again no gender differences were observed in the effects of education.

Discussion

The primary objective of this study was to assess the impact of mass media on male and female intentions to use the female condom, after an intervention which included mass media promotion of the female condom, peer education about the female condom and provider's explanation of how to use the female condom was implemented in Dar es Salaam. A secondary objective was to evaluate the impact of peer education and provider's explanation on intentions to use the female condom. We used a path analytic approach that allowed us to assess the impact of the different components on the female condom program on male and female intentions to use the female condom.

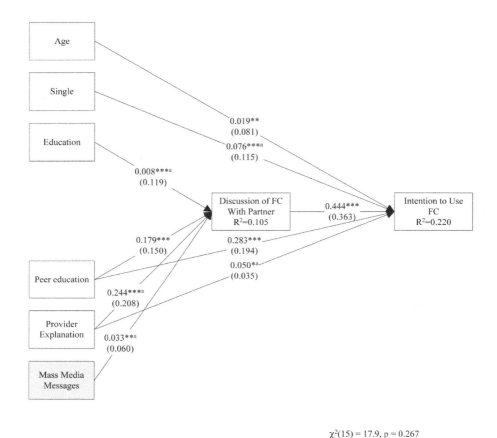

$\chi^2(15) = 17.9$, p = 0.267
RMSEA = 0.012
NNFI=0.995

Figure 3

Mass media had a significant positive impact on intentions to use the female condom—even after controlling for socio-demographic variables. Our findings are consistent with the interpretation that mass media promotion of the female condom motivated sexual partners to discuss use of the female condom, and that discussion of condom use exerted a strong influence on their intention to use the female condom. This pattern was observed for both men and women. Because lack of discussion of condoms between partners can be a significant barrier to condom use, mass media promotion of condoms is likely to have a positive impact on safer sex behavior.

Mass media was, however, only one of the program variables that had an impact on discussion of the female condom with a partner. Among women, a provider's explanation had a powerful impact on the likelihood of discussing the female condom with a partner. Among men, both peer education and a provider's explanation encouraged discussion of the female condom with a partner. These findings show that interpersonal interventions that encourage men and women to use condoms are, in part, successful because they increase discussion of condom use between partners.

The findings also show that an intervention that promotes the discussion of the female condom with a partner may be particularly successful in motivating men to use condoms (since the effect of discussion on intentions was significantly greater among men). For these reasons, peer education had a particularly strong impact on male intentions to use condoms.

Unlike mass media promotion, which had an indirect effect on the intention to use the female condom, peer education had a powerful direct impact on male and female intentions to use the female condom. These findings are consistent with previous research showing that peer education interventions are important in motivating individuals to adopt safer sex behaviors.

The impacts of the peer education and the provider component of the female condom program on intentions to use the method were larger than the impact of the mass media component. However, a relatively small proportion of respondents were reached by either a peer educator or by a provider: 6% of respondents were exposed to peer education and 6% were given an explanation about female condom use by a provider. In contrast, about 38% of respondents were reached by the mass media campaigns. Thus, mass media may have a less powerful impact on an individual's motivation to use a method than either peer education or provider explanation, but it is likely to have a substantial impact at the population level because of its considerably greater reach.

Studies have shown that the combination of interpersonal interventions and mass media campaigns are likely to have a measurable impact on reproductive behavior (Agha, 2000; Ashford, 2000). The findings of this study are consistent with previous research and show that interpersonal and mass media interventions have independent effects on intentions to use condoms.

One limitation of the present study is that its findings can only be generalized to higher socioeconomic status individuals who visit retail outlets such as pharmacies. Additional analyses, using data that is representative of the general population (i.e. from household surveys), should be conducted to confirm the findings of this study.

These findings also suggest that it would be useful to compare the cost-effectiveness of different components of a social marketing program using path analysis. Such analyses could help determine the optimal allocation of communication resourcesbetween the interpersonal and mass media components of an intervention. Finally, the results of this study support the strategy of including mass media promotion, peer education, and provider explanation of condom use in programs designed to promote use of the female condom.

Acknowledgements

This research was funded by AIDSMark/USAID and by PSI (which has core support from the British Department of International Development). The authors are grateful to Dominique Meekers for his comments on an earlier version of this report, and to Megan Klein for editing.

References

Agha S, An Evaluation of Adolescent Sexual Health Programs in Cameroon, Botswana, South Africa and Guinea, PSI Research Division Working Paper Number 29, Washington D.C.: Population Services International, 2000.

Agha S and Meekers D, The Availability of Social Marketed Condoms in Urban Tanzania, 1997 to 1999, PSI Research Division Working Paper Number 36, Washington D.C.: Population Services International, 2000.

Agha S, Intentions to use the female condom following a mass-marketing campaign in Lusaka, Zambia, American Journal of Public Health, 2001, 91(2): 307–310.

Agha S, Patterns of use of the female condom after one year of mass-marketing, AIDS Education and Prevention, 2001, 13(1): 55–64.

Bandura A. Social Foundations of Thought and Action. A Social Cognitive Theory, New Jersey: Prentice Hall, 1986.

Curtis SL and Westoff CF, Intentions to use contraceptives and subsequent contraceptive behavior in Morocco, Studies in Family Planning, 1996, 27: 239–250.

Duncan OD, Path analysis: sociological examples, The American Journal of Sociology, 1966, 72(1): 1–16.

Ezeh, AC, The influence of spouses over each other's contraceptive attitudes in Ghana. Studies in Family Planning, 1993, 24(3): 163–174.

Forrest K, Female Condom Acceptability Study Final Report, Population Services International Tanzania, 1997.

Jato MN, Simbakalia C, Tarasevich JM, Awasum DN, Kihinga CNB and Ngirwa-mungu E, The impact of a multimedia family planning promotion on the contraceptive behavior of women in Tanzania, International Family Planning Perspectives, 1999, 25(2): 60–67.

Jones ES, Social marketing of the female condom in Dar es Salaam, Tanzania, Thesis submitted to the Department of International Health Emory University, in partial fulfillment of the requirements for the degree of Master of Public Health, 1999.

Jöreskog K and Sörbom D, LISREL 8: Structual Equation Modeling with the SIMP-LIS Command Language, Chicago: Scientific Software International, 1993.

Jöreskog K and Sörbom D, PRELIS 2: User's Reference Guide, Chicago: Scientific Software International, 1996.

Jöreskog K and Sörbom D, LISREL 8: User's Reference Guide, Chicago: Scientific Software International, 1996.

Kabira WM, Kanyi W, Ruminjo J, Njau W, Nduati R, Hayman J and Ankrah M, The Female Condom as a Woman Controlled Protective Method: Summary of Research Project, Nairobi: AIDSCAP Women's Initiative, 1997.

Kane TT, Gueye M, Speizer I, Pacque-Margolis S and Baron D, The impact of a family planning multimedia campaign in Bamako, Mali, Studies in Family Planning, 1998, 29(3): 309–323.

Kim YM and Marangwanda C, Stimulating men's support for long-term contraception: A campaign in Zimbabwe, Journal of Health Communication, 1997, 2: 271–297.

Kim YM, Kols A, Nyakauru R, Marangwanda C and Chibatmoto P., Promoting Sexual Responsibility Among Young People in Zimbabwe, International Family Planning Perspectives, 2001, 1: 11–19.

Kincaid DL, Social networks, ideation, and contraceptive behavior in Bangladesh: a longitudinal analysis, Social Science and Medicine, 2000, 50: 215–231.

Kincaid DL, Merritt AP, Nickerson L, Buffington SC, de Castro MPP, de Castro BM, Impact of a mass media vasectomy promotion campaign in Brazil, International Family Planning Perspectives, 1996, 22(4): 169–175.

Klapper JT, The Effects of Mass Communication, New York: Free Press, 1969.

Meekers D, Patterns of Use of the Female Condom in Urban Zimbabwe, PSI Research Division Working Paper Number 28, Washington D.C.: Population Services International, 1999.

Meekers D and Ogada E, Explaining Discrepancies in Reproductive Health Indicators from Population-Based Surveys and Exit Surveys: a Case from Rwanda. Health Policy and Planning, 2001, 16(2): 137–143.

Mwale G and Burnard P, Women and AIDS in Rural Africa, Vermont: Ashgate Publishing Company, 1992.

PSI Tanzania Quarterly Report, January to March 1998. Dar es Salaam: PSI Tanzania, 1998.

PSI Tanzania Quarterly Report, January to March 1999. Dar es Salaam: PSI Tanzania, 1999.

PSI Tanzania Quarterly Report, July-September 1999. Dar es Salaam: PSI Tanzania, 1999.

Rogers EM, Vaughan PW, Swalehe RMA, Rao N, Svenkerud P and Sood S, A radio soap opera's effects on family planning behavior in Tanzanai, Studies in Family Planning, 1999, 30(3): 193–211.

Schoepf BG, Women and AIDS and economic crisis in Central Africa, Canadian Journal of African Studies, 1988, 22(3): 625–644.

Sherry JL, Prosocial soap operas for development: A review of research and theory, Journal of International Communication, 1997, 4(2), 75–101.

Ulin PR, African women and AIDS: negotiating behavior change, Social Science and Medicine, 1992, 34(1): 63–73.

Westoff CE and Rodríguez G, The mass media and family planning in Kenya, International Family Planning Perspectives, 1995, 21(1): 26–31.

Taipei's Use of a Multi-Channel Mass Risk Communication Program to Rapidly Reverse an Epidemic of Highly Communicable Disease

Muh-Yong Yen, Tsung-Shu Joseph Wu,
Allen Wen-Hsiang Chiu, Wing-Wai Wong,
Po-En Wang, Ta-Chien Chan and Chwan-Chuen King

ABSTRACT

Background

In September 2007, an outbreak of acute hemorrhagic conjunctivitis (AHC) occurred in Keelung City and spread to Taipei City. In response to the epidemic, a new crisis management program was implemented and tested in Taipei.

Methodology and Principal Findings

Having noticed that transmission surged on weekends during the Keelung epidemic, Taipei City launched a multi-channel mass risk communications program that included short message service (SMS) messages sent directly to approximately 2.2 million Taipei residents on Friday, October 12th, 2007. The public was told to keep symptomatic students from schools and was provided guidelines for preventing the spread of the disease at home. Epidemiological characteristics of Taipei's outbreak were analyzed from 461 sampled AHC cases. Median time from exposure to onset of the disease was 1 day. This was significantly shorter for cases occurring in family clusters than in class clusters (mean±SD: 2.6±3.2 vs. 4.39±4.82 days, p = 0.03), as well as for cases occurring in larger family clusters as opposed to smaller ones (1.2±1.7 days vs. 3.9±4.0 days, p<0.01). Taipei's program had a significant impact on patient compliance. Home confinement of symptomatic children increased from 10% to 60% (p<0.05) and helped curb the spread of AHC. Taipei experienced a rapid decrease in AHC cases between the Friday of the SMS announcement and the following Monday, October 15, (0.70% vs. 0.36%). By October 26, AHC cases reduced to 0.01%. The success of this risk communication program in Taipei (as compared to Keelung) is further reflected through rapid improvements in three epidemic indicators: (1) significantly lower crude attack rates (1.95% vs. 14.92%, p<0.001), (2) a short epidemic period of AHC (13 vs. 34 days), and (3) a quick drop in risk level (1–2 weeks) in Taipei districts that border Keelung (the original domestic epicenter).

Conclusions and Significance

The timely launch of this systematic, communication-based intervention proved effective at preventing a dangerous spike in AHC and was able to bring this high-risk disease under control. We recommend that public health officials incorporate similar methods into existing guidelines for preventing pandemic influenza and other emerging infectious diseases.

Introduction

The viral illness known as acute hemorrhagic conjunctivitis (AHC) is frequently accompanied by a highly transmissible acute eye infection. This infection is most often caused by the adenovirus, enterovirus 70, and Coxsackie's virus. Coxsackie A24 infection was first reported in 1969 in Ghana and has since appeared around the world [1], [2], [3], [4], [5].

Since late 2002, several AHC epidemics have occurred in Asian countries such as Korea, Malaysia, and Singapore [6], [7], [8]. In September 2007, southern China's Coxsackie A24 AHC epidemic spread to Hong Kong after first appearing on the mainland in early summer. On September 18th, a cluster of cases with AHC-like symptoms was first unofficially reported by the media in Keelung, a harbor city bordering Taipei (816 km away from Hong Kong), in northern Taiwan. Because AHC was not on Taiwan's list of reported communicable diseases at the time, it was difficult for public health officials to collect adequate epidemiological data until October 4th, when a dramatic spike in AHC cases was reported by the mass media. At that time, the Keelung Department of Health reported 2722 cases of pink eye disease among public school students. Although general control measures were taken, case numbers continued to increase rapidly in Keelung, particularly during weekends.

Also on Oct. 4th, Taipei City Department of Health was alerted to its first AHC cluster (20 cases from a primary school) in Neihu, a Taipei district neighboring Keelung (Figure 1). Taipei was more prepared for the AHC outbreak as its alertness was raised by media coverage of outbreaks in nearby Keelung. The local Department of Health was also able to identify clusters quickly because it had made school reporting of influenza-like illness clusters (or other unusual clinical presentations) a mandatory practice since 2003.

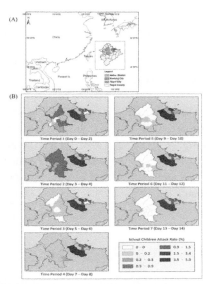

Figure 1. Spatial Distribution of the 2007 AHC Attack Rates in Taipei City and Keelung City. Geographical location of Taipei City and Keelung City and their spatial relationship was shown in panel A. Spatial and temporal changes of AHC attack rates (AR) between Taipei City and Keelung City were plotted according to their place in the outbreak timeline (panel B). Day 0 is used to indicate the days that cluster cases were first identified in Taipei or in Keelung cities. Darker colored areas indicate regions with higher AR.

Taipei's Department of Health had reorganized its disease control and prevention system against emerging infectious diseases (EID) after 2003's severe acute respiratory syndrome (SARS) epidemic but had not yet tested the system under real life circumstances. In launching countermeasures to bring the AHC outbreak under control, the Taipei Department of Health was also able to test its system and fine-tune its public health response for future EIDs. To evaluate the effectiveness of these intervention measures, daily surveillance was conducted to analyze the incidence rate and temporal-spatial distribution of new AHC cases. In addition, students' parents were sent questionnaires to capture their experience with these preventative measures.

Materials and Methods

Setting

Taipei City, the largest city in Taiwan, is located in northern Taiwan and directly borders Keelung City (Figure 1). In 2007, Taipei, a city of 2.6 million people occupying 271.8 km^2, had a student population of 277,159 (10.53%). Taipei City has a larger population size and density than neighboring Keelung City (Table 1), and is, thus, exceedingly vulnerable to microbial transmission and EID outbreaks.

Table 1. General Information on the AHC Outbreak in Taipei City and Keelung City in 2007.

Demographic Information	Taipei City	Keelung City
Duration of the AHC Outbreak (days) 13		34
Population Size		
Reported AHC Cases in School Children 5,414		6,154
Total Number of School Children	277,159	41,244
Crude Attack Rate (%)*	1.95%	14.92%
Total Population	2,632,242	390,084
Population Density (per **Km^2**)	9684.5	2937.4
Geographic Area (Km^2)	271.8	132.8

*$p<0.001$.

Ethics

This study was approved by the Advisory Committee for Infectious Diseases Control of Taipei City's Department of Health, Taipei City Government. Informed consent was obtained from the parents of participating schoolchildren in writing before they were asked to complete the questionnaire.

Surveillance Methods

In response to a large outbreak of SARS in 2003, Taipei's Department of Heath established a new crisis management system with the goals of detecting EIDs early, implementing appropriate and timely public health responses, and administering effective risk management [9], [10]. At the start of Taiwan's 2007 AHC outbreak, local health departments in all of Taiwan's cities were engaged in a passive surveillance system in which schools reported cases as they occurred. On October 4th, Taipei's Department of Health urged schools and kindergartens with clusters of more than three AHC cases to actively report cases to the local Department of Health twice weekly. Age-specific incidence rates of AHC among school-aged children during the outbreak were also calculated using the collected surveillance data.

When total AHC cases in Taipei reached close to 500 on October 11, 2007, an active school-based surveillance system was launched by the city to monitor trends in the spread of AHC and evaluate the effectiveness of intervention measures. Schools were required to make daily reports to Taipei's Department of Education, regardless of whether there were any new cases on a given day. As the incidence rate of the last reported AHC cases in Keelung (on October 22) was 0.14%, we set this rate as a cut-off point for comparing the effectiveness of the countermeasures used by the two cities. Tailing data, i.e., data that fell below the 0.14% incidence rate was excluded from our analysis. We used this cut-off to define the duration of the AHC epidemics for both cities. According to our definition, the AHC epidemics for each city began from the date of the first reported cluster and ended on the date that rates of new case incidence dropped to 0.14% or below.

Epidemiological Design and Data Analysis

Study Subjects

We analyzed 461 reported AHC cases from ten Taipei schools (totaling 18,134 students). Students from six of the ten schools, three elementary schools and three junior high schools, made up most of the reported AHC case numbers. Two elementary schools and two junior high schools that were also included in the research reported continuous AHC occurrences during the week that our field epidemiological study was conducted. For each of the ten schools, we randomly selected one class that had had occurrences of AHC and one class where there had been no occurrence of AHC as our case and control groups, respectively. Data collected from these individual school groupings were gathered and divided into one study and one control group for data analysis.

Case Definition of AHC and Clusters (Family, School)

The AHC cases in this study all involved an acute conjunctiva inflammation that included eye redness (pink eye) accompanied with pain, swelling, tearing, or discharge from one or both eyes. Family clusters were defined as two or more cases of AHC occurring in one family within 14 days. Class clusters were defined as three or more AHC cases in one class of students within 7 days. Both family clusters and class clusters were charted through epidemiological investigation.

Tempo-Spatial Data Analysis

District-specific AHC attack rates were calculated by dividing the number of reported cases for each district by the total number of schoolchildren under its supervision. The Kriging method [11], [12], a statistical mapping technique utilizing data collected at each location, was used to interpolate each grid cell over a spatial domain. In this study, the centroid of each grid designated the attack rate in each district. In order to observe spatio-temporal spreading, Kriging assessed the spatio-temporal interactions in a diffusion map. We made a surface plot of daily time series as a gradient interpolated between adjacent days and district data points. Distance in the map symbolizes relative geographic relationship rather than actual distance. Townships were ordered from East to West and from North to South.

Control Measures used by Taipei City

To identify the possible etiologic agent of the outbreak, health care professionals were required to administer eye swabs and conduct laboratory testing. Local health workers were then able to match the epidemiological characteristics for the confirmed agent, Coxsackie A24, with appropriate and specific prevention and control measures. Government officials of the Taipei City Department of Health informed the media of the outbreak through press releases and used a variety of health education methods to reach the public. Beginning on October 5, public service messages were delivered to kindergartens, primary schools, middle schools, and high schools to encourage children to avoid touching their eyes, wash their hands routinely, and participate in disinfecting the school environment. Within schools, health education programming during daily morning assemblies provided updates to students and teachers regarding the current status of the epidemic and additional measures that were needed to reduce infections. A special telephone hotline was also established to improve case reporting and provide up-to-date disease counseling from health care institutions.

These measures, though helpful, had also been used in Keelung and had, thus far, proven inadequate at containing the epidemic. In early October 2007, Taipei City government decided to adopt a more aggressive campaign against the epidemic by implementing an "incident management system." This system required various administrative agencies to follow an integrated disaster response plan. Although school closures and class cancellation were not required for schools with reported AHC cases, schools were encouraged to persuade symptomatic students to stay home and provide guidance on how to prevent the spread of the infection in the home environment. In addition, schools were authorized to keep symptomatic students from entering the school in case parents insisted on their attendance. If infected students were able to gain entry to school premises, the school was authorized to prevent them from joining public activities (such as swimming). School absenteeism was also reported and recorded daily.

The Taipei City Department of Health devised backup plans should the above-mentioned measures not succeed. These plans included separate care facilities for AHC patients at ophthalmic clinics, more intensive segregation of symptomatic students from classmates (in the classroom, at public washbasins, and during outdoor student activities), and quarantines that required symptomatic students to stay at home for seven days.

Mass Risk Communication Program (MRCP)

Monday incidence reports (Figure 2) exhibited tremendous increases in AHC case incidence during weekends in Keelung. Mindful of these weekend spikes, Taipei implemented a multi-channel risk communication prevention program during the weekend of Friday, October 12 (2,253 new cases of AHC were reported in Taipei on that date). This risk communication program focused on communicating directly to the public through three routes: (1) schools delivered a Taipei Department of Health letter signed by the mayor (that detailed AHC information and prevention methods) for students to take home to their parents, (2) the mayor held a press conference to discuss the epidemic and offer guidance to citizens for preventing the spread of the disease, and (3) over 2.2 million short message services (SMS) messages, a communication tool for exchanging short text messages between mobile telephonic devices, were delivered to all Taipei mobile phone numbers. The messages briefed Taipei residents on the current status of the epidemic and recommended citizen-level control measures. All communications suggested that symptomatic students stay at home, apart from other members of the family, and recommended household disinfection.

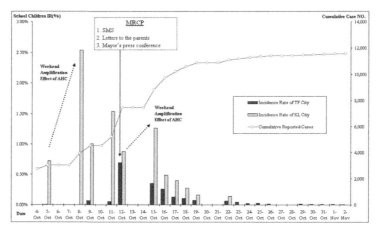

Figure 2. Incidence Rate (IR) and Cumulative Number of AHC Cases among School Children in Taipei City and Keelung City, October - November 2007. The figure's arrow indicates the weekend in which children stayed at home instead of attending school. The MRCP was launched on October 12th in Taipei City, causing the incidence rate (IR) of AHC to decline more rapidly in Taipei City than in Keelung City, where AHC cases continued to increase.

Evaluating the Effectiveness of the Control Measures

On October 31st, all Taipei students involved in the study were asked to give their parents a questionnaire devised to collect epidemiological data and assess their opinions regarding Taipei City's infection control measures. The questionnaire asked about the clinical symptoms/signs of children with AHC, school attendance, and inquired on parents' sources of disease prevention information. Parents were also asked to comment on their degree of satisfaction with Taipei City's public health efforts and provide suggestions for improving future SMS alerts.

We evaluated the effectiveness of the control measures based on the duration of the epidemic and the attack rate of the disease among school students in both Taipei and Keelung. As Keelung was without a risk communications program, and had only applied the general control measures recommended by Taiwan's Center for Disease Control (Taiwan CDC), the effectiveness of the special measures taken by Taipei City could be readily calculated through direct comparison.

Results

Because this study utilized risk communication methods used to minimize the public health threat of an unusual outbreak, we briefly describe the 2007 AHC epidemic below and analyze the effectiveness of the chosen methods using epidemiological measures.

The 2007 AHC Epidemic

AHC Attack Rates in Taipei and Keelung Cities

At the beginning of the epidemic, the etiologic agent of this AHC outbreak was unknown. On October 12th, based on culture and sequencing analysis performed at Taiwan CDC, the pathogen was identified as the A24 variant of the Coxsackie virus [13]. The epidemic lasted 13 days in Taipei (5,414 cases), and 34 days in Keelung (6,154 cases) (Table 1). Keelung City applied general control measures and Keelung CDC monitored daily reported new cases as suggested by Taiwan's CDC. However, there was no further assessment by Keelung on the effectiveness of its control measures. The crude attack rate of AHC in Keelung was significantly higher than in Taipei (14.92% vs. 1.95%; p<0.001). After the risk communication program was implemented in Taipei the overall incidence in the city decreased significantly (0.093% before vs. 0.056% after; p<0.001) while the incidence rates in Keelung continued to increase almost every weekend (Figure 2).

The greatest number of AHC cases in Taipei City occurred on a Friday (October 12), signaling an upcoming weekend spike in infections. However, on that day, Taipei City government launched the multi-channel risk communication program, greatly reducing the incidence rate and, in effect, causing a sharp weekend drop in new cases. Because of such measures, the epidemic ebbed much earlier in Taipei than in Keelung (Figure 3).

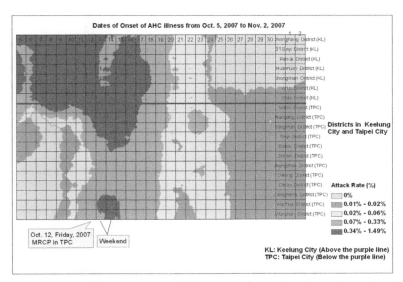

Figure 3. Spatio-temporal Diffusion Patterns of AHC Outbreaks from Keelung City to Taipei City, 2007. The X-axis reflects the temporal scale, while the Y-axis displays district names ordered by geographical correlation from North to South, East to West. The horizontal purple line marks the border between Keelung City and Taipei City.

Epidemiological Characteristics

The outbreaks began in Keelung in September of 2007. Due to the high frequency of transportation from Keelung to Taipei, the epidemic gradually reached Taipei. Districts in Taipei City closest to Keelung City began to see an increase in their attack rates on October 8th (Figure 3). The wave of new infections moved steadily from the northeast districts to the southwest districts of Taipei. In both cities, the disease spread citywide within a short period (4 days), as shown in Figure 1, and the median time between exposure and onset of disease was as short as 1 day [mean ± standard deviation (SD): 2.6±3.2 days, range 0 to 16 days] [Figure 4]. The mean time from exposure to onset of AHC was significantly shorter in family clusters than in school cluster cases (mean ± SD: 2.6±3.2 vs. 4.39±4.82 days, p = 0.03). The mean and range of time between exposure and disease onset was also significantly shorter in larger family clusters (>3 AHC cases per family) than in smaller ones (< = = 3 AHC cases) (1.2±1.7 days, range 0 to 6 days vs. 3.9±4.0 days, range 0 to 16 days, respectively) (p<0.01).

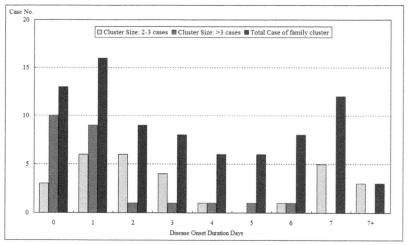

Figure 4. Distribution of AHC Illness Duration as Related to Family Cluster Size. Onset duration tended to be shorter when cluster size was more than 3 family members. (1.2±1.7 days, range 0 to 6 days, vs. smaller cluster size 3.9±4.0 days, range 0 to 16 days, p<0.01).

In terms of risk factors (Table 2), boys were at significantly higher risk for AHC-related pink eye than girls (OR = 2.14, p<0.001), and older children (over 10 years old) were generally at higher risk for pink eye both at home (OR: 2.56, p = 0.008) and at school (OR 3.51, p<0.001). In general, children at northeastern Taipei schools, located closest to Keelung, were at greater risk for pink eye (OR = 2.26, p-value = 0.003) both at home (OR = 3.93, p-value <0.001) and at school

(OR = 2.46, p-value = 0.001), than those at schools located in districts further away (Figure 1). In addition, school children were identified as the index cases in 75.5% of fifty-three family clusters (40/53), demonstrating their high risk for transmitting the disease to other family members.

Table 2. Demographic Information of Participating School Children Presenting/Not Presenting Pink Eye Illness (Within/Outside Family or School Clusters) during the AHC Outbreak in Taipei City, 2007.

	Red Eye Illness			Family Cluster			School Class Cluster		
	Present	Absent	OR	Yes	No	OR	Yes	No	OR
Gender									
Male	55	164	2.17*	32	187	1.45	53	166	2.15*
Female	28	181		22	186		27	182	
Age (Years)									
<10	15	128		10	133		12	131	
≥10	68	211	2.75*	45	234	2.56*	68	211	3.51*
School Grades									
1–3	5	131		4	132		2	134	
4–6	21	65	8.46*	13	88	4.87*	21	65	21.64*
7–9	57	181	8.25*	38	200	6.27*	58	181	21.47*
School Areas									
Northeast	63	215	2.26*	47	231	3.93*	62	216	2.46*
Southwest	21	162		9	174		19	163	
Index Case in Family									
1st case	61	11	11.71*	40	32	4.13*	59	13	9.58*
Not 1st case	18	38		13	43		18	38	

*$p < 0.05$.

Effectiveness of the Mass Risk Communication Program

Home Confinement of Symptomatic School Children

On Friday, October 12th (a day marked for its dramatic spike in new cases) the multi-channel mass risk communication program was launched in Taipei just prior to the weekend. On that day, three containment measures were urgently implemented: (1) the mayor addressed the press about the outbreak, (2) a letter written by the Taipei City Department of Health and signed by the mayor was given to students to take home to their parents, and (3) SMS messages were sent to all Taipei citizens with mobile phones. The collective message of all three channels emphasized the severity of the outbreak and outlined preventive measures, including home confinement. According to results obtained from the questionnaire (Table 3), home confinement of symptomatic students increased from a rate of 10% prior to the implementation of the risk communication program to 60% afterwards (p<0.05).

Disease Containment

As mentioned above, Taipei launched its mass risk communication program on October 12th. This was also the day that the epidemic reached its highest peak. As demonstrated in Figure 2, the pre-weekend case surge was reduced by almost half by October 15th (following the mass risk communication campaign in Taipei).

In Keelung, where no such risk communication program was launched, the epidemic lasted for thirty-four days and had fourteen days of high attack rates within that period. In contrast, the epidemic lasted thirteen days in Taipei and had less than five days of high attack rates following the implementation of the risk communication program.

The diffusion map in Figure 3 further illustrates the limited scope and short duration of high AHC attack rates (labeled in red) in Taipei districts. By October 17, attack rates in all Taipei districts reduced to moderate levels (labeled in yellow) and then further reduced to low levels (labeled in green) on October 26 (Figure 3).

Sources of Information Related to Control Measure Compliance and Satisfaction Evaluation of the SMS Program

According to Taipei City's parents' responses to the questionnaire, primary sources for AHC information included TV news broadcasting (54.45%), daily school health education programs during morning assemblies (34.92%), and the Taipei City Department of Health letter signed by the Mayor (29.28%) (Table 4). Approximately fourteen percent (14.32%) of parents surveyed identified the short message service (SMS) issued by the Taipei City Department of Health as their primary source of AHC information.

Based on a five-point scale, parents who received the SMS communication felt more satisfied with this method as a means of public health communication than those who did not receive SMS messages (3.89 vs. 3.01; p<0.05).

Table 4. Parents' Primary Sources for Control Measure Information from Taipei City Government.

Information Sources / Knowledge Content (%)	Absent from School and stay Home while Pinkeye (N = 461)	Household Segregation for Pinkeye Illness (N = 461)	Household Environmental Disinfection (N = 461)
TV Broadcasting	54.45%	50.54%	47.94%
Schools' Prompt Daily Morning Assembly Education Program	34.92%	34.49%	35.79%
Letter to Schoolchildren's Parents	29.28%	27.98%	28.42%
Newspaper	24.95%	23.21%	22.34%
Mobile Phone SMS*	14.32%	10.20%	10.85%
Parent's own Decision (from Regular Public Health Resources)	7.81%	19.52%	22.56%
Radio News	5.64%	6.29%	5.42%
Taipei City Mayor's Announcements	3.90%	4.77%	4.56%

Discussion

Prompt and effective prevention and control measures to combat EIDs are imperative to maintaining public health and safety. In this study, we found that the multi-channel risk communication program launched midway through the 2007 AHC epidemic in Taipei City increased the number of students confined to their homes, reduced total duration and affected areas of the epidemic, and decreased the number of dangerous, high attack days. By interrupting the prevailing transmission route between school and home, the program effectively inhibited the spread of this highly communicable disease in the community.

AHC has been identified as a highly contagious disease, capable of far-reaching, epidemic spread, since its first reported case in 1970 [2], [14] The Coxsackie virus A24 (CV-A24) variant in particular has been the causing agent of several difficult outbreaks. It has also been a significant challenge to sensitivity and timeliness efforts in disease surveillance systems [13], [15]. In addition, the virus's eye-related symptoms [16], [17], [18] are not easily differentiated from other infections (i.e. the human strain of Netherland's 2003 avian influenza, H7N7) [19], [20], [21], [22]. During the 2007 AHC epidemic in Taiwan, schools were found to be epicenters of transmission. By focusing disease control efforts in the school system, Taipei was more effective than neighboring Keelung (which relied on traditional control strategies) at interrupting the school-family-community cascade of transmission.

Because AHC was not initially listed as a reportable disease when this outbreak first occurred, accessible data was initially unavailable for cases before October 4, 2007. Several characteristics of the 2007 outbreak suggest a foreign source for Taiwan's AHC epidemic. The introduction of the outbreak in Keelung, a port city, and the genotype II status of the 2007 CV-24 virus (all CV-24 viruses isolated in Taiwanese outbreaks prior to 2007 had belonged to genotype III [13]) strongly suggest that the virus was imported in the summer of 2007. The spread worsened in Taiwan after schools returned to session in September. Although health officials in Keelung had advocated for hand washing, eye protection, and disinfection, new cases continued to rise after October 8. The CV-24 virus, spread primarily through person-to-person contact and contact with infected fomites, may also have spread through contact with respiratory droplets and fecal-oral routes, resulting in rapid and widespread transmission [13], [15]. Older children were more likely to be members of case clusters at home and at school. The reasons for this increased likelihood is unknown, though it may be related to higher rates of participation in team sports and/or less compliance with rules of hygiene. Research may be needed to fully understand this phenomenon. In essence, school children serve as index cases in around seventy-five percent of family clusters (Table 2) and are, indisputably, the largest transmitters of the virus. The findings of the study illustrate that schools serve as epicenters of CV-24 transmission and are effective intervention targets for containing the virus before its introduction to the general population.

The large weekend increases of CV-24 infection that occurred in Keelung may have resulted from a lack of preventive measures at home, e.g. ineffectiveness at keeping symptomatic children separate from other family members and/or improper disinfection of the home environment. Because the median time from exposure to onset is short (median 1 day in Figure 4), AHC is able to spread quickly from one index case to other family members, many of whom might take it back to schools and larger communities over the weekend. This creates a highly efficient family-school-community transmission cascade that is capable of spreading quickly throughout a city. Therefore, measures that effectively reduce and isolate infections at home and at school would contribute greatly to breaking the transmission cycle.

In the face of an unexpected outbreak of EID, risk communication and management are essential for keeping infection and mortality rates under control. The large disparity between mortality rates of the 1918 influenza pandemic in Philadelphia and St. Louis in the United States was due to distinct differences in the preparedness and timeliness of their respective local public health responses [23], [24]. This example serves to illustrate the importance of preventing and containing EIDs in a systematic and timely manner.

As the Capital of Taiwan, Taipei City has a much larger population size and density than Keelung City (Table 1). In addition, Taipei is a highly dynamic city with frequent economic, cultural, and social change. This inconstancy, coupled with its status as a large international travel hub, makes the city particularly vulnerable to EID. Much of Taipei's preparedness was the result of the city's experience as Taiwan's epicenter of the SARS outbreak in 2003. After the SARS outbreak, Taipei City Government initiated a new public health plan using an integrated infection control system against EID. This new system integrated early detection of outbreaks (particularly in hospitals and schools), epidemiological investigation, and epidemiologically based public health prevention and control policies. The renovated Division of Disease Control and Prevention (Taipei's CDC) also became the core operational unit for implementing crisis management procedures and facilitating policy. These systematic upgrades allowed for quick enactment of multi-channel risk communication measures during the 2007 outbreak of conjunctivitis.

The 2007 AHC outbreak provided the perfect opportunity for Taipei health authorities to test the effectiveness of the newly renovated system. Measures that were used to contain this epidemic may also, in turn, serve as a practice model for dealing with future influenza pandemics. There are many similarities between AHC and novel influenza: (1) there is currently no available vaccine for the circulating virus strain and anti-viral treatment is limited, (2) time from exposure to onset is very short, (3) the disease is highly contagious and easily contracted through contact with contaminated aerosols/droplets or fomites, and (4) schools serve as epicenters for the spread of the virus to households and, eventually, to the larger community.

It has been previously demonstrated that home confinement of symptomatic children can dramatically limit the spread of AHC and influenza in the community [25], [26], [27]. The timely launch of our multi-channel risk communication program to all Taipei citizens on Friday, October 12, allowed us to provide clear instructions to families on how to prevent the infection at home over the course of weekend, when infection rates would normally increase. These direct communication methods successfully convinced parents to keep their symptomatic children at home (from 10% to 60% in Table 3). With contagious students confined to their homes, school transmissions decreased dramatically and public health officials were able to contain the Taipei outbreak quickly. The effectiveness of these innovative methods in the heavily populated metropolitan area of Taipei City was evidenced by how quickly the epidemic, which had infected 5414 students, subsided after 2 weeks. This can be compared with the two months that were needed to control Taipei's previous CV-24 epidemic in 1987 [28].

The importance of appropriate risk communication in response to disasters has often been overlooked by public health officials in Taiwan. Traditionally, the mass media has helped disseminate epidemic information and increase awareness on how health risks may be reduced. However, the modern mass media has, at times, had a negative impact on public health efforts by encouraging public indifference or sensationalizing incomplete and inaccurate information. The media's reporting of the SARS outbreak contributed to unnecessary chaos in the early phases of the epidemic [29].

Rather than rely on the media alone to convey productive messages regarding the epidemic, Taipei's CDC was able to implement its Multi-Channel Mass Risk Communication Program to reach the public directly during critical points in the epidemic. We believe the SMS messaging component of the program was integral to the success of the 2007 AHC intervention and will continue to explore the use of this tool. We know from our questionnaire that fourteen percent of parents who confined their affected children at home during 2007's AHC outbreak reported that their decision to comply with this preventive measure was based on the SMS messages they received. Although the effects of the cell phone method cannot be fully isolated from the multi-channel risk communication system in this study, we believe that future interventions that utilize SMS exclusively will provide more insight on the effectiveness of this method. Taipei's CDC has since conducted a SMS campaign on Chinese Valentine's Day in 2009 to reach high-risk groups for Human Immunodeficiency Virus (HIV). The message asked the public to answer an AIDS-related trivia question and also provided information on free, anonymous HIV testing. After this exploratory campaign, Anonymous HIV screening rates went up 20% from the same time the year before. As SMS messaging is still an emerging approach to wide-scale information dissemination, we believe that further examination into the effectiveness of cell phone-based risk communication methods will need to be done at the local, national, and international level.

Taipei's ability to launch such a large-scale SMS campaign was a direct result of Taiwan's Communicable Disease Act (2006). This act allowed government officials to override the people's right to privacy when responding to epidemic disasters. In this case, the Taipei city government held a contract with Taiwan's six major mobile phone companies and committed all of them to allowing six free public service messages (per year) to be sent to their users if deemed necessary by the proper authorities. The SMS message in response to the AHC epidemic was sent to 2.2 million registered mobile phone users in Taipei City. Public satisfaction with the SMS campaign was high, especially amongst parents of school children. While this mass communication method has been advocated for use in many Asian countries, Taiwan's large-scale employment of SMS technology was, to the best of our knowledge, the first such attempt in the world. While it was, overall, an effective means of communication, the efficacy of this method was limited by several factors. First, the sudden influx of over two million messages put a large burden on the network system and resulted in a long delay (many received their message around midnight). Second, many Taipei mobile phones users are registered in other cities and did not receive the messages. Third, consumer weariness may have caused some people to ignore the long, unsolicited message before they read it. To reduce technical limitations, we suggest that SMS surge capacity be increased and tested at both non-epidemic and pre-pandemic stages. Other limitations to the SMS tool and alternative mass communication prevention methods can be fine-tuned with more experience, frequently updated guidelines, an efficient system for risk management, an integrated public health plan, and extra training for public health personnel [30], [31]. Another important challenge is reaching diverse populations, particularly those with low socioeconomic status that may not be able to afford mobile phone service (and reside in less affluent, high-risk areas) [32]. This may be less of problem in Taiwan than in other countries.

This study had several limitations, including a lack of early data on pink-eye cases in Keelung. After the conclusion of the outbreak, there was also no further assessment on the effectiveness of control measures in Keelung. This study was non-randomized and missing epidemiological information for calculating secondary attack rates, age-specific asymptomatic ratios, and geographical diffusion of AHC cases outside Taipei and Keelung. Seroepidemiological studies in the future should be able to obtain more accurate secondary attack data with the use of comprehensive infection and disease exposure data.

In conclusion, the timely launch of the multi-channel risk communication program described in this study greatly reduced the duration and number of cases of Taiwan's 2007 AHC epidemic. These efforts effectively avoided a potentially large-scale epidemic of AHC in Taipei City. In encountering challenges such as outbreaks of influenza pandemic, or other EIDs with short incubation periods, public health officials need to prepare an integrated and timely administrative public health response. Urgent intervention and education must reach the community directly through multi-module channels, like SMS, for rapid communication.

Geographical variations in epidemiological characteristics, as described in our comparison analysis of the AHC epidemic in Keelung versus Taipei, are similar to variations in swine-origin H1N1 outbreaks in Mexico versus United States. Such similarities support this intervention's potential applicability to the prevention and control of other EIDs. Based on the findings of this study, we believe that the success of this risk communication method is dependent on: (1) the timeliness of the communication, (2) simplicity and consistency of the message, (3) appropriateness of the channels of dissemination, (4) transparency of the information, and (5) public faith in the communicator; in this instance the mayor of Taipei. While we found that the use of SMS significantly contributed to the effectiveness of the risk communication program, more SMS-based campaigns and research, like the HIV testing campaign mentioned in our manuscript, are needed to fully evaluate its effectiveness at communicating public health messages to the public.

Acknowledgements

We greatly appreciate local public health professionals who helped coordinate and implement efforts for controlling the 2007 AHC outbreak. We are also grateful to the Taiwan CDC for their laboratory support. The authors would also like to thank two English editors, Mr. James Steed and Ms. Peggy Lee, for their assistance in the final edits of this manuscript.

Authors' Contributions

Conceived and designed the experiments: MYY AWHC WWW PEW. Performed the experiments: MYY AWHC WWW PEW CCK. Analyzed the data: MYY TSJW TCC CCK. Contributed reagents/materials/analysis tools: MYY TCC. Wrote the paper: MYY TSJW TCC CCK. Initiated this study: MYY. Implemented risk communication methods: MYY. Facilitated outbreak control: MYY. Spearheaded the writing of this manuscript: MYY. Responsible for all data analysis: TSJW. Prepared the tables and figures: TSJW. Contributed several important ideas regarding the structure of this paper: TSJW. Supervised the study: AWHC. Suggested citywide SMS risk communication: AWHC. Monitored AHC outbreak control efforts: AWHC. Responsible for case definition, administration, and coordination for contact tracing in Taipei City: WWW. Implemented several clinical and epidemiological investigations: WWW. Applied general control measures: PEW. Collected epidemiological data on AHC cases in Keelung during the 2007 epidemic: PEW. Conducted geographical diffusion data analysis using a geographical information system: TCC. Responsible for designing the epidemiological study: CCK. Formulated questionnaire questions: CCK. Selecting focus areas for data analysis: CCK. Revised this manuscript: CCK.

References

1. Chatterjee S, Quarcoopome CO, Apenteng A (1970) Unusual type of epidemic conjunctivitis in Ghana. Br J Ophthalmol 54: 628–630.

2. Mirkovic RR, Kono R, Yin-Murphy M, Sohier R, Schmidt NJ, et al. (1973) Enterovirus type 70: the etiologic agent of pandemic acute haemorrhagic conjunctivitis. Bull World Health Organ 49: 341–346.

3. Christopher S, Theogaraj S, Godbole S, John TJ (1982) An epidemic of acute hemorrhagic conjunctivitis due to coxsackievirus A24. J Infect Dis 146: 16–19.

4. Brandful JA, Yoshii T, Addy ET, Adiku TK, Osei-Kwasi M, et al. (1990) Epidemic acute haemorrhagic conjunctivitis due to Coxsackie virus A24 variant in Ghana. East Afr Med J 67: 878–886.

5. Yin-Murphy M, Goh KT, Phoon MC, Yao J, Baharuddin I (1993) A recent epidemic of acute hemorrhagic conjunctivitis. Am J Ophthalmol 116: 212–217.

6. Ghazali O, Chua KB, Ng KP, Hooi PS, Pallansch MA, et al. (2003) An outbreak of acute haemorrhagic conjunctivitis in Melaka, Malaysia. Singapore Med J 44: 511–516.

7. Park K, Lee K, Lee J, Yeo S, Lee S, et al. (2006) Acute hemorrhagic conjunctivitis epidemic caused by coxsackievirus A24 variants in Korea during 2002–2003. J Med Virol 78: 91–97.

8. Leveque N, Amine IL, Cartet G, Hammani AB, Khazraji YC, et al. (2007) Two outbreaks of acute hemorrhagic conjunctivitis in Africa due to genotype III coxsackievirus A24 variant. Eur J Clin Microbiol Infect Dis 26: 199–202.

9. (2004) Control of Communicable Diseases in Taipei City. Taipei City: Department of Health.

10. Yen M-Y, Wong W-W, Sung Y-J (2007) Strategies for Preparedness of Responding to Possible Pandemic of Novel Influenza in Taipei Metropolitan Area. Taiwan Epidemiology Bulletin 23: 16–18.

11. Carrat F, Valleron AJ (1992) Epidemiologic mapping using the "kriging" method: application to an influenza-like illness epidemic in France. Am J Epidemiol 135: 1293–1300.

12. Sakai T, Suzuki H, Sasaki A, Saito R, Tanabe N, et al. (2004) Geographic and temporal trends in influenzalike illness, Japan, 1992–1999. Emerg Infect Dis 10: 1822–1826.

13. Lin TL, Huang CW, Hsu CC, Li YS, Lin YC, et al. (2008) "Pink Eyes": Confirmation of Pathogens and Investigation and Analysis of Molecular Epidemiology. Taiwan Epidemiology Bulletin 23: 303–318.

14. Palacios G, Oberste MS (2005) Enteroviruses as agents of emerging infectious diseases. J Neurovirol 11: 424–433.

15. Kuo PC, Lin JY, Chen LC, Fang YT, Cheng YC, et al. (2009) Molecular and immunocytochemical identification of coxsackievirus A-24 variant from the acute haemorrhagic conjunctivitis outbreak in Taiwan in 2007. Eye.

16. Madhavan HN, Malathy J, Priya K (2000) An outbreak of acute conjunctivitis caused by Coxsackie virus A 24. Indian J Ophthalmol 48: 159.

17. Oh MD, Park S, Choi Y, Kim H, Lee K, et al. (2003) Acute hemorrhagic conjunctivitis caused by coxsackievirus A24 variant, South Korea, 2002. Emerg Infect Dis 9: 1010–1012.

18. (2004) Acute hemorrhagic conjunctivitis outbreak caused by Coxsackievirus A24–Puerto Rico, 2003. MMWR Morb Mortal Wkly Rep 53: 632–634.

19. Du Ry van Beest Holle M, Meijer A, Koopmans M, de Jager CM (2005) Human-to-human transmission of avian influenza A/H7N7, The Netherlands, 2003. Euro Surveill 10: 264–268.

20. Nguyen-Van-Tam JS, Nair P, Acheson P, Baker A, Barker M, et al. (2006) Outbreak of low pathogenicity H7N3 avian influenza in UK, including associated case of human conjunctivitis. Euro Surveill 11: E060504 060502:

21. Belser JA, Lu X, Maines TR, Smith C, Li Y, et al. (2007) Pathogenesis of avian influenza (H7) virus infection in mice and ferrets: enhanced virulence of Eurasian H7N7 viruses isolated from humans. J Virol 81: 11139–11147.

22. Sandrock C, Kelly T (2007) Clinical review: update of avian influenza A infections in humans. Crit Care 11: 209.

23. Bootsma MC, Ferguson NM (2007) The effect of public health measures on the 1918 influenza pandemic in U.S. cities. Proc Natl Acad Sci USA 104: 7588–7593.

24. Hatchett RJ, Mecher CE, Lipsitch M (2007) Public health interventions and epidemic intensity during the 1918 influenza pandemic. Proc Natl Acad Sci USA 104: 7582–7587.

25. Patriarca PA, Onorato IM, Sklar VE, Schonberger LB, Kaminski RM, et al. (1983) Acute hemorrhagic conjunctivitis Investigation of a large-scale community outbreak in Dade County, Florida. Jama 249: 1283–1289.

26. Yasuda H, Yoshizawa N, Kimura M, Shigematsu M, Matsumoto M, et al. (2008) Preparedness for the spread of influenza: prohibition of traffic, school closure, and vaccination of children in the commuter towns of Tokyo. J Urban Health 85: 619–635.

27. Zhao H, Joseph C, Phin N (2007) Outbreaks of influenza and influenza-like illness in schools in England and Wales, 2005/06. Euro Surveill 12: E3–4.

28. Chou MY, Malison MD (1988) Outbreak of acute hemorrhagic conjunctivitis due to coxsackie A24 variant–Taiwan. Am J Epidemiol 127: 795–800.

29. Berry TR, Wharf-Higgins J, Naylor PJ (2007) SARS wars: an examination of the quantity and construction of health information in the news media. Health Commun 21: 35–44.

30. Pitrelli N, Sturloni G (2007) Infectious diseases and governance of global risks through public communication and participation. Ann Ist Super Sanita 43: 336–343.

31. Thomas JC, MacDonald PD, Wenink E (2009) Ethical decision making in a crisis: a case study of ethics in public health emergencies. J Public Health Manag Pract 15: E16–21.

32. Pitrelli N, Sturloni G (2007) Infectious diseases and governance of global risks through public communication and participation. Ann Ist Super Sanita 43: 336–343.

Egypt Violence Against Women Study Media Coverage of Violence Against Women

Dr. Enas Abu Youssef, Dr. Awatef Abdel Rahman,
Dr. Nagwa Kamel, Dr. Mehrez Ghally, Dr. Hanaa Farouk,
Doaa Hamed El Ghawabi, Marwa Radwan, Amal Hussein,
Asmaa Fouad and Ahmed Hussein

Executive Summary

This study attempts to identify the nature of the coverage of violence against women in the Egyptian mass media with the aim of introducing an effective media mechanism that will help expand interest in this issue beyond the limited academic community and dedicated authorities, and expanded to the general public.

This report was written by Dr. Enas Abu Youssef and the Cairo University Center for Research on Women and Media. The National Council for Women (NCW) selected Dr. Abu Youssef to conduct this secondary analysis of the NCW

Media Watch Unit's previously published reports. The study was conducted within the framework of the NCW's multidimensional study of violence against women in Egypt, funded by the United States Agency for International Development (USAID) through the Combating Violence Against Women project.

This study is based on a secondary analysis of six reports published by the NCW's Media Watch Unit from April 2005 to March 2006 and from February 2007 to February 2008. The theoretical framework of the study is based on the social cultural analysis model of monitoring the direct relationship between the media discourse and the prevalent culture and the social and political discourses in society.

The findings of the analytical study indicate that the media did not give sufficient attention to publishing information related to violence against women. Issues related to violence against women comprised only 17.4 percent of its total coverage of women's issues, based on the study sample. The representation of community violence was covered more often (66.1 percent of cases of media coverage of violence against women), compared to domestic violence (33.9 percent). Both print media and television were similar in their coverage of community violence (70 percent and 60.2 percent coverage of violence against women, respectively), and in their coverage of domestic violence (30 percent and 39.8 percent, respectively). Radio programs had an equal interest in domestic and community violence (50.1 percent and 49.9 percent coverage of violence against women, respectively).

The findings confirm that media discourse tends to focus negatively on sexual harassment of women at work and in the street. However, on the issue of political involvement of women, media discourse was divided between supporting and opposing women in politics. Of particular note is the media's general agreement with the idea that a woman does not have the right to be nominated for the presidency.

The review of the target audiences indicates that media messages do not differentiate by audience categories — rural/urban, age categories, and economic levels. Rather, media discourse is oriented primarily elite audiences.

In dramatic representation of violence against women on radio and television, the analysis shows that violence against women is one of the main sources for conflict in plots for broadcast dramas. Of the 48 percent of radio dramas that presented issues of violence against women, 86.8 percent depicted domestic violence and 13.2 percent depicted community violence. Of the 45 percent of television dramas presenting violence against women, 69.5 percent depicted domestic violence and 30.5 percent depicted community violence.

The qualitative analysis of the dramatic productions shows that, when these programs portray violence, the family's disintegration or malfunctioning is mostly the woman's fault and only she is to be blamed. In addition, in these productions, justifiable reasons are given for violence against women.

Introduction

Violence against women stems from Egypt's cultural heritage. The country's male-dominated culture reveres patriarchal authority in its current social relations. Exacerbating the negative effects of this male-dominated culture on Egyptian women is the relationship of violence against women to the deteriorating economic situation and the gap between different social categories and classes. However, with the increasing involvement of organizations concerned with women's rights, the issue of violence against women has attracted the attention of the Egyptian mass media in the past decade — especially the emerging media, such as privately owned newspapers, private television channels, and other media. Violence against women takes several forms, and is categorized as follows:

- Violence against women within the family (domestic violence)
- Violence against women within the society (community violence)
- Violence against women by the state

Each category may include subcategories, such as physical or psychological violence. Civil society organizations concerned with women's causes and rights are keen to monitor the role of Egyptian media in the representation of women's issues and images in the media. Foremost in this effort is the NCW, which signed an agreement with UNICEF in December 2003 to establish a Media Watch Unit concerned with the image of women in the Egyptian mass media. This agreement fit within one of NCW's main objectives — to propose general policies that contribute to the integration of Egyptian women in different fields of development.

The Media Watch Unit presented an evaluation of methods used by mass media to addressing issues related to Egyptian women, values included in the media discourse, and how this representation affects the formation of images of women in the media. The report was designed to acquaint policy-makers, media experts, and those concerned with women's issues with its findings. A major issue that the Media Watch Unit has analyzed in its six reports is violence against women and how it is addressed in print media and radio and television programs and dramas.

This study, produced under the direction of the Egyptian NCW and funded by USAID through the Combating Violence Against Women project, will shed light on the role of the mass media in influencing attitudes towards women in general and the representation of violence against women in particular. It is based a secondary analysis of the Media Watch Unit's reports on the Egyptian mass media's representation of violence against women. Therefore, this study includes the following:

1. A quantitative and qualitative analysis of the media coverage of violence against women during the past two years

2. An analysis of methods adapted by the media when addressing violence against women compared to the results of previous research in the same area during the past decade

3. Identification of the priority given to the issue of violence against women compared with other issues addressed by the media

4. Identification of patterns of violence against women on which the media has focused

Literature Review of Egyptian Media

Studies related to the mass media's coverage of women's issues during the past decade can be divided into three categories:

1. Studies that addressed women's issues in general (74 studies)

2. Studies that focused on violence as a main topic (18 studies)

3. Studies that focused only on violence against women (2 studies)

Media Studies that Addressed Women's Issues in General (74 Studies)

Covering the period from 1996 to 2007, the media studies that addressed women's issues in general included a sample from every type of mass media (print media, radio, television, and cinema). This research included both analytical and field studies. The field studies were based on samples from rural and urban districts in Upper and Lower Egypt and on random samples of media leadership in high administrative and management positions, including media figures in the Egyptian Radio and Television Union, in addition to communications experts from Egyptian newspapers. To analyze women's issues addressed by the mass media, these studies applied utilization and satisfaction assessments, survey research methods, comparative methods, quantitative and qualitative analysis methods, and discourse analysis.

A review of these studies reveals several findings:

1. The mass media are now more interested in social issues; traditional issues are of less importance. Also, the support of the mass media for participation of women in the political process has increased; women are encouraged to vote and to run for seats in the parliament and local councils. There is also a positive relationship between exposure to television and interest in women's political participation.

2. Print media communications experts are still dominated by stereotypical and traditional views of women, although some progress has occurred. Although an image of modern and creative working women has emerged, this image was nevertheless lost amid other images of women. Newspaper "crimes and incidents" sections and caricatures still typically focus on the image of a woman as unfaithful, a murderess, a mistress, a tyrant, an exploiter, a chatterbox, and an opportunist. These stereotypes cast women as the cause of family conflicts, while men are shown as providers and dominant members of the household. A similarity is suggested between the wife and the state, showing them both as supervisory authorities who may engage in coercion and, sometimes, violence. The image of women in social marketing campaigns differs from that in advertisements and music videos. While social marketing campaigns portray women positively and equal to men, advertisements and music videos usually exploit women as provocative symbols. In the cinema, portrayal of women is more often negative than positive, with women often associated with sexuality and the commission of illegal acts. Some studies have shown some improvement in the image of women as reflected in radio and television dramas.

3. Some media still portray women as negative, as weak creatures who are unable to make decisions or think logically, as emotional and superficial, with no initiative, and shying away from problems. Women were depicted in some dramatic works as caring only for appearances and formalities. Egyptian newspapers, television dramas and advertisements still focus on the traditional and stereotypical roles of women as mothers, wives, employees, victims, mistresses, and provocateurs. Although there is an increase in positive roles for women, the attention given to negative roles is nevertheless still greater. For example, mass media is usually keener to emphasize women committing illegal acts than men. Although the mass media is well aware of the productive role of women and the importance of including them in development processes for education, health, culture, economics, and politics through topics that deal with adult literacy, women's political participation and equality at work, this occurs only on political occasions with direction from political authorities.

4. The public's perception of women varies; it is positive when associated with the constructive role of women in the family but negative when associated with the mass media's distorted and superficial portrayal that focuses on women's femininity as an element of seduction and attraction to men. Rural women are portrayed as weak and inferior, a stereotypical and traditional image that marginalizes them and their issues. Some studies described female media professionals' disapproval of the image of women as portrayed by the mass media, concluding that these professionals' acceptance the prevalent traditional perceptions influences their work. Some studies noted the need for a media strategy that aims to change the negative image of women prevalent in the mass media.

5. The views of media professionals are affected by their affiliations and experience as well as their stereotypical images of women's role and status in society. These views affect what is printed or broadcast about women in the mass media. Some studies commented on female media professionals' lack of cultural and social awareness as well as their failure to understand the psychological dimensions that prevent them from fully understanding and effectively reporting on violence against women.

6. Media professionals of both genders are affected by limitations to their freedom in the field of media and the rights and obligations imposed on them by legislation that regulates journalism. In addition, like other egyptian women, female media professionals experience the same limitations in employment opportunities, travel, and training. Specific to their profession, they lack opportunities to advance to management positions in print media organizations to serve on editorial boards or in central editorial departments.

7. Media discourse does not focus equally on all values in its communication to the public. Although participation of both men and women in family life and responsibilities was the most prominent value revealed in daily newspapers (particularly national papers but also some political newspapers) and radio and television broadcasts, equality was the most prominent value discussed in some private and party newspapers and some radio and television programs. One study concluded that the egyptian public perceives equality between men and women in a stereotypical way, whether in daily life or through the symbolic reality reflected on television; findings revealed the projection of positive qualities on men and negative qualities on women. Some advertisements focus on equality between men and women and equal opportunities for their participation in public and family life. The values of loyalty and cooperation are depicted in some radio drama, but of freedom, forgiveness, and independence are rare. The value

of work appears in the content of some private, daily, and party newspapers.

8. Some publications still promote intellectual intolerance and extremism, demanding that women revert to the social, political and cultural backwardness typical of earlier centuries

9. The studies revealed the absence of a general mass media strategy for women's issues; radio and television programs and much writing for print media, present dual messages: at the same time that they urge women to participate in politics, they marginalize their political role and depict their responsibilities as limited to household chores. Similarly, the media presents contradictory images of women: one that is more traditional, showing women as obedient, submissive, helpless, self-sacrificing, and passive; and more modern image of independent, constructive women who are capable of making decisions and contributing to Egypt's development. Ms. Magda Omar believes that by adopting a media strategy that reflects male logic in the development process, women's contributions are marginalized.

10. The media discourse lacks clear social depth in addressing some important social issues, leading to misunderstandings. For example, a woman's right to retail the option of divorcing her husband is regarded superficially. Where the media could correct misinterpretations of this right by explaining the benefits to women, it instead portrays the only benefit as a woman denying her husband a say in the procedure.

11. Media discourse focuses on women of child-bearing age and ignores young girls, adolescents, and older women. The media also gives greater attention to urban women, whether by presenting their issues or portraying their stereotypical images, and ignoring poor and rural women.

12. The mass media addresses women's issues in incidental news rather than providing in-depth commentary that would provide context for these incidents and give news stories greater significance. Study findings reveal that in cinema and television drama address women's topics as secondary issues. However, women are depicted more than men in commercial advertisements.

13. International gender issues have influenced the media in Egypt, and some of these issues were linked to issues addressed in the Egyptian media. One example is equal rights for men and women. Coverage also emphasizes personal status issues such as restriction of the number of wives a man takes, the concept of judges presiding over divorce cases, providing houses for divorcees, female genital mutilation, and violence against women.

14. The media gives positive coverage to topics that are important to women in general, reflecting priorities and interests identified by the female public. Programs addressing women's appearance ranked highest, followed by topics related to health, children, and religion. The number of female viewers is higher for programs about women and families — more so in rural than urban districts. Television's agenda is similar to that of women, as women are interested in literacy, spinsterhood, early marriage, poverty, and violence against women, and drama reflects these priorities to some extent.

15. Studies concurred that television is the most common mass medium accessed by Egyptian women, followed by newspapers and radio, and that women prefer dramatic programs, especially television drama. Because drama attracts the largest audiences, it is a considerable and effective cultural force in the formation of mental images.

16. In terms of evaluating good gender-specific/women's magazines, the study notes that women's magazines are no longer concerned only with women's issues and the liberation of women, but resemble magazines that target broader audiences, with a feminine perspective.

17. Based on the total percentages gathered, the contributions of female media professionals in television and radio are far greater than in print media organizations or in management positions.

Media Studies that Focused on Violence as a Main Issue (18 Studies)

Covering the period from 1999 to 2005, the studies that focused on violence as the main issue included a sample from every type of mass media (print media, radio, television, and cinema). They included both analytical and field studies. The field studies were based on samples from rural and urban districts in Upper and Lower Egypt and on random samples of leadership in high administrative and management positions, including media figures in the Egyptian Radio and Television Union and communication experts at Egyptian newspapers. To analyze issues of violence addressed by the mass media, these studies applied utilization and satisfaction assessments, survey research methods, comparative methods, quantitative and qualitative analysis methods, and discourse analysis.

These studies found that the media still continues to portray women in a negative manner, portraying her as the main reason behind violence. Some of the results are as follows:

1. The studies confirmed that the print media focuses on violence committed by women. Although El Goumhoreya newspaper had discussed a case of violence against women, it was also interested in crimes committed by women and portrayed them as unfaithful, culprits, mistresses, and murderers.

2. The Egyptian cinema often denigrates the image of women, restricting their roles to sexual relationships with me, and typically presenting exaggerated images of corrupt women who violate taboos or appear as murderers, drug dealers, drug abusers, and prostitutes without any positive traits.

3. During the past five years, the mass media has shown a tendency to discuss some topics that were previously kept quiet, such as violence against women and female genital mutilation.

4. Field studies of media leadership reveal that the violence against women did not receive adequate media coverage.

5. Some studies confirmed that cases of violence against women are at the top of the Egyptian print media's priority list, although sexual harassment is at the bottom.

6. Newspapers have reported that violence often accompanies elections, and this restricts women from voting in public elections.

7. Studies suggest that addressing violence against women in the mass media offers benefits to the public by developing awareness of these issues. However, programs that discussed these issues tended to do so in a traditional and repetitive manner.

8. The studies concluded that it is important to improve the image of women in mass media by developing a media strategy that can enhance the image of women; focus on violence (such as beating, sexual harassment, and female genital mutilation) and discrimination against women; and increase the legal and social awareness that will guarantee the elimination of all forms of violence against women.

9. A study compared the communication agenda of nongovernmental organizations print media agenda over the period from June 2003 to May 2004. The study found that violence against women leads the communication agenda for nongovernmental organizations. Issues such as female genital mutilation had the highest priority, followed by psychological violence, rape, and sexual harassment. In contrast, the highest priority of the national newspapers was wife-beating, followed by rape and female genital mutilation.

Studies that Focused only on Violence against Women (2 Studies)

The studies that focus on violence against women are relatively recent; only two studies were done between 2003 and 2007. The first, a study of television drama, analyzes 30 Arabic movies, 10 evening dramatic series, and three Arabic drama series broadcast on Channel 1 during from September through November 1998. The study findings were based on a random sample of 400 episodes in Cairo governorate.

The second study, using media theory and frame analysis, was conducted on a sample from the newspapers El Ahram, El Akhbar, El Gomhoureya, El Messa, El Wafd, El Masry El Youm, El Dostour, El Osbou', and El Ahaly newspaper editions, published from October 23 to November 23, 2006. The study also examined everything that was published regarding a sexual assault case that occurred on November 23, 2006, the first day of the Bairam feast. In addition, a field study was conducted on a sample of 100 stories divided equally among the media and academic elites.

The study of television drama focused on violence between men and women as portrayed in Arabic drama. This study examined the perceptions and views of individuals toward violence in male/female relationships and the association of these views with what they saw portrayed in television dramas.

The television drama study concluded that:

1. The most common form of violence portrayed in the relationship between men and women was verbal violence (59.88 percent), followed by physical violence (21.14 percent), then both types in combination (18.98 percent).

2. Men commit physical violence most often (30.7 percent) in television drama; women committed verbal violence more often (70.59 percent).

3. Violence between men and women as portrayed in television drama occurs in rural districts (79.84 percent) more often than in cities 20.16 percent).

The print media study focused on identifying how Egyptian newspapers addressed sexual harassment.

The most important analytical and field results from the print media study are:

1. The study revealed that there are differences in print media coverage of sexual harassment. These differences not only were based on the different types of newspapers (national, party, or independent) but also were found among newspapers of the same type. Independent newspapers addressed

sexual harassment and assault most frequently (52.3 percent, followed by party newspapers at 30.8 percent and national newspapers at 16.9 percent). These newspapers addressed sexual harassment as a general issue in society by introducing an issue, presenting causes for its occurrence, and making recommendations for solving the problem. These findings conform with both the field study measuring feedback on the interest newspapers demonstrated in reporting on sexual harassment and the researchers' observations of the newspapers' level of interest in addressing the issue. El Dostour was most interested, followed by El Masry El Youm, El Ahaly, El Wafd, El Gomhoureya, El Ahram, El Mesaa, El Akhbar, and El Osbou'.

2. In comparing national newspapers' coverage of sexual harassment cases, El Gomhoureya gave the greatest amount of coverage. This newspaper is one that makes use of appealing editorial content, catchy titles, pictures, and colored headlines. Nevertheless, its perspective is similar to the other national newspapers, varying between criticism and caution regarding sexual harassment. In contrast, private newspapers focus more on the causes of sexual harassment (36.9 percent of total coverage of this issue), while national newspapers focused on the causes in 27.9 percent of coverage. Party newspapers were somewhere in the middle, focusing on the causes of sexual harassment in 32.2 percent of the coverage.

3. The newspapers under study show both differences and similarities in addressing the main themes, causes, and suggested solutions for issues of violence against women. With regard to general or main themes, the national newspapers opted to focus on sexual assault as the most dangerous form of violation of human rights, whereas party and private newspapers focused on sexual abuse of children attending primary and preparatory schools. In terms of the news media's views on the causes of sexual harassment, both the national and party newspapers blamed unemployment and delay in the age of marriage; the private newspapers focused on the lack of police security in congested areas. In proposing solutions to issues related to sexual harassment, the national newspapers were elimination of unemployment and removal of marriage prerequisites; the party and private newspapers focused on the elimination of the phenomenon of street children and the role of the National Council for Childhood and Motherhood.

4. The private newspapers elicited the greatest trust from the public (63 percent) regarding information on sexual harassment; party newspapers received 31 percent trust and the national newspapers 23 percent.

The study reveals the importance of conducting scientific research on the issues of sexual harassment and assault to evaluate their current status more comprehensively. The hazards of this issue do not lie only in its extent, nature, and frequency, but in what it suggests for the future with regard to disorders in the current social structure as well as what it reveals of the demise of traditional values in Egyptian society.

Main Study Concepts

Challenge

Based upon the findings discussed above, the challenge of this report is to develop and investigate scientific hypotheses in an effort to answer the following question: What is the nature, interest, and limitations of the Egyptian media in dealing with issues of violence against women in governmental, private, and specialized media?

This study is important because:

1. Few studies focus on this subject
2. The issue is becoming increasingly important in Arab societies in general and in Egypt in particular
3. Interest in women's rights has increased
4. The occurrence of severe human rights violations against women in Egypt necessitates that the media play a critical role in both documenting these incidents and mounting public awareness campaigns

Objectives

The main objective of this study is to identify the nature and limitations of the Egyptian mass media in all its material forms (print media — newspapers and magazines, radio, and television); forms of ownership (state, independent/private, party); audience type (for the general public or specialized); frequency of publication or broadcast; and content type (talk shows, drama, advertisements, print media articles) with regard to the issue of violence against women.

Several secondary objectives emerge from this main objective:

1. Defining issues of violence against women on which various mass media channels focuses — domestic, community, or state violence
2. Conducting a qualitative analysis of mass media coverage of violence against women
3. Comparing types of coverage of violence against women in the mass media

4. Analyzing the image of women in the mass media in relation to issues of violence against women with particular attention to the source and justifications of violence and reactions to it

Building on this study, the aim is to introduce an effective media mechanism to addresses violence against women in a way that extends the scope of interest to the entire Egyptian society rather than being limited to academic researchers and relevant, specialized authorities.

Hypotheses

Hypothesis 1

Significant statistical differences exist among different types of Egyptian mass media regarding coverage of violence against women. These include:

- Level of interest

- Forms and types of violence

- Justifications (arguments)

- Reaction and methods of addressing violence

- Geographical areas targeted by the media when addressing issues of violence

Hypothesis 2

Significant statistical differences exist among different types of Egyptian mass media regarding coverage of violence against women based on ownership of the media (state, private or party).

Hypothesis 3

Significant statistical differences exist among different types of Egyptian mass media regarding coverage of violence against women based on specialization of the media (for the general public or specialized).

Inquiries

1. What is the mass media's interest in violence against women in relation to its interest in Egyptian women's issues in general?

2. What is the most common form of violence against women as depicted in the Egyptian mass media?

3. What persuasive arguments (whether supporting or opposing) are made regarding violence against women as presented by the mass media?

4. What are the aspects of agreement or disagreement in the Egyptian mass media's representation of violence against women?

5. What is the source of violence against women presented in radio and television dramas?

6. What reactions to violence against women are presented in radio and television dramas?

7. What solutions do the Egyptian media introduce to combat violence against women?

Study Framework and Methodology

Theoretical Framework

The theoretical framework of the study is the social cultural analysis model of monitoring the direct relationship of media discourse to the prevalent cultural, social, and political discourses in society. The analysis assumes that this discourse truly affects the media and its outputs as it acts as a means for consolidation or obstruction of women's rights. Special attention is also is given to the role of religious speech as a fundamental influence on and its role in changing, consolidating, or critiquing this discourse.

Type of Study

This study is an analytical description that aims to monitor, describe, and analyze the representation of violence against women in the Egyptian mass media (print, television, and radio) according to its content type (print media articles, talk shows, drama, advertisements); extent of specialization (for the general public, specialized); and ownership pattern (state, party, or private).

Study Methods

Media Survey

The study is based on a survey methodology — the most suitable scientific methodology for descriptive studies in general. The aim is to record, analyze, and explain the current condition of a phenomenon. After collecting the necessary and sufficient data on the phenomenon and its elements, they are analyzed using a set of procedures that define the type of data, their source, and their method of collection55. The survey methodology is divided into two parts: a descriptive part that attempts to describe the phenomenon and the object of the study and an analytical part that attempts to explain and analyze the phenomenon under study and its causes.56 Within this framework, media messages related to violence against women were surveyed in the different Egyptian mass media.

Comparative Method

Researchers compared different intellectual perspectives of violence against women as addressed by mass media channels; they also compared the results of previous studies against one another.

Analysis Tools

This study relied on statistical quantitative analysis obtained using the statistical program SPSS and secondary qualitative analysis of the results of the monitoring and content analysis from the six reports previously published by the Media Watch Unit.

Study Scope and Survey Sample

This study is based on a secondary analysis of the Media Watch Unit's six reports. These reports include the findings of quantitative and qualitative monitoring and content analysis of 20,160 hours of television broadcasting and 20,160 hours of radio broadcasting (excluding news bulletins and movies).

The Egyptian print media sample encompassed 672 issues of Egyptian daily newspapers and magazines (national, party, and private) and 96 issues of Egyptian weekly newspapers (national, party, and private) and magazines. The drama sample included 64 television and radio series that were analyzed from April 2005 to March 2006 and from February 2007 to February 2008, based on the rotation method to specify the sample period and an artificial month (by selecting the first week of the first month, the second week of the second month, and so on until an artificial month is completed for analysis). The sample of the media material that the Media Watch Unit analyzed over the past two years included 10,648 occurrences of women's issues in print media; 6,469 occurrences in television productions and 643 in television dramas; and 3,899 occurrences in radio productions and 636 in radio dramas.

Procedural Definitions

Definition of Violence

The study used the definition of violence against women in the United Nations Declaration on the Elimination of Violence against Women, issued in December 1993 (resolution 48/104), which was adopted by the United Nations General Assembly. The declaration defines violence against women as any act of gender-based violence [that] results in, or is likely to result in, physical, sexual, or psychological harm or suffering to women, including threats of such acts, coercion, or arbitrary deprivation of liberty, whether occurring in public or in private life…

Violence against women shall be understood to encompass, but not be limited to, the following:

a. Physical, sexual and psychological violence occurring in the family, including battering, sexual abuse of female children in the household, dowry-related violence, marital rape, female genital mutilation, and other traditional practices harmful to women, non-spousal violence and violence related to exploitation;

b. Physical, sexual, and psychological violence occurring within the general community, including rape, sexual abuse, sexual harassment, and intimidation at work, in educational institutions and elsewhere, trafficking in women, and forced prostitution;

c. Physical, sexual and psychological violence perpetrated or condoned by the State, wherever it occurs.

Study Findings

Based on the sample drawn, violence against women was the subject of approximately one-third of the material published in Egyptian print media about Egyptian women (Table 1). This suggests that violence against women was present on the agenda of the Egyptian media.

Table 1. Print Media and Violence Against Women

Type of Issue	Quantity	Percentage
Issues of violence against women	3,096	29.1
Other women's issues	7,552	70.9
Total	**10,648**	**100**

The findings showed that community violence is the Egyptian media's first priority in its agenda regarding violence (Table 2). Domestic violence is the second priority, suggesting that the print media still exercises some caution in its coverage of domestic violence

Table 2. Print Media and Coverage of Violence Against Women

Forms of Violence in the Print Media	Quantity	Percentage
Discrimination and community violence	1,708	67
Domestic violence	8,41	33
Total	2,549	100

Forms of Domestic Violence against Women in the Print Media

The study's quantitative results indicate that the journalistic coverage addressed several forms of physical and psychological domestic violence against women. Psychological violence was a topic in 654 of 841 instances (77.7 percent) and physical violence in 187 (22.3 percent).

Print media covered various forms of psychological domestic violence (Table 3). The most attention was devoted to obstinacy in divorce, followed by insulting wives and the discrimination against girls within the family. Subjects such as polygamy and coercing girls into marriage receive the least coverage despite their harmful social consequences.

Table 3. Psychological Domestic Violence in the Egyptian Print Media

Psychological Domestic Violence Addressed in the Print Media	Quantity	Percentage
Obstinacy in divorce	163	19.4
Husband verbally insults wife	155	18.4
Family members are cruel to girls / mistreat girls	117	14
Wife portrayed as a tyrant	72	8.6
Marital infidelity	71	8.4
Polygamy	37	4.4
Girls coerced into marriage	27	3.2
Women are the main cause of marital problems and corruption of children	12	1.4
Total	654	100

An article in Ein magazine, "Have mercy on us," condemned psychological and physical domestic violence against girls by portraying the tragedy of a girl, not yet 16 years old, whose family tortured and humiliated her and whose father forced her to drop out of school and ordered her to marry her cousin. As a result, she killed herself. "Save me," an article in El Goumhoreya newspaper presented a girl's complaint in the form of a call to help from Egyptian society. To punish the girl's mother for divorcing him, her father prevented the girl from finishing school. El Akhbar newspaper printed a report on Nage Banan, the first Egyptian village to refuse to circumcise girls, and El Ahram newspaper printed an article by Dr. Hassan Noaman, a professor at Cairo Medical University, confirming that "forcing wives to have sexual intercourse is another form of physical domestic violence; it is one form of violence difficult to prove."

These examples reveal that Egyptian newspapers condemn the increase in violence against women and consider it a main indicator of family disintegration.

Table 4. Physical Domestic Violence in the Egyptian Print Media

Physical Domestic Violence Addressed in the Print Media	Quantity	Percentage
Wife beating	84	33.3
Female genital mutilation	75	29.8
Early marriages	21	8.3
Forcing woman to have an abortion	72	8.6
Total	252	100

Discrimination and Community Violence against Women in the Print Media

The analytical study's findings indicate inconsistency in print media coverage of discrimination against women and community violence: coverage appeared to reject all forms of violence against women at work and in the street but was divided between support and opposition of discrimination against women on the issue of participation in the political process (Table 5).

Community Violence against Women at Work in the Print Media

El Wafd newspaper confirmed that several hired men sexually harassed and attempted to rape female journalists and women who participated in a demonstration against the referendum to amend Clause 76 in the Egyptian Constitution. Journalist Abbas El Tarabeily condemned this behavior in El Wafd, saying "the state has reached a level where it pays its men to rape and harass women and girls."

Table 5. Discrimination and Violence Against Women in the Community

Discrimination and Violence Against Women in the Community	Quantity	Percentage
Focusing on portraying women as criminals	882	51.6
Invasion of privacy of female celebrities	313	18.3
Weak political participation of women	114	6.7
Treatment of women as commodities or merchandise	92	5.4
Rape	86	5
Absence of women in judicial positions	45	2.6
Harassment or verbal abuse of women	17	1
Absence of women in leadership positions	16	0.9
Difficulty of women to be nominated for presidency	8	0.5
Sexual harassment	75	4.4
Crimes against women	60	3.5
Total	**1,708**	**100**

El Akhbar newspaper printed a condemnation of the Arab Journalist Union regarding an incident of rape and sexual harassment of female journalists in front of the syndicate, noting "the district attorney was unable to identify the culprits who violated the female journalists."

The print media addressed some issues of physical community violence against women, such as sexual harassment at work (4.4 percent). Coverage is low because this is sensitive topic is considered taboo in Egyptian society. On the other hand, the print media never addressed the exposure of less fortunate women, such as farm or factory workers, to sexual harassment.

The print media portrayed the rape of women as a physical act of community violence in 5 percent of the total coverage of community violence against women, and it condemned sexual harassment of women in public transportation, demanding the separation of men and women in public transportation to protect women against all forms of physical sexual harassment. The print media discourse confirmed the importance of supporting rape victims, providing them with all means of protection, and attempting to change society's view of them. The newspapers condemned the increase of rape in general, and Sot El Omah newspaper condemned murders committed in the name of honor. Sot El Omah reported the story of a farmer who killed his wife because he was suspicious of her behavior and her ambition. The print media also addressed the exposure of women to verbal harassment and offenses to their modesty as a form of psychological community violence on 17 occasions (1 percent).

Discrimination against Women Participating in the Political Process in the Print Media

The state-owned El Ahram newspaper reported that the governing National Democratic Party nominated 60 businessmen as party representatives, but only six of the 160 women who had submitted their papers to the electoral committee. In the same newspaper, Ms. Ekbal Baraka questioned the National Party's position towards women running in parliamentary elections and criticized other political parties for their regressive views on women in Parliament.

The print media discourse attacked discrimination against women in the field of political participation (6.7 percent of cases), but it was also skeptical of women's capacity to be an eligible candidate for presidency (5 percent of cases).

Egyptian newspapers of all types of ownership — the national newspapers taking the lead — launched an organized campaign against marginalizing the participation of women in political life. In its presentation at a seminar conducted by the El Ahram Regional Institute on Egypt's experience in the elections in light of political plurality, El Ahram newspaper criticized and blamed the government for the low number of Egyptian women in the Egyptian Parliament in 2005.

The state-owned newspaper, El Gomhoureya, vigorously opposed the idea of a female presidential candidate. This position reflects the state's vision, because the state owns this publication.

El Gomhoureya newspaper discussed the nomination of women in the presidential elections, commenting that "Eve herself refuses to assume the president's position." A female columnist asked "if it was logical to give her vote in the presidential elections to Ashgan, Nageya, or Hamdeya running against President Hosny Mubarak with his long experience. Is it logical to risk supporting women who had never run in any elections and never performed any political work in their lives?"

The newspaper also printed an interview with Dr. Fawzeya Abdel Sattar, former chair of the Parliament's legislative committee. Dr. Sattar confirmed that women are not permitted to nominate themselves for the presidential elections because men are more capable, Egypt does not lack male presidential candidates, and men are the caretakers of women."

Relationship between Gender of Sources and Coverage of Violence in the Print Media

The attitudes of a journalist's sources used by a journalist affect the print media coverage of violence. Many studies have shown that using both genders as sources has the greatest effect on the representation of issues. The studies also show that male sources may be more persuasive when addressing certain topics might have a more persuasive effect.

The quantitative results indicate that the use of both genders as sources varies, depending on the topic (Table 6). Male sources are most often used in discussions of subjects related to violence (34.7 percent), followed by female sources (27.4 percent), sources whose gender is not identified (19.6 percent), and sources of both genders (18.3 percent).

Table 6. Gender of Source

Gender of Source	Quantity	Percentage
Men only	883	34.7
Women only	707	27.4
Gender not identified	500	19.6
Men and women together	459	18.3
Total	2,549	100

Detailed findings revealed that men were more common sources on neglect of wives by husbands (62 percent) than female sources (19.7 percent). Regarding exposure of women to sexual harassment, men were sources more frequently (50 percent) than women (16.7 percent).

The statistical analysis confirmed that men were more often sources on topics that denigrate women's images and portray them as criminals (64.9 percent) and tyrants (42.1 percent). Men were the only source who provided bad examples of women at work (100 percent).

Meanwhile, female sources exceed male sources on topics such as cruelty of stepmothers (40 percent), marital infidelity (27.5 percent) and problems facing working women (46.7 percent).

Both men and women were sources on topics such as coercing girls into marriage (42.9 percent), women's daily sufferings (46.2 percent), and legal aspects of violence against women (91.9 percent).

Respondents noted two positive points regarding the media's persuasiveness related to VAW issues: first, that both males and females (experts and members of the public) took part in addressing some issues of domestic and community violence, and second, that male sources served as sources who were against some issues of domestic violence, thus emphasizing that both men and women disagree with domestic violence. Male journalists more often addressed violence against women in the Egyptian print media (55.2 percent) than female journalists (23.2 percent).

Male and female journalists worked together to address issues related to violence at a very low rate (0.6 percent).

Table 7. Gender of Journalist Addressing Violence Against Women

Gender of Journalist	Quantity	Percentage
Men	1,407	55.2
Women	591	23.2
Journalist not mentioned / gender not apparent	535	21
Both together	16	0.6
Total	2,549	100

Detailed analytical results reveal that only male journalists addressed some topics related to VAW, such as Coptic women's right to civil divorce, loss of trust between married couples, denigration of women's images in media, poor examples of women at work, and social pressure on women. Only female journalists addressed male chauvinism toward women.

Male journalists more often addressed other issues related to violence, such as marital infidelity (60 percent), neglect of women by men (69 percent), cruelty of stepmothers (80 percent), coercing girls into marriage (71.4 percent), problems facing working women (44 percent), and exploitation of women in music videos (50 percent)

Print media coverage by male journalists took a negative perspective of some topics, such as portrayal of women as criminals (72 percent) or tyrants (60.5 percent), and invasion of privacy of female celebrities (41.2 percent compared to 19.6 percent by females).

Female journalists more often addressed the marital problems of female celebrities (40 percent compared to 26.7 percent by males) and the daily sufferings of women (61.5 percent). Coverage of sexual harassment by male and female journalists was equal (50 percent each).

The general public was most often the target of the cases addressing violence (59.2 percent), followed by the entire family (26.2 percent), women (11.1 percent), a specific audience (1.4 percent), children (0.7 percent), and youth (0.2 percent).

Table 8. Target Audience for Print Media Discourse on Violence against Women

Target Audience	Quantity	Percentage
General public	1,509	59.2
Family	668	26.2
Women	283	11.1
Specific audience	36	1.4
Men	29	1.2
Children	18	0.7
Youth	6	0.2
Total	**2,549**	**100**

Coverage of different forms of violence against women most often targets the general public. This is a positive indicator, emphasizing that these issues do not concern women alone but are social problems that need the combined efforts of society to solve them.

Nevertheless, ignoring the different environments of the targeted audiences (Table 9) is an indication that the print media has the urban districts and elites at the top of its agenda — revealing a primarily elite-oriented discourse. Marginalization of audiences in crowded neighborhoods, rural districts, and Bedouin areas suggests that print media discourse is not concerned with the uniqueness of the different areas; therefore, it does not address the separate problems of each area.

Table 9. Environment of Target Audience

Environment of Target Audience	Quantity	Percentage
Entire society	2,022	79.3
Rural and urban districts	208	8.1
Urban districts (upper-class neighborhoods)	143	5.6
Urban districts (middle-class neighborhoods)	113	4.4
Urban districts (low-income neighborhoods)	39	1.5
Rural districts	21	0.8
Bedouin areas		0.1
Total	**2,549**	**100**

General Analysis

The print media discourse has included the issue of violence on its agenda, at least quantitatively (29.1 percent). This quantitative indicator does not reflect in-depth coverage or regular campaigns combating different forms of violence against women; rather, it reflects the fact that most coverage was sporadic and in response to particular incidents or as part of coverage of public events, not a newspaper's initiative to combat violence as a social phenomenon.

The analysis showed that print media still tackles issues of domestic violence hesitantly and omits mention of issues considered taboo and not to be addressed. As such, issues related to family violence (domestic violence) ranked in second place in reporting after community violence. Analysis of the print media coverage of community violence confirmed that print media discourse has contributed to creating a type of psychological violence against women by denigrating the image of women in discussions of crime-related issues, diminishing them through caricatures, or objectifying them as mere bodies or symbols of provocation and attraction in advertisements. Commenting negatively and denigrating the image of women when reporting on community violence occurred more frequently (75.3 percent) than reporting on community violence against women in general. The numbers bring into question the journalists' awareness of the forms of violence against women.

As a result of sporadic coverage of violence and insufficient awareness of violence against women, journalistic discourse is very general and does not reflect unique environments or social classes. In addition, coverage was primarily oriented toward elites, the upper class, and upper segments of the middle class, with rare exceptions. As a result, forms of violence that are prevalent among the poorer social classes, such as sexual harassment in factories and fields, incest in slum areas, and trading of girls through so-called summer marriages, are absent from the print media discourse agenda.

The print media did not offer solutions to issues of either domestic or community violence against women addressed in the print media discourse. Rather, print coverage only requested separation of men and women in public transportation to minimize harassment of women. However, plenty of attention was given to the absence of political participation by women, leading to demands by the print media to strengthen laws and legislation guarantee fair representation of women in the Egyptian Parliament.

Television Programs and Violence against Women

Approximately 20 percent of the total occurrences of women's issues on television addressed violence against women during the sample period, thus affirming the existence of this issue on the agenda of Egyptian television (Table 10).

Table 10. Women's Issues on Television

Type of Issue	Quantity	Percentage
Violence against women	1,164	18
Other women's issues	5,305	82
Total	6,469	100

Forms of Violence Against Women on Television Programs

Discrimination and community violence against women were more frequently addressed on television compared to domestic violence (56.3 percent versus 43.7 percent, respectively) (Table 11). Interest in community violence is attributable to the broadcast of political programs that discuss participation of women in political life and the many topics and events covered on television during the monitoring period, such as constitutional amendments and legislative and local council elections.

Table 11. Forms of Violence Against Women on Television

Forms of Violence	Quantity	Percentage
Discrimination and community violence	431	56.3
Domestic violence	335	43.7
Total	766	100

In addressing domestic violence, television programs focused on some forms of psychological domestic violence, such as husbands insulting wives verbally (27.5 percent); portraying wives as tyrants (11.3 percent), obstinacy in divorce (10.9 percent), accusing women of causing marital problems and corrupting children (8.9 percent), polygamy (6.9 percent), marital infidelity (3.6 percent), and coercing girls into marriage (3.3 percent). Television programs also covered some forms of physical domestic violence among domestic violence issues that were addressed, such as wife-beating (9.9 percent), female genital mutilation (8.9 percent), early marriage (7.2 percent), and forcing women to have medically unnecessary abortions (2.1 percent) (Table 12).

Discrimination and Community Violence against Women on Television Programs

The Dream2 television channel condemned both psychological and physical domestic violence against Egyptian women. The programs Sayedati Anysati and El 'ashera Masaan presented many acts of violence against Egyptian women, such as marital infidelity, beatings, and insults to wives. The channel noted that 43 percent of women in Egypt are beaten by their husbands and 30 percent of those women suffer from physical and psychological effects that require medical attention.

Table 12. Forms of Domestic Violence Against Women on Television

Domestic Violence Against Women	Quantity	Percentage
Husbands insulting wives verbally	92	27.5
Portrayal of wife as a tyrant	38	11.3
Obstinacy in divorce	35	10.9
Wife-beating	33	10.4
Accusing women of causing marital problems and corrupting children	30	8.9
Female genital mutilation	30	8.9
Early marriage	24	7.2
Polygamy	23	6.9
Marital infidelity	12	3.6
Coercing girls into marriage	11	3.3
Abortion (when medically unnecessary)	7	2.1
Total	**355**	**100**

Television programs covered some forms of discrimination and community violence against women at work, in political participation, and in the streets, while some television programs focused on psychological violence against women (Table 13).

Discrimination against Women at Work and in Political Participation

The Arab House program considered the lack of political participation by women and the weakness of representation of women in Parliament as a sign of the government's indifference to women and women's rights. The program demanded support for women's political rights and representation in Parliament.

Magalet El Mara'ah and Good Morning Egypt called for a search for a legal solution that would result in fair representation of Egyptian women in Parliament. Channel 8 highlighted the decline in women's political participation and the weak representation of women in Parliament, suggesting that the government, all political parties, and civil society organizations search for radical solutions to this problem.

Table 13. Discrimination and Violence Against Women in the Community

Discrimination and Violence Against Women in the Community	Quantity	Percentage
Weak political participation by women	130	30.2
Absence of women in leadership positions	87	20.2
Rape	46	10.7
Failure of women to occupy judicial positions	44	10.2
Treating women as a commodity or merchandise in advertisements and music videos	43	10
Focusing on portraying women as criminals	31	7.2
Invasion of the privacy of female celebrities	30	6.9
Difficulty for women to be nominated for presidency	10	2.3
Sexual harassment	10	2.3
Crimes against women	0	0
Sexual abuse	0	0
Total	**431**	**100**

Television programs focused on two types of psychological community violence against women — disparaging women's capacity to occupy leadership positions (20.2 percent) and judicial positions (10.2 percent).

Television programs addressed discrimination against political participation by women in 30.2 percent of cases and skepticism of women's capacity as presidential candidates in 2.3 percent of cases.

Community Violence against Women in the Streets

Television programs addressed issues of physical community violence against women such as rape (10.7 percent) and exposure of women to verbal harassment and offending their modesty (2.3 percent each).

The West El Balad program presented by Ms. Shafky El Moneiry on Channel 1 condemned rapes of large numbers of women and girls. According to the program, some statistics revealed 34 rapes every six months. The program condemned all community violence against women and characterized it as a form of tyranny that causes Egyptian women all ages to commit suicide. The El kessa we ma fiha program presented by Ms. Rola Kharsa noted increased sexual harassment of

Egyptian women and girls. The program argued that a large percentage of women and girls in Egypt are sexually harassed on public transportation due to the absence of security measures that could end such crimes.

Gender of Guests and Violence in Television Programs

In television programs that discuss issues of violence against women, those whose only featured guests were female were the most common (52.3 percent), followed by programs with only male guests (23.2 percent) and programs in which guests of both genders appeared together (15.6 percent) (Table 14).

Detailed results reveal that female guests were invited to participate in programs that discussed problems of working woman and other problems, such as wife-beating, polygamy, balancing work and family, the right to occupy leadership and judicial positions, political empowerment of women, female genital mutilation, and traditions that lead to discrimination against women at work. Men were invited as guests on programs discussing the role of women in marital problems, family conflicts, and boredom in marital life.

Table 14. Gender of Guests

Gender of Guests	Quantity	Percentage
Women only	400	52.2
Men only	178	23.2
Both men and women together	120	15.6
No Guests	68	9
Total	766	100

Programs dealing with violence confirmed that had only male presenters (50 percent) were more common than those with only female presenters (35.1 percent), or with male and female co-presenters (14.9 percent) (Table 15).

Men were presenters of programs focusing on several related issues, such as passing over women for work trips abroad, a woman's right to be nominated to the presidency, increased unemployment among women, employers' preference for male workers, denying women training opportunities, forcing women to work in unsuitable conditions, institutional violence, depriving women of free expression opinions, objectifying women as commodities, and incompatible marriages.

Women were the only presenters for programs addressing female celebrities' marital problems, rape, early marriage, polygamy, and Coptic women's right to divorce. Men were presenters on programs addressing marital infidelity, verbal abuse of women by their husbands, portrayal of women as tyrants and criminals, exploitation of women in music videos, sexual harassment, polygamy, accusing women of causing marital problems and corrupting children, a women's right to occupy leadership positions, and forced abortions. Men were also the presenters on programs regarding the habits, traditions and customs that disempower women, such as depriving women of their inheritances and the restricting the participation of women in public life and at work.

Female presenters were active in television programs addressing problems of working woman and their ability to combine work and family, women occupying leadership positions, allocation of Parliament seats for women, inclusion of women on election lists, obstinacy in divorce, paternity suits, a woman's right to travel abroad without her husband's permission, rape, and customs that reinforce women's inferior status. Men and women were commonly co-presenters on television programs on the selection of males over females in the field of education, verbal harassment, wife-beating, early marriage, and customs and traditional values that oppose women working.

Table 15. Gender of the Program Presenters and the Representation of Violence

Gender of Program Presenter	Quantity	Percentage
Male only	383	50
Female only	269	35.1
Male and female co-presenters	114	14.9
Total	**766**	**100**

The statistical analysis confirmed that the television programs addressing violence targeted the general public (46.2 percent), women (32 percent), and the entire family (17 percent); while the targeting of men was very weak (4.2 percent). Television programs also targeted children (0.3 percent), specific audiences (0.2 percent) and youth (0.1 percent) (Table 16). The categories of children and youth need special attention because they are most susceptible to changing social ideas and harmful behaviors. It is easy to shape their attitudes toward women by refuting the social and cultural heritage that helps to spread violence.

Table 16. Target Audience of Television Programs Regarding Violence Against Women

Target Audience	Quantity	Percentage
General public	353	46.2
Women	245	32
Family	130	17
Men	32	4.2
Children	3	0.3
Specific audience	2	0.2
Youth	1	0.1
Total	**766**	**100**

The statistical analysis confirmed that the entire Egyptian society was the main target of programs addressing issues of violence against women (91.9 percent), while 7.6 percent of such programs targeted rural societies and 0.4 percent of the programs targeted urban societies (Table 17).

Rural districts were targeted by programs addressing issues such as male domination, depriving women of education, early marriage, polygamy, female genital mutilation, customs that reinforce the inferior status of women, and harmful social practices. This confirms that the television programs support uniqueness local environments and that the media discourse aims to change customs and traditions that oppress women's rights. The programs targeting the entire society discussed all issues related to different forms of violence, whether domestic — such as marital infidelity, wife-beating, polygamy, and early marriage — or community violence, such as discrimination against women at work, portrayal of women as criminals, and restriction of women's participation in public life.

Table 17. Focus of Target Audience

Focus of Audience	Quantity	Percentage
Entire society	704	91.9
Rural districts	58	7.6
Urban districts	4	0.4
Total	**766**	**100**

General Analysis

Although the issue of violence against women is present on the agenda of television programs, the issue still does not attract the expected attention in Egyptian television. Television is considered one of the most important means of affecting awareness among the Egyptian population. As shown by the analytical findings described above, television programs address issues of violence only periodically, and they avoid discussions of critical issues such as domestic violence, which is last on agenda of interests of television programs.

The analysis also indicated that Egyptian television programs concerned with women's issues typically oppose community violence. In contrast, programs usually represented domestic violence as a result of the general spread of violence, unemployment, and disintegration of the family. Television programs did not often suggest solutions to these problems or encourage society to combat violence.

Radio Productions and Violence against Women

Radio programs addressing violence against women did not exceed 15 percent of the total radio coverage of women's issues during the sample period (Table 18). This suggests the low priority of this issue on the agenda of the Egyptian radio.

Table 18. Type of Issue Addressed

Type of Issue	Quantity	Percentage
The issue of violence against women	573	14.7
Other women's issues	3,326	85.3
Total	3,899	100

Radio programs more commonly addressed domestic violence (58.5 percent) than community violence (41.5 percent) (Table 19). This is in contrast to the print media and television, which were more concerned with community violence than domestic violence.

Table 19. Forms of Violence Against Women Addressed

Form of Violence	Quantity	Percentage
Domestic violence	196	58.5
Discrimination and community violence	139	41.5
Total	335	100

Radio Productions of Domestic Violence against Women

Media discourse in radio leans toward combating domestic violence generally, the violence is whether physical or psychological. Acts of psychological violence were addressed in 72.4 percent of programs on domestic violence; acts of physical violence were addressed in 27.6 percent of such programs (Table 20).

Table 20. Forms of Violence by Radio Programs Addressing Domestic Violence

Forms of Violence in Radio Programs	Quantity	Percentage
Psychological violence	142	72.4
Physical violence	54	27.6
Total	196	100

Radio programs most frequently covered mistreatment of girls by family members (18.4 percent), husbands verbally insulting thief wives (15.3 percent), female genital mutilation (14.3 percent), and early marriage (8.2 percent) (Table 21). Radio programs also focused on problems related to a women's right to obtain alimony as a form of violence against women. Discussion of other issues was neglected, which suggests that the Egyptian radio needs to discuss forms of violence more broadly, especially domestic violence, as many studies have indicated an increase in the number of listeners in rural areas who might not have other sources of news and information.

Table 21. Forms of Domestic Violence Addressed by Radio Programs

Forms of Domestic Violence Against Women in Radio Programs	Quantity	Percentage
Mistreatment of girls by family members	36	18.4
Husband verbally insulting wife	30	15.3
Female genital mutilation	28	14.3
Obstinacy in divorce	17	8.7
Early marriages	16	8.2
Wife-beating	9	4.6
Portraying wife as a tyrant	9	4.6
Coercing girls into marriage	7	3.5
Total	196	100

The For Men Only program discussed the tyranny of men obtaining divorces. The For Housewives program discussed the dangers of polygamy, the fight for women's rights, and the struggle to combat discrimination against women. On the Al Quran Al Karim station, in response to a question about the right to divorce, a guest stated that the reason that divorce is a man's decision and that women do not have the right to divorce is that God made men responsible for women.

Discrimination and Community Violence Addressed by Radio Programs

Discrimination Against Women in the Field of Political Participation

Some radio programs addressed discrimination against women in the field of political participation in general (18.7 percent) (Table 22) without addressing a woman's eligibility to be nominated for the presidency in particular, even though this issue was addressed in print and on television during the two-year sample period. Radio, on the other hand, addressed women's right to participate in political life, emphasizing the role of the state in removing obstacles restricting women's participation, such as efforts of the state and political parties to include women on elections list and the introduction of laws that enable the effective political participation of women.

Discrimination against Women at Work

Radio programs addressed two types of discrimination against women at work: doubting their ability to occupy leadership positions (6.5 percent) and judicial positions (3.6 percent) (Table 22).

Community Violence against Women in the Streets

Radio programs discussed rape in 5.8 percent of programs addressing community violence (Table 22), a low percentage that indicates that radio programs are still reluctant to tackle the taboo subjects that are usually kept quiet.

On programs that addressed issues of violence against women, those with only female guests were most common (44.2 percent), followed by programs with no guests (31.9 percent), only male guests (23.4 percent), or both male and female guests (0.5 percent) (Table 23). The presentation of only a woman's point of view is not enough when discussing issues of violence; these issues should be discussed in the presence of both genders to give a complete picture. In addition, presenting only a women's point of view encourages audience prejudices, leading to superficial attention to these issues. In several cases, the absence of guests was due to the short time provided for the discussion of the issue.

Table 22. Discrimination and Violence Against Women in the Community

Discrimination and Violence Against Women in the Community	Quantity	Percentage
Invasion of privacy of female celebrities	71	51.1
Weak political participation of women	26	18.7
Treating women as commodities or in music videos	15	10.7
Absence of women in leadership positions	9	6.5
Rape	8	5.8
Absence of women in judicial positions	5	3.5
Portrayal of women as criminals	5	3.5
Sexual abuse	0	0
Crimes against women	0	0
Harassment or verbal abuse of women	0	0
Preventing women from being nominated for the presidency	0	0
Total	**139**	**100**

Table 23. Gender of Guests and Issues of Violence in Radio Programs

Gender of Guests	Repetition	Percentage
Women only	148	44.2
No guests	107	31.9
Men only	78	23.4
Women and men together	2	0.5
Total	**335**	**100**

Female presenters were concerned with the issues of divorce, marital infidelity, verbal abuse of wives by husbands, cruelty of families towards girls, gender discrimination in all aspects of life, female genital mutilation, sexual harassment, paternity cases, and obstacles to the inclusion of women on elections lists.

Male presenters were more concerned with crimes committed by women, polygamy and the reasons behind it, discrimination against women at work, and passing over women for training opportunities and work trips abroad.

Table 24. Gender of Program Presenter and Issues of Violence

Gender of Program Presenter	Quantity	Percentage
Women only	205	61.1
Men only	109	32.5
Women and men together	21	6.4
Total	335	100

Target Audience of Radio Programs Regarding Violence Against Women

Radio programs addressing issues of violence targeted the general public (57 percent), women (24.6 percent), the entire family (15.5 percent), children (0.9 percent), specific audiences (1 percent), and youth (1 percent) (Table 25).

Table 25. Target Audience for Programs on Violence Against Women

Target Audience	Quantity	Percentage
General public	191	57
Women	79	24.6
Family	52	15.5
Youth	5	1
Specific audience	5	1
Children	3	0.9
Total	335	100

All of Egyptian society was the main target of radio programs addressing issues of violence (94.9 percent); 4.7 percent of these programs targeted rural audiences and 0.4 percent targeted urban audiences. Rural districts were targeted by programs addressing issues such as early marriage, polygamy, female genital mutilation, and depriving girls of education. These topics confirm that the programs support unique local environments and that radio discourse aims to change customs and traditions that oppress women's rights.

General Analysis

Radio programs address controversial issues only marginally, focusing mainly on the official international agenda that places women's political participation at the top of its priorities. Radio could have an important role in shaping public awareness of the dangers of and possible solutions to violence against women. For example, broadcasts could mention success stories and role models for combating violence against women.

Radio and Television Drama and Violence against Women

Violence against Women in Radio Drama

Radio dramas focused on domestic more than community violence (Table 26). Radio dramas also presented different points of view on combating violence, consistent with the nature of dramatic work that usually attempts to present a conflict and a solution. Domestic violence was more commonly depicted in radio drama (90.9 percent) than community violence (9.1 percent).

Table 26. Forms of Violence Against Women in Radio Drama

Type of Violence	Quantity	Percentage
Domestic violence	159	90.9
Discrimination and community violence	16	9.1
Total	**175**	**100**

Based on the qualitative analysis, radio drama has been supportive of women and has condemned forms of domestic violence.

Table 27. Forms of Domestic Violence Against Women in Radio Drama

Domestic Violence Against Women in Radio Drama	Quantity	Percentage
Wife-beating	24	15.1
Coercing girls into marriage	22	13.8
Polygamy	20	12.6
Marital infidelity	13	8.2
Portrayal of wives as tyrants	12	7.5
Depriving girls of choice of life partners	11	6.9
Early marriage	5	3.1
Husband using wife to achieve certain objectives	10	6.3
Obstinacy in divorce	10	6.3
Husband's greed for wife's inheritance	8	5
Female genital mutilation	7	4.4
Stepfather's cruelty and misuse of stepdaughters	5	3.1
Coercing girls to drop out of school	5	3.1
Abortion (when medically unnecessary)	4	2.5
Limiting women's role to breeding	3	1.9
Total	**159**	**100**

Radio drama marginalized issues of community violence and discrimination against women, with only 16 shows addressing the topic during the two years when programs were sampled. Issues of violence represented included rape (62.5 percent), treating women as commodities (18.8 percent, 3 occasions), exploitation of women in music videos in (12.5 percent, 2 occasions), and depriving women of the right to receive pensions (6.2 percent, a single occasion) (Table 28).

Table 28. Discrimination and Community Violence Against Women in Radio Dramas

Violence against Women in the Community	Quantity	Percentage
Rape	10	62.5
Treating women as commodities	3	18.8
Exploitation of women in music videos	2	12.5
Depriving women of the right to receive pensions	1	6.2
Total	16	100

Methods of Combating the Forms of Violence Presented in Radio Drama

Radio drama did not present a vision for combating violence that would lead to strengthening the image of women (for example, how to endure or attempt to fight psychological and physical harm). Radio dramas also did not present ways to legally combat violence or motivate public opinion against the phenomenon. Nor did they provide an enlightened vision for tackling other issues of violence against women, such as coerced marriage, except through individual interventions by a parent.

Source of Violence in Radio Drama

Men were the source of violence in 54.5 percent of radio dramas and while women in 45.5 percent. Violence directed toward women by men was most frequent (40.6 percent), followed by violence directed toward men by women (26.6 percent) and violence directed at women by other women (9.7 percent). Both categories of violence by women summed to 36.3 percent, almost equal to the level of violence directed at women by men. Violence directed at men by men was 8.6 percent, followed by self-inflected violence by women (5.3 percent) by parents toward children (4.3 percent), by the police (3.9 percent), and self-inflicted violence by men and violence by children toward parents (both 0.5 percent).

Violence against Women in Television Drama

Domestic violence dominated (71.3 percent) in television dramas dealing with the issue of violence against women, compared to community violence (28.7 percent) (Table 29).

Table 29. Forms of Violence Against Women in Television Drama

Type of Violence	Quantity	Percentage
Domestic violence	206	71.3
Discrimination and community violence	83	28.7
Total	289	100

Forms of Domestic Violence against Women in Television Drama

Acts of psychological domestic violence against women in television drama are numerous, including portraying women as the main cause of marital problems and corruption of children (18.4 percent), portraying a wife as a tyrant (17 percent), obstinacy in divorce (9.7 percent), polygamy (8.3 percent), marital infidelity (7.3 percent), neglect of wives by husbands (5.3 percent), and coerced marriage (2.9 percent). These were followed by cruelty of family members towards girls; depriving women of free expression of opinions, attitudes, and thoughts; incompatible marriages (2.6 percent each); and men's right to insult women (1.5 percent) (Table 30)

Forms of Physical Domestic Violence against Women in Television Drama

The acts of physical domestic violence against women are numerous in television drama, including instances of wife-beating (14 percent), abortion when medically unnecessary (3.4 percent), early marriage (2.9 percent), and female genital mutilation (2.4 percent) (Table 30). The latter indicates that the issue of female genital mutilation still does not appear in television drama, although some writers have adopted an enlightened attitude toward this issue.

The television series A Women's Outcry addressed female genital mutilation when Tharwat, the father of a girl who was going to be genitally mutilated by a barber, feels sorry that she is crying and says he doesn't want the procedure done to his daughter. His mother-in-law replies "What are you saying? This is our tradition, and circumcision is for the chastity of girls." Afifi responds, "Chastity should be embedded in our children as part of their upbringing, and there is no evidence in the Quran and Prophet Mohammed's sayings about the obligation to perform this act. It's a Pharonic custom, not to mention that it is barbaric. So why should we uphold it?" Tharwat's mother-in-law replies, "All the women in the family were circumcised." The girl is circumcised, and she bleeds to death.

Table 30. Forms of Psychological Domestic Violence in Television Drama

Violence against Women in the Family	Quantity	Percentage
Women considered the main cause of marital problems and corruption of children	38	18.4
Wife portrayed as a tyrant	35	17
Wife-beating	29	14
Obstinacy in divorce	20	9.7
Polygamy	17	8.3
Marital infidelity	15	7.3
Neglect of wives by husbands	11	5.3
Abortion (when medically unnecessary)	7	3.4
Coercing girls into marriage	6	2.9
Early marriage	6	2.9
Cruelty of family members toward girls	5	2.4
Female genital mutilation	5	2.4
Depriving women of free expression of opinions, attitudes, and thoughts	5	2.4
Incompatible marriage	4	1.9
Husband's right to verbally insult wife	3	1.5
Total	**206**	**100**

The acts of community violence against women in television drama are numerous, including rape and the negative view of the society toward the raped woman as scandalous and a disgrace (35 percent), followed by portraying women as criminals (19.3 percent), denying women their inheritance (14.5 percent), sexual touching (12 percent), and illiteracy and considering girls the cause of anxiety and problems (6 percent each) (Table 31).

Table 31. Discrimination and Community Violence Against Women in Television Drama

Discrimination and Violence against Women in the Community	Quantity	Percentage
Rape and the negative view of the rape victim	35	42.2
Focusing on portraying women as criminals	16	19.3
Denying women their inheritance	12	14.5
Sexual touching of women	10	12
Considering girls the cause of anxiety and problems	5	6
Women illiteracy	5	6
Total	**83**	**100**

Methods of Combating the Different Forms of Violence in Television Drama

Two television series A Case of Public Opinion and A Woman's Outcry, showed support for the right of women to combat violence against them by all means, legally and in the media. Both series offered reasonable and logical justifications for the need to combat violence and address taboo subjects — particularly in the face of fear of scandal and threats of negative images of female victims of violence. The programs also emphasized that rape victims are not responsible for these assaults.

Sources of Violence in Television Drama

Men were portrayed as the source of violence in 63.8 percent of television dramas and women in 36.2 percent. In 35 percent, men were violent toward women. This violence is often portrayed in drama as justified by showing women as raging and screaming tyrants who force men to resort to violent responses. Violence was directed at men by other men (22.5 percent), at men by women (19.8 percent), by women toward each other (12.2 percent), by parents toward children (4.8 percent), by children toward parents (2.4 percent), by the police (1.9 percent), self-inflected by women through suicides and abortions (0.8 percent), and self-inflicted violence men (0.6 percent) (Table 32).

In A Case of Public Opinion, Nadia's husband learns that her her sister Abla was raped, and tells his wife not to allow Abla to stay at their house because her situation is a catastrophe, and scandalous among his colleagues at school. Dr. Abla replies, "you should know that I am protecting the future generations."

Table 32. Sources of Violence in Television Drama

Source of Violence	Quantity	Percentage
By man to woman	164	35
By man to man	105	22.5
By woman to man	93	19.8
By woman to woman	57	12.2
By parents to children	22	4.8
By children to parents	11	2.4
Self-inflicted by woman	4	0.8
By police	9	1.9
Self-inflicted by man	3	0.6
Total	**468**	**100**

General Analysis

The findings discussed above indicate that radio and television dramas use domestic violence as the principal material for their work. Although some dramatic works discuss issues of violence against women and support women's causes — such as defending rape victims and criticizing the immorality of coerced marriage —the quantitative analysis shows that radio and television dramas depicting family conflict usually present women as solely responsible for family disintegration. Moreover, television and radio dramas suggest that the best way to reform a woman is to reproach or hit her, and such violence is always presented in a justifiable manner that will appear to viewers as the appropriate solution. Therefore, it is vital to recommend the broadcasting of enlightened drama productions like the television series A Woman's Outcry and A Case of Public Opinion.

Hypothesis Testing

Non-parametric tests were used for hypothesis testing using the statistical program SPSS, as follows:

1. The Kruskal-Wallis test was used to measure variations in types of violence, issues of violence, targeted audiences, supporting and opposing arguments, and gender of media personnel and guests

2. The chi-squared test was used to determine the relationship between variables related to violence for each type of mass media separately

Hypothesis 1

Significant statistical differences exist in Egyptian mass media coverage of issues of violence against women. The areas of difference include:

1. Level of interest (as measured by the frequency that issues are included in media content)

2. Forms and types of violence covered/portrayed

3. Justifications (arguments)

4. Reaction and methods of addressing violence against women

5. Geographic areas targeted by the media when addressing issues of violence

The Kruskal-Wallis test was used to test the accuracy of the hypothesis. Test results confirmed the existence of significant statistical differences regarding types of violence (Table 33).

Table 33. The Correlation between VAW Coverage and Different Types of Mass Media

Mass media	Mean	Chi-squared	Degree of Freedom	Level of Significance
Print Media	778.67			
Television	757.34	99.5	2	<0.001
Radio	477.43			

As shown in Table 33, it is obvious that significant statistical differences exist regarding the types of violence addressed by the different mass media. As indicated by the means for each group, the print media was more interested than television and radio in violence of all types. As indicated by the qualitative and quantitative analysis, this result is due to the variety of newspapers, with their diverse intellectual perspectives, variety of ownership, extent of specialization, amount of freedom allowed to discuss different types of violence, frequency of publication, and dedicated print space for these issues.

The results of the Kruskal-Wallis test indicate the existence of significant statistical differences regarding media personnel (chi squared calculated as 583.32 at a level of significance p<0.001), gender of guests (chi squared calculated as 219.9 at a level of significance p<0.001), nature of targeted audience (chi squared calculated as 448.7 at a level of significance p<0.001), environment of targeted audience (chi squared calculated as 32.88 at a level of significance p<0.001), and opposing arguments (chi squared calculated as 69.006 at a level of significance p<0.001).

Hypothesis 2

Significant statistical differences exist in the Egyptian mass media in their coverage of violence against women based on ownership patterns (state, private or party).

To test the accuracy of this hypothesis, a chi-squared test of independence was used for each medium separately and in comparison with other media, as discussed below.

Print Media

The results of the chi-squared test indicate the existence of significant statistical differences in coverage of types of violence against women based on the type of newspaper ownership. The calculated chi-squared is 41.04 and the level of significance is p<0.001.

State newspapers had the greatest coverage of all forms of violence — primarily domestic violence (93.9 percent) compared to 3.9 percent coverage by private newspapers and 2.5 percent by party newspapers. State newspapers also covered community violence to a greater extent (87.4 percent) compared to party news-papers (11.5 percent) and private newspapers (1.1 percent). State newspapers also provided greatest coverage of state violence (98.4 percent) compared to private newspapers (1.6 percent); coverage of state violence was absent from party news-papers.

Accordingly, significant statistical differences were seen among newspapers based on the frequency of publication and the presence of specialized, permanent pages for women's issues. Many newspapers also now have daily pages dedicated to crimes; unfortunately, this has led to increased portrayal of women as criminals by publicizing crimes in which women are involved in a provocative, exaggerated, accusatory, and biased fashion — usually even before a woman accused of a crime is found guilty(the level of coverage is 85.3 percent).

The national newspapers devoted more coverage to all types violence against women, including infidelity, portrayal wives as tyrants, problems of working women, violation of the privacy of female celebrities, and violence against women —specifically the legal aspects of these issues.

The statistical analysis did not prove any statistically significant relationship between type of ownership of newspaper and coverage of violence of these con-troversial issues, such as sexual harassment. The calculated chi-squared is 9.426 at a significance level of $p=0.051$, which is not statistically significant.

Television

Significant statistical differences exist in television's representation of violence against women based on pattern of ownership (state or private). The statistical results obtained using the chi-squared test confirmed the existence of significant statistical differences in coverage of controversial types of violence against women based on ownership of the television channels (calculated chi-squared is 21.609, degree of freedom 2, at a level of significance of $p<0.001$). This shows a relation-ship between coverage of controversial issues on television and type of ownership. Private satellite channels cover these issues more often than state-owned chan-nels.

The state-owned channels had the greatest coverage of all forms of violence, primarily community violence, (63.7 percent) compared to private channels (36.3 percent). State-owned channels also focused on issues such as employers' preference for hiring males over females, rape, the right to travel, and custody of children.

The state-owned television channels also covered state violence (71.4 percent) more often compared to private channels (26.8 percent). Accordingly, the pro-grams focused on several issues, such as the women's right to occupy judicial and leadership positions, nomination to presidency, and political participation of women, in addition to discrimination against women in the laws.

Finally, television coverage focused on domestic violence, with greater interest shown by public stations (57.1 percent) compared to private channels (42.9 percent). This coverage addressed issues such as wife-beating, polygamy, early marriage, women as the main cause of marital problems, female genital mutilation, divorce, and temporary marriage to a second man (mohalel).

Accordingly, significant statistical differences appear in favor of state-owned television channels. However, there is less coverage of domestic violence in comparison with the forms of violence against women. This lesser coverage is logical in light of the state's insistence on the family as the basic unit of society and its insistence that any deviation from this pattern violates the ethics, values, and religion that govern Egyptian society. This has led to the hushing-up of many negative developments in current Egyptian society, particularly as they relate to increased violence and the spread of practices such as incest.

With regard to other, non-controversial, women's issues, findings obtained through the chi-squared test confirmed the existence of significant statistical differences for types of violence against women based on ownership of the television channels: calculated chi-squared is 9.791, degree of freedom 1, at a level of significance of $p=0.002$.

The state-owned television channels covered all non-controversial violence related to women —primarily the negligence of wives by husbands, portraying wives as tyrants, problems of working women, female school drop-outs, portraying women as criminals, and invasion of privacy. The private channels addressed sexual harassment, invasion of female celebrities' privacy, and the marital problems of celebrities.

Radio

The chi-squared test confirmed a lack of significant statistical differences in coverage of different types of violence in women's issues and topics based on the type of ownership of the radio stations. The calculated chi-squared is 0.199, degree of freedom 1, at a level of significance of $p=0.656$, which is not statistically significant.

With regard to controversial issues, statistical analysis confirmed that only state-owned radio stations discussed controversial issues of violence; private stations did not (e.g., Negoum FM).

Accordingly, the statistical analysis only partially proved the accuracy of the second hypothesis; it applies to print media and the television but not to radio.

Therefore, for accuracy, the hypothesis should be amended as follows: Significant statistical differences exist between the representation of issues of violence against women by print media and television based on the pattern of ownership (state, party, or private).

Hypothesis 3

Significant statistical differences exist in Egyptian mass media coverage of violence against women based on the extent of specialization of the media (for the general public or specialized).

To test this hypothesis, a chi-squared test of independence was used for each method separately and in comparison with the other methods, as discussed below.

Print Media

Findings obtained using the chi-squared test indicate significant statistical differences among the controversial types of violence against women covered based on the specialization of the newspaper. The calculated chi-squared is 17.992 at a level of significance of $p<0.001$.

Public newspapers had greater coverage of the different forms of violence (85.6 percent), compared to for specialized publications (14.4 percent), represented by Hawaa and Nesf El Donya magazines.

Public newspapers also had greater coverage of community violence (91.5 percent) compared to specialized publications (8.5 percent). Public newspapers also had more extensive coverage of state violence against women (84.1 percent) compared to specialized media (15.9 percent), and also covered more domestic violence (73.7 percent) than specialized publications (26.3 percent).

These differences are related to the frequency of publication of the public newspapers (mostly daily, as in the sample), whereas the specialized magazines are published weekly. Additionally, specialized magazines — particularly women's magazines —usually devote a greater amount of space to traditional topics such as cooking, décor, cosmetics, and fashion, with little mention of controversial issues, especially violence against women. Specialized magazines focused primarily on the importance of women's education and social attitudes that limit access to education, paternity suits, early marriage, women's to combine work and family responsibilities, and success stories.

With regard to non-controversial women's issues, the statistical analysis confirmed the existence of significant statistical differences between the extent of a publication's specialization and its coverage of violence in topics related to women. The calculated chi-squared is 115.969 at a significance level of p<0.001.

The public newspapers covered marital infidelity, husband's neglect of their wives, portrayal wives as tyrants or criminals, problems of working women, invasion of privacy of female celebrities, and legal violations against women. In contrast, specialized newspapers focused on the marital problems of female celebrities.

Findings obtained using the chi-squared test confirmed the existence of significant statistical differences between the type of violence coverage of controversial issues of violence based on the type of publication (newspaper or magazine); the calculated chi squared is 15.318 at a level of significance ofp<0.001.

Newspapers primarily covered community violence (91.3 percent) compared to magazines (8.9 percent), state violence (newspapers: 83.5 percent; magazines: 16.5 percent), and domestic violence (newspapers: 74.7 percent; magazines: 25.3 percent).

With regard to controversial issues, newspapers covered female genital mutilation, women's political participation, divorce, and crimes committed by women.

Regarding non-controversial issues related to women, statistical analysis confirmed the existence of significant statistical differences between the type of publication and coverage of issues of violence related to women. The calculated chi-squared is 104.701 at a significance level of p<0.001.

Television

Data gathered supports that there are significant statistical differences among television channels' representation of violence against women based on the extent of the channel's specialization (i.e., public or private channels).

The chi-squared test confirmed the existence of significant statistical differences among coverage of non-controversial types of violence based on a channel's specialization (calculated chi-squared is 8.925 at a level of significance of p=0.003). This indicator is statistically significant.

Public channels had more extensive coverage of different forms of violence, primarily community violence (91.6 percent) compared to specialized channels (8.4 percent) and focused on issues such as rape, employers' preference for hiring males over females, inheritance, crimes committed by women, sexual harassment, female drop-outs, invasion of privacy of female celebrities, marital problems of female celebrities, and problems of working woman. Coverage of state violence against women by public channels (87.5 percent) was much higher than coverage by specialized channels (12.6 percent) and addressed issues such as a woman's right to hold judicial and leadership positions, representation on election lists, impediments to political participation, and women's rights to travel abroad. Coverage of domestic violence by public channels (81.3 percent) contrasts with that of specialized channels (18.7 percent) and focused on issues such as husbands' neglect of their wives and portrayal of wives as tyrants. The specialized channels also covered coercion of girls into marriage, Coptic women's right to civil divorce, verbal harassment, and exploitation of women in music videos.

Regarding controversial issues related to women, statistical analysis confirmed the existence of statistically significant differences between a television channel's specialization and its coverage of controversial women's issues. Calculated chi-squared is 123.072 at a level of significance of $p<0.001$.

The public channels covered wife-beating, polygamy, customary marriages, women's ability to combine family and work responsibilities, women as the primary cause of marital problems and corruption of children, the right of women to occupy leadership positions and to travel abroad, female genital mutilation, employers' preference for hiring men, abortion, effects of illiteracy, deprivation of women's rights, and women's political empowerment. Specialized channels covered paternity suits, child custody, women's right to travel without a husband's approval, and early marriage.

Radio

Regarding controversial issues related to women, the statistical analysis confirmed the lack of significant statistical differences between a radio station's specialization and its coverage violence against women. The calculated chi-squared is 0.175 at a level of significance of $p=0.676$; this is not a significant indicator.

Regarding issues and subjects related to women, the statistical analysis also confirmed the lack of significant statistical differences between a radio station's specialization and its coverage of violence against women. The calculated chi-squared is 1.537 at a level of significance of $p=0.216$).

Accordingly, the statistical analysis proved the accuracy of the third hypothesis only partially, as it was applicable to the print media and television on controversial issues and cases of violence against women, and not applicable to the radio. Therefore, to be accurate, the hypothesis would need to be amended as follows:

Significant statistical differences exist between the representation of violence against women by the print media and television based on the specialization of the media channel (for the general public or specialized).

Conclusion and Recommendations

Conclusion

Issues of Violence in the Egyptian Media's Agenda

In media channels, issues of violence against women occupied 23 percent of the space allocated to women issues. Print media addressed violence against women more often than did television or radio. Community violence constituted 61.5 percent of media focus on violence against women in the media — more than any other issue.

Discriminating between Domestic and Community Violence in Media Channels

Community violence was covered most frequently by print media (66 percent), followed by television (20 percent), and radio (13.4 percent).

Domestic violence was covered most frequently by print media (67.8 percent), followed by television coverage of domestic violence (20.8 percent), and radio programs (11.4 percent). Psychological domestic violence issues constituted 74.1 percent of domestic violence issues covered, compared to 25.9 percent coverage of physical domestic violence.

Quantitative results confirmed that print media still enjoys a margin of freedom in its coverage of issues of violence against women. An examination of issues of domestic violence covered by print media reveals that print media led (or, in one case, equaled) coverage of four following issues, followed by television and radio.

- Beatings of wives by their husbands (print media: 66 percent of cases; television: 26.2 percent; radio: 7.2 percent)
- Circumcision (print media: 56.4 percent; television: 22.5 percent; radio: 21.1 percent)
- Forced abortion (print media: 46.6 percent; television and radio: 6.8 percent each
- Early marriage problems (print media and television: 34.4 percent each; radio: 26.4 percent

In presenting community violence issues the inferior image of women occurred at a rate of 68 percent, violence against women in the work place at a rate of 14.2 percent; psychological community violence against women within the framework of political participation and showing women as second-class citizens at a rate of 12.5 percent; and various forms of violence on the street at a rate of 5.3 percent.

In addressing issues of violence against women, the media portrayed women as criminals at a rate of 40 percent and discussed dealing with women as mere bodies in television advertisements and music videos at a rate of 6.8 percent.

Media channels only timidly discussed some silent issues, such as sexual harassment, which was addressed at a rate of 5.5 percent. Media channels gave only minimal coverage to incest, psychological consequences of circumcision, wife-beating, forced marriages and marriage between rich men and young girls. However even this low rate of coverage is considered the first step in raising awareness about such issues.

Issues of Violence against Women in Radio and Television Drama

Radio and television dramas presented against women differently from other programs, in that the dramas used manifestations of violence against women as basic focal points of plot conflicts.

Unlike other media, television and radio dramas focused on domestic violence more than community violence and presented different visions for confronting violence. This is in line with the usual dramatic structure, which presents a problem followed by its solution.

Men appeared the source of violence in 36 percent of television and radio dramas and women as the source of violence in 29.9 percent.

Target Audiences of Media on Issues of Violence

The general public was most often the main target audience of media (89.9 percent) followed by the urban upper class area audience (3.4 percent), the public in rural areas (3 percent), the middle class in urban areas (2.5 percent), the public in average areas (0.8 percent), Bedouins (0.6 percent), and the public in Upper Egypt (0.3 percent).

The Main Problem in the Research is the Overlap between Discrimination and Violence

This research raises a major problem from the researchers' point of view because of the overlap between issues of discrimination and violence, especially within the framework of the United Nations definition, because discrimination could be among the main causes of psychological violence.

Can we consider the laws, which are based on inequality between men and women, to be direct psychological violence against women? Or are they a main cause for subsequent psychological or physical violence against women? The research team and its consultants believe precise definition is required — one that identifies patterns of violence and clarifies the dividing lines between violence and discrimination.

Recommendations

An analysis of the conclusions and previous quantitative and qualitative indicators leads to the following recommendations:

Capacity Building

1. Develop a training program for communications professionals. Such a program should extend over a period of five years and aim to upgrade the skills of personnel working in the various media to better address issues of violence against women, rectify concepts of violence, and emphasize new aspects of violence (including the human rights dimension), culminating in the formation of a media lobbying group to address issues of violence against women.

2. Raise awareness of media personnel pertaining to violence against women through competitions and other mechanisms.

3. Raise awareness of violence against women through media channels.

4. Establish a mechanism for monitoring of violence against women in the various Egyptian media channels.

5. Plan a media campaign on the national level to raise citizens' awareness of the impact of violence against women on the family and community.

6. Develop a media strategy to combat all forms of violence in the community, primarily violence against women and girls, while urging media policymakers to implement this strategy and to reconsider media messages that conflict with the strategy.

References

1. Awatef Abde Rahman—Media and the modern woman, a research published in the book on media and women in the age of technology (El Tobgy Publication, Cairo, 2005)

2. Nagwa Kamel and others: Media and woman in rural and urban areas, Applicable study on Egypt and Bahrain, Gulf Centre for Strategic Studies and

Centre for Research and Studies on Women and Media, Faculty of Mass Communication—Cairo University, 2006.

3. Laila Abdel Megeid and others: The Egyptian women and media, Cairo University, Faculty of Mass Communication, Egyptian Women's Issues Center, 2007.

4. Adel Abdel Ghaffar, Cultural discrimination against women in television series, National Council for Women, Cultural Committee, 2006.

5. Hossam Aly Aly Salama. Ethics for addressing women's issues in the Egyptian Cinema: Analytical study. Seminar on media ethics between theory and implementation. 4th part (Cairo: Faculty of Mass Communication—Cairo University, May 2003) pp 1563–1664.

6. Raghda Mohamed Eissa. Factors affecting the female media leaderships in the Egyptian Radio and Television Union and its reflection on media planning. Unpublished master degree thesis. (Cairo: Faculty of Mass Communication—Cairo University, 2005)

7. Mohamed Shuman: Political participation of women as portrayed in the caricatures in the Egyptian press—Parliament elections 2000 model, Faculty of Arts' magazine, University of Zagazig, June 2004.

8. Mohamed Zein Abdel Rahman: Journalistic coverage of the women's participation in Parliament elections 2000—Analytical study of women's magazines and women's daily pages—master degree thesis—unpublished—Faculty of Mass Communication—Cairo University—2002.

9. Omaima Omran, the role of mass media in the women's participation in political life, Global Media Journal, Cairo University, Faculty of Mass Communication, Issue (11), 2001, p 211, 275.

10. Amira Mohamed El Abbassi, Egyptian's women political participation and the role of media in activation of her participation: field study, Egyptian journal of public opinion research, Faculty of Mass Communication, Cairo University, 2nd Volume, 1st Issue, January-March 2001.

11. Nadia Mostafa Abdo, The communication role in the political participation of Egyptian women: field study, unpublished master degree thesis, Faculty of Mass Communication, Cairo University, 2000.

12. Mohamed Shuman: Political participation of women as portrayed in the caricatures in the Egyptian press—Parliament elections 2000 model, Faculty of Arts' magazine, University of Zagazig, June 2004.

13. Mohamed Zein Abdel Rahman: Journalistic coverage of the women's participation in Parliament elections 2000—Analytical study of women's magazines and

women's daily pages—master degree thesis—unpublished—Faculty of Mass Communication—Cairo University—2002.

14. Omaima Omran, the role of mass media in the women's participation in political life, Global Media Journal, Cairo University, Faculty of Mass Communication, Issue (11), 2001, p 211, 275.

15. Enas Abu Youssef, Image of the Arabic family in Egypt's women's press—January—September 1998, unpublished research, 1999 (quoting: Wael Maher Aref: Image of Egypt in the journalistic discourse for news reporters, and Arab News Agencies working in Egypt during the period from 1990-1996, unpublished master degree thesis, (Cairo University: Faculty of Mass Communication, 2002)

16. Mohamed Shuman: Political participation of women as portrayed in the caricatures in the Egyptian press—Parliament elections 2000 model, Ibid.

17. Atta Hassan Abdel Reheim, Mohamed Metwally Afifi, Advertisements and changing values, Media research journal, issue 97/98, January/March 2000.

18. Hamdy Hassan, Cultural content in advertisements: comparitive study on a sample of television advertisements in the Arab World, Arab research and studies, issue (33), July 2000.

19. Nagwa Mohamed El Gazzar, The women's image in television advertisements: content analysis of Egyptian television advertisements in Ramadan, National Council for Women, 2001.

20. Somaya Arafat, Extent of respecting our ethics in Arabic music videos, Analytical study of music videos on Dream Channel, Media research journal, El Azhar University, Issue 12, October 2002.

21. Ashraf Galal, Arab values as reflected in the music videos and the repercutions on youth values. 10th Scientific Convention, Faculty of Mass Communication, Cairo University, May 2004.

22. Magda Bagnied, The image of Arab Women in music videos, Arab Reform Forum, Alex, Egypt, December, 11–13, 2006.

23. Mahmoud Youssef. The image of Egyptian women in cinema movies presented on television. In: Global media journal, issue 10, January. March 2001, pp 49–107.

24. Abdel Reheim Ahmed Soliman Darwish. Egyptian cinema movies presented on television addressing social issues and its effect on youth. Unpublished PhD thesis. (Cairo: Faculty of Mass Communication, Cairo University, 2002).

25. Adel Abdel Ghaffar, The women's image in television drama broadcasted in Ramadan, National Council for Women, 2001.

26. Adeeb Khadour, The women's image in Arab media, Media library, 1st Ed., Damascus, 1997.

27. Suzan El Keleiny. The women's image in Egyptian mass media. In: Broadcasting Art Quarterly, Issue 172—October 2003. pp 101–106.

28. Ashraf Galal, The women's image in the drama on Arab satellite channels and its effect on audience perception of social reality, 1st Scientific Convention for International Academy for Media Science, Egyptian-Lebanese Publishing House, Cairo, 2004.

29. Laila Abdel Megeid and others: Egyptian women and media, Cairo University, Faculty of Mass Communication, Egyptian Women's Issues Center, Ibid.

30. Ahmed Zakareya Ahmed: Editing public women's magazines in Egypt, and its effects on journalistic performance during 96-97—survey study of Hawaa and Nesf El Donia magazines, master degree thesis, Faculty of Mass Communication, Cairo University, 2001.

31. Azza Abdel Azim, The impact of the television drama on the perception of the Egyptian family, unpublished PhD thesis, Faculty of Mass Communication, Cairo University, 2000.

32. Mona Helmy Refaii, Exploring the Egyptian drama on television and the relationship between both sexes as percepted by the Egyptian youth, unpublished master degree thesis, Faculty of Mass Communication, Cairo University, 2003.

33. Amany Abdel Raouf, The social status of the Egyptian woman as presented on the Egyptian television and its relevance to real life: An applied analytical study, unpublished PhD thesis, Faculty of Mass Communication, Cairo University, 2004.

34. The women's image in Egyptian newspapers and magazines (2004), Cairo, Development Support Communication Center, Media Watch Unit, 2005.

35. Awatef Abde Rahman—Media and the modern woman, a research published in the book on media and women in the age of technology, (El Tobgy Publication, Cairo, 2005).

36. Nagwa Mohamed El Gazzar, The women's image in television advertisements: content analysis of Egyptian television advertisements in Ramadan, National Council for Women, 2001.

37. Hossam Aly Aly Salama. Ethics for addressing women's issues in the Egyptian Cinema: Analytical study. Seminar on media ethics between theory and implementation. 4th part (Cairo: Faculty of Mass Communication—Cairo University, May 2003) pp 1563–1664.

38. Abdel Reheim Ahmed Soliman Darwish. Egyptian cinema movies presented on television addressing social issues and its effect on youth. Unpublished PhD thesis. (Cairo: Faculty of Mass Communication, Cairo University, 2002).

39. Laila Abdel Megeid and others: The Egyptian women and media, Cairo University, Faculty of Mass Communication, Egyptian Women's Issues Center, Ibid.

40. Nagwa Kamel and others: Media and woman in rural and urban areas, Ibid.

41. Mohamed Zein Abdel Rahman: Journalistic coverage of the women's participation in Parliament elections 2000—Analytical study of women's magazines and women's daily pages—master degree thesis—unpublished—Faculty of Mass Communication—Cairo University—2002.

42. Gehan Youssry, College girls' opinion of the presentation of their image in the Arab television drama, Egyptian journal of public opinion research, Faculty of Mass Communication, Cairo University, 3rd Volume, 4th Issue, October/December 2002.

43. Radio and Television Union: Research on female audient attitudes regarding women's and family programs in television, General Assembly, Cairo, 2003.

44. Amany Abdel Raouf, The social status of the Egyptian woman as presented on the Egyptian television and its relevance to real life: An applied analytical study, unpublished PhD thesis, Faculty of Mass Communication, Cairo University, 2004.

45. Gehan Youssry, The view of the college girl of the image presented of her in the Arab television drama, Egyptian journal of public opinion research, Ibid.

46. Amany Abdel Raouf, The social status of the Egyptian woman as presented on the Egyptian television and its relevance to real life, Ibid.

47. Azza Abdel Azim, The impact of the television drama on the perception of the Egyptian family, Ibid.

48. Mona Helmy Refaii, Exploring the Egyptian drama on television and the relationship between both sexes as percepted by the Egyptian youth, Ibid.

49. Abdel Reheim Ahmed Soliman Darwish. Egyptian cinema movies presented on television addressing social issues and its effect on youth, Ibid.

50. Magda Ahmed Amer (2002): —The rural women's image in the Egyptian cinema: survey study.

51. Awatef Abdel Rahman and others, Egypt women in Upper Egypt, Cairo University, Faculty of Mass Communication and UNESCO, 2007.

52. Ragia Ahmed Kandil: ―The role of the Egyptian press in the elimination of forms of gender discrimination against women ‖, National Council for Women, 2002.

53. Margaret Samir Sawiris: Factors affecting the occupational satisfaction of the female communication experts in the Egyptian press, master degree thesis, unpublished, Faculty of Mass Communication, Cairo University, 2005.

54. Nahed Ramzy, Women and media in a changing world, (Egyptian-Lebanese Publishing House, Beirut, 2001).

55. Azza Kamel, The image of women in the Egyptian press (report 2002-2003), Ibid.

56. Study by Awatef Abdel Rahman: Egyptian female media figures between the professional responsibilities and the social role, Media research journal, Issue 2, 1997.

57. Farouk Abu Zeid. Women and media. In: Broadcasting Art Quarterly, Issue 185, January 2007. pp 28–33

58. Raghda Mohamed Eissa. Factors affecting the female media leaderships in the Egyptian Radio and Television Union and its reflection on media planning, Ibid.

59. Ragia Ahmed Kandil: ―The role of the Egyptian press in the elimination of forms of gender discrimination against women ‖, Ibid.

60. Nagwa Kamel, Media legislations and its affect on the professional performance of the female media figures, research published in the book on media and women in the age of technology (El Tobgy Publication, Cairo, 2005).

61. Naglaa Mahmoud Abu Samra, Restraints on the media performance of the Egyptian female journalists, a field study on a sample of journalists working in regional national and party newspapers, unpublished master degree thesis, Faculty of Mass Communication, Cairo University, 1995.

62. Margaret Samir Sawiris: Factors affecting the occupational satisfaction of the female communication experts in the Egyptian press, Ibid.

63. Awatef Abdel Rahman: Egyptian female media figures between the professional responsibilities and the social role, Ibid.

64. Laila Abdel Megeid and others: The Egyptian women and media, Cairo University, Faculty of Mass Communication, Egyptian Women's Issues Center, Ibid.

65. Laila Abdel Megeid and others: The Egyptian women and media, Cairo University, Faculty of Mass Communication, Egyptian Women's Issues Center, Ibid.

66. Laila Hussein Mohamed El Sayed, same as previous.

67. Nagwa Mohamed El Gazzar, The women's image in television advertisements: content analysis of Egyptian television advertisements in Ramadan, Ibid.

68. Laila Abdel Megeid and others: The Egyptian women and media, Cairo University, Faculty of Mass Communication, Egyptian Women's Issues Center, Ibid.

69. Nagwa Kamel: Egyptian press and women's issues: implementation on the International conference on population, and women's conference, Global media journal, Faculty of Mass Communication, Cairo University, 1st issue, January 1997, pp 53–96.

70. Laila Abdel Megeid and others: The Egyptian women and media, Cairo University, Faculty of Mass Communication, Egyptian Women's Issues Center, Ibid.

71. Laila Abdel Megeid and others: The Egyptian women and media, Cairo University, Faculty of Mass Communication, Egyptian Women's Issues Center, Ibid.

72. Samia Hassan El Saati. The women's issues in the Egyptian media discourse between tradition and social change. In: Arab Radio Broadcast, Issue 2—2003, pp 6–10.

73. Amira Mohamed El Abbassi, Egyptian's women political participation and the role of media in activation of her participation, Ibid.

74. Omaima Omran, the role of mass media in the women's participation in political life, Ibid.

75. Magda Ahmed Amer, —The modern attitudes for studying rural women's issues in the media research ‖, a research published in the book on media and women in the age of technology (El Tobgy Publication, Cairo, 2005)

76. Omaima Omran: The women's issues addressed in the regional press, published research, Faculty of Arts' magazine, Issue (8), 2nd part (Assiut University: Faculty of Arts, October 2001).

77. Ahmed Zakareya Ahmed: Editing public women's magazines in Egypt, and its effects on journalistic performance during 96-97—survey study of Hawaa and Nesf El Donia magazines, master degree thesis, Faculty of Mass Communication, Cairo University, 2001.

78. Azza Kamel, The image of women in the Egyptian press (report 2002-2003), Ibid.

79. Hossam Aly Aly Salama. Ethics for addressing women's issues in the Egyptian Cinema: Analytical study, Ibid.

80. Mahmoud Youssef. The image of Egyptian women in cinema movies presented on television, Ibid.

81. Adel Abdel Ghaffar, The women's image in television drama broadcasted in Ramadan, Ibid.

82. Wessam Ahmed Mohamed Nasr. Role of awareness campaigns in radio and television in the health education of Egyptian women. Unpublished PhD thesis (Cairo: Faculty of Mass Communication—Cairo University, 2006).

83. Mona El Hadidi. Egyptian media and women's issues. In: 1st Opinion Forum: Women and media. Conducted on May 11, 2000 (Cairo: National Council for Women) pp 35–42.

84. Adel Sadek Mohamed Rezk: The role of women's press in setting the priorities of interest for Egyptian women regarding women's issues, analytical field study, unpublished master degree thesis—Faculty of Mass Communication—Cairo University—1999.

85. Omaima Omran: The women's issues addressed in the regional press, published research, Faculty of Arts' magazine, Issue (8), 2nd part (Assiut University: Faculty of Arts, October 2001)

86. Mona El Hadidi. Egyptian media and women's issues, Ibid.

87. Ahmed Mohamed Sabek: —The role of the daily Egyptian press in forming the religious awareness of youth for women's issues, Ibid.

88. Farida Marey. Divorced women in the Egyptian cinema. In: Egyptian cinema and human rights. Editor and Presenter: Hesham El Nahas. (Cairo Center for Human Rights, 200).

89. Hossam Aly Aly Salama. Ethics for addressing women's issues in the Egyptian Cinema: Analytical study, Ibid.

90. Ehsan Said Abdel Megeid. —The Egyptian women's image in the cinema 1990-1997 ‖ unpublished master degree thesis. (Cairo: Faculty of Arts—Ein Shams University, 2000)

91. Ashraf Galal, The women's image in the drama on Arab satellite channels and its effect on audience perception of social reality, Ibid.

92. Nagwa Mohamed El Gazzar, The women's image in television advertisements: content analysis of Egyptian television advertisements in Ramadan, Ibid.

93. Nagwa Kamel: Egyptian press and women's issues: implementation on the International conference on population, Ibid.

94. Hossam Aly Aly Salama. Ethics for addressing women's issues in the Egyptian Cinema: Analytical study, Ibid.

95. Somaya Arafat, Extent of respecting our ethics in Arabic music videos, Ibid.

96. Ashraf Galal, Arab values as reflected in the music videos and the repercussions on youth values. 10th Scientific Convention, Faculty of Mass Communication, Cairo University, May 2004.

97. Nawal Abdel Aziz El Safty: The journalistic discourse in Africa with regard to rural women's problems—Critical-analytical study, Global media journal, Issue (11), (Cairo University: Faculty of Mass Communication, 2001), pp 1–73.

98. Seham Nassar, The Egyptian women's use of women's magazines and the satisfaction achieved from it, Egyptian journal of public opinion, 1st issue, Cairo University, Faculty of Mass Communication, 2002, p 231, 304.

99. Mahitab Mohamed Ahmed, The reasons why female Upper Egyptians watch Egyptian television and the satisfaction achieved from it, unpublished master degree thesis, Menya University, Faculty of Arts, 2003.

100. Samy Said El Naggar, The women's attitudes towards addressing her issues in Egyptian newspapers in light of the ethical and professional regulators, Research submitted to the 9th Conference of the Faculty of Mass Communication, Cairo University, 2nd Volume, 2003, p 385, 462.

101. Adel Sadek Mohamed Rezk: The role of women's press in setting the priorities of interest for Egyptian women regarding women's issues, Ibid.

102. Radio and Television Union: Research on female audient attitudes regarding women's and family programs in television, Ibid.

103. Nagwa Kamel and others: Media and woman in rural and urban areas, Applicable study on Egypt and Bahrain, Ibid.

104. Gehan Youssry, College girls' opinion of the presentation of their image in the Arab television drama, Ibid.

105. Magda Ahmed Amer and Hala Kamal Nofal, The rural audience's attitude towards family planning campaign, field study on a sample of rural women in the villages of Giza governorate, Global media journal, Issue (16), September 2002, p 255.

106. Mahitab Mohamed Ahmed, The reasons why female Upper Egyptians watch Egyptian television and the satisfaction achieved from, Ibid.

107. Amira Mohamed El Abbassi, Egyptian's women political participation and the role of media in activation of her participation, Ibid.

108. Samia Desouky Eid —The television's role in providing Egyptian women with environmental information, a study based on the knowledge-gap hypothesis theory, unpublished master degree thesis, Faculty of Mass Communication, Cairo University, 2005.

109. Amira Samir Taha, the role of Arabic television series in the perception of social problems by Egyptian youth, unpublished master degree thesis, Faculty of Mass Communication, Cairo University, 2001.

110. Nevine Ghobashy, The role of opinion leaders in the social marketing campaigns targeting rural women and implementation in the field of family planning, unpublished master degree thesis, Faculty of Mass Communication, Cairo University, 1996.

111. Seham Nassar, The Egyptian women's use of women's magazines and the satisfaction achieved from it, Ibid.

112. Awatef Abdel Rahman: —Media and the modern women, a survey study (issues—media discourse for women—human cadres), a research published in the book on media and women in the age of technology (El Tobgy Publication, Cairo, 2005)

113. Gehan Reshty. Egyptian media and women: Women and media forum, under the slogan: Towards an interactive media space (Cairo, 2002) p 230.

114. Nawal Abdel Aziz El Safty: The journalistic discourse in Africa with regard to rural women's problems, Ibid.

115. Ehsan Said Abdel Megeid. —The Egyptian women's image in the cinema 1990–1997 ||, Ibid.

116. Laila Abdel Megeid and others: Egyptian women and media, Ibid.

117. Fada Fouad Abdel Fattah Salem (2002) titled —Regional media and social issues of modern women ||, Ibid.

118. Raghda Mohamed Eissa. Factors affecting the female media leaderships in the Egyptian Radio and Television Union and its reflection on media planning, Ibid.

119. Maha Mohamed Kamel El Tarabeishy: The Egyptian media representation of rural women's problems, Ibid.

120. Ghada Moussa Sakr: The relation between exploring printed press and the political participation of women in the Egyptian Parliament election 2005, Ibid.

121. Hemat Hassan Abdel Megeid, The difference of gained knowledge from mass media by implementing on violence against women, Ibid.

122. Mona El Hadidi. Egyptian media and women's causes, Ibid.

123. Maysa El Sayed Taher Gamil. Violence in the relations between man and woman as presented in the Arabic drama on the Egyptian television: an analytical field study, unpublished master degree thesis, Faculty of Mass Communication, Cairo University, 2003

124. Abdel Gawad Said Mohamed, Journalistic representation of sexual harassment—Analytical and field study based on the theory and frame analysis, Egyptian journal of public opinion research, Volume 8—2nd Ed. (Cairo University: Public Opinion Research Center—Faculty of Mass Communication, April/June 2007) pp 9-10, 47-50. Cases of violence against women in the television and radio drama appeared in 57.7 percent of the total representation of women's issues in both types of drama.

What are the Roles and Responsibilities of the Media in Disseminating Health Information?

Gary Schwitzer, Ganapati Mudur, David Henry,
Amanda Wilson, Merrill Goozner, Maria Simbra,
Melissa Sweet and Katherine A. Baverstock

BACKGROUND TO THE DEBATE

In December 2004 three news stories in the popular press suggested that the side effects of single-dose nevirapine, which has been proven to prevent mother-to-child transmission of HIV, had been covered up. Many HIV experts believed that the stories were unwarranted and that they would undermine use of the drug, leading to a rise in neonatal HIV infection. The controversy surrounding these stories prompted the PLoS Medicine editors to ask health journalists, and others with an interest in media reporting of health, to share their views on the roles and responsibilities of the media in disseminating health information.

Gary Schwitzer: The Agenda-Setting Role of Health Journalists

Some journalists say that their role and responsibility is no different in covering health information than it is in covering politics, business, or any other topic. These journalists say that their primary concern is accurate, clear reporting— they are less concerned about the consequences of their story once it is published [1]. But that approach may result in shoddy journalism and potential harm to the public [2]. I assert that it isn't sufficient to be accurate and clear when covering health news. Journalists have a responsibility to mirror a society's needs and issues, comprehensively and proportionally [3]. Often that doesn't happen in health news.

Recently, I led an effort by the Association of Health Care Journalists to publish a statement of principles [4]. "Journalists have a special responsibility in covering health and medical news," the statement reads. "Association members know that readers and viewers may make important health care decisions based on the information provided in our stories."

In our current era of entanglement, journalists must investigate and report the possible conflicts of interest among sources of health information and those who promote a new idea or therapy. Such conflicts may not be readily apparent, so journalists must look for them as a routine part of story research and interviews. They must investigate and report the possible links between researchers and private companies, researchers and public institutions, patient advocacy groups and their sponsors, celebrity spokespersons and their sponsors, and nonprofit health and professional organizations and their sponsors. To fail to do so may mean that journalists become unwitting mouthpieces for incomplete, biased, and imbalanced news and information.

Journalists face unique challenges in covering health news. Some specialized skills, knowledge, and judgment are helpful. For example, some information based on poorly designed or poorly powered studies should not be reported unless the flaws are emphasized.

Editors, reporters, and writers need to scrutinize the terminology used in health news. Vague, sensational terms (such as "cure," "miracle," and "breakthrough") may harm news consumers by misleading and misinforming [5]. At the core of journalism's values, such terms should not be used because they are meaningless.

It is not the role of journalists to become advocates for causes. However, I believe that journalists have a responsibility to investigate and report on citizens' needs as they struggle to understand and navigate the health-care system. People need help in understanding the ways in which scientists and policymakers reach conclusions. In that sense, there is an inherent educational role that journalists must assume.

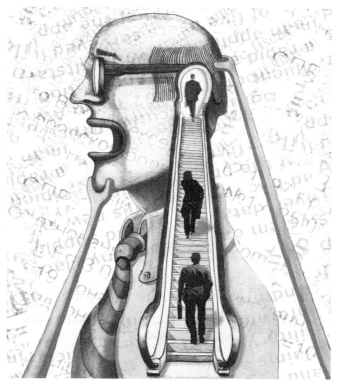

Figure 1: Journalists risk becoming unwitting mouthpieces for those with vested interests in their story (Illustration: Scott Mickelson)

I have a special interest in how television journalists cover health and health policy news. Surveys consistently show that many Americans get most of their health news and information from television. One study documented troubling trends of brevity (an average of 45 seconds per story), absence of reporter specialization, sensational claims not supported by data, hyperbole, commercialism, disregard for the uncertainty of clinical trials, baseless predictions of treatments based on basic science studies, single-source stories, and a paucity of coverage of health policy [6].

Television viewers are likely to see many more one-sided political ads about health policy issues than balanced, comprehensive news stories about such issues. In my current research, I am analyzing health policy news coverage on three award-winning TV stations in three different parts of the United States in 2004. Despite the fact that American voters ranked health care as their third leading concern (after war and the economy) [7], the three stations I monitored devoted little time to health policy issues. My analysis shows that in ten months (326 hours of stations' key late night newscasts) on these three stations, there was only one story on the uninsured. Presidential candidates' health policy platforms drew a combined total of seven minutes of news—an average of 23 seconds per story, or about 15 seconds per station per month of the 2004 campaign. Whether it is preclinical news that is not ready for prime time, or clinical news that oozes optimism over unproven ideas, or a disdain for health policy news, television journalists seem to have abdicated their possible agenda-setting role.

Journalists must weigh the balance between the amount of attention given news about medicine and the attention given news about health and the social determinants of health. There may be too much news about the delivery of medical services and not enough news about the cost of, quality of, and evidence for those services. The current imbalance may contribute to the nation's health-care cost crisis, driving up demand for expensive, unproven ideas. These are responsibilities journalists may not encounter in covering other topics. In health news, they are everyday issues.

Ganapati Mudur: The Media may be the most important Source of Health Information for the General Public

Health reporting does involve "telling a story," but it also requires writers to take on additional responsibilities through the story cycle—finding the story, collecting information, and writing it.

Standard news criteria such as timeliness and impact may be used to pick stories. But in health reporting, context is crucial. Research advances to be reported need to be placed in context. This may be achieved by citing earlier research on the topic and seeking out comments from independent experts who could put a new finding in perspective. Sometimes health research throws up contradictory findings. Is a gene linked to a disease? One study finds a link. Another does not. Such situations demand interpretative and analytical skills on the part of health writers. Otherwise, writers may mislead readers, or leave them confused.

Health reporters need to find out who has funded the research and who might be likely to gain. And reporters must always double-check claims or else they may end up in embarrassing situations. Let me illustrate with an example. A top international science magazine last year reported that a novel stem cell therapy had cured patients with chronic aplastic anemia in Bombay, India [8]. The story was apparently based on claims made by the developers of the therapy, a private British company. A little more patience and investigation would have led the magazine to the real story: none of the patients had responded to the treatment, and the clinical collaborators in India had terminated the study [9].

In Health Reporting, Context is Crucial

When a public health situation is involved, health writers and the media can certainly play a role in quickly delivering important messages to the public. In a sense, then, they do serve as a component of the health provider community. And this makes it all the more important for health writers to ensure that they get it absolutely right. Given that most people do not interact with their doctors on a regular basis, the media is possibly the most significant source of health information for the general public. But health information in the media cannot substitute for personal medical advice. It is important that the public understands this.

Regulatory mechanisms may be lax in some developing countries. India, for instance, has had a long history of unethical or illegal clinical trials. Drug regulatory authorities in India allow the sale of drugs—including pediatric formulations—that have never been approved in Western countries. This opens up opportunities for investigative health journalism, an opportunity for reporters to take up the traditional watchdog role of the press to find and report wrongdoing.

David Henry and Amanda Wilson: Health Journalists should Discuss Benefits and Harms of New Treatments and use Independent Expert Sources

Health reporting is a major growth area for the media, probably because it is in demand by the public and it is profitable. However, media coverage of medical news is generally of poor quality, particularly stories about new treatments [10–12].

Media Doctor is a Web site where the quality of stories in the Australian press is reviewed (www.mediadoctor.org.au). We rate articles using ten evaluation criteria (www.mediadoctor.org.au/content/ratinginformation.jsp). In February/ March 2005 articles that we rated achieved an average of only 52% on our "satisfactory" score (www.mediadoctor.org.au/content/sourceinfo.jsp). This was an improvement on the score from one year ago, but it is still inadequate. North American analyses of the quality of health reporting have had similar results [11]. The print media are clearly superior to the online news services [12]. The greatest differences between print and online services are in the use of independent information sources, and the quantification of the benefits and the coverage of potential harms of new treatments.

We recognise that there are different depths of journalism and that journalists face constraints, including commercial pressures and deadlines that give little time to reflect on stories, which are usually written on the same day as the press release arrives. Some journalists argue that the media are the messengers and not the message, and it is up to others to interpret their reporting. To a reporter who might otherwise exercise more caution, a well-written media release from a large public relations company describing a new pharmaceutical product must be attractive when a deadline is imminent. There is no danger that the company will allege plagiarism if it appears, almost intact, under the journalist's by-line.

Researchers and Medical Journal Editors have Responsibilities Too

And even when they do have the time, journalists face two major challenges—understanding the clinical science and epidemiology, and dealing with powerful vested interests. Vested interests are not unique to medicine, but reporting on a new drug is different from, say, an MP3 player or a dishwasher. People will be intensely interested in a story about a new drug if it purports to treat a condition that they or their relatives have, and the story may become the basis of discussions with their physician and subsequent treatment decisions. We believe that in writing this type of story journalists have special responsibilities to ensure that they provide balanced information for their readers. In Australia, the Press Council believes the matter is of sufficient importance to provide advice to journalists [13].

In our view journalists will meet their responsibilities if they cover certain key issues when writing stories about new medical treatments. These include the accurate reporting of the comparative benefits, harms, and costs of the treatment and the extent to which their informants have ties with the manufacturer. It is helpful if journalists use independent expert sources to answer questions about the novelty of the treatment and the availability and efficacy of alternatives, although we acknowledge the practical difficulties in finding independent sources when time is limited. Journalists have indicated to us that they are concerned about these issues and are prepared to look critically at their own practices. It is unclear whether their editors and producers hold the same views and will provide the necessary resources, particularly time to do the job properly.

But researchers and medical journal editors have responsibilities too. When reading medical news stories it is sometimes possible to tell whether the researchers and journals have done a good or bad job in communicating the essential facts to journalists. A number of medical journals issue press releases, and these have been found wanting [14]. Researchers should consider carefully what they wish to convey about the results of a new study and should ask to see and edit any press releases. We believe the criteria used by Media Doctor to evaluate news stories are a good starting point for researchers and editors.

Criteria used by Media Doctor to Evaluate News Stories

- Whether the treatment is genuinely new
- The availability of the treatment in Australia
- Whether alternative treatment options are mentioned
- If there is evidence of disease mongering in the story
- If there is objective evidence to support the treatment
- How the benefits of the treatment are framed (in relative or absolute terms)
- Whether harms of the treatment are mentioned in the story
- Whether costs of the treatment are mentioned in the story
- Whether sources of information and any known conflicts of interest of informants are disclosed in the article
- Whether the journalist relied only on the press release for the story

Merrill Goozner: Medical Reporters Must Get Beyond the Hype and Hope when Reporting on the Latest "Breakthrough"

When I broke into the news business, the financial desk's primary source of breaking news was a Dow Jones wire clack-clack-clacking in the corner of the room. A bell rang whenever a major story broke. Sometimes two bells would go off, signaling a really big story. The day the stock market crashed in 1987, the newsroom sounded like St. Peters Square on Easter.

I imagine something comparable occurs these days when the advance copies of leading medical journals cross science editors' computer screens. Stories from the frontiers of medical research can make it onto page one—the most coveted real estate in daily journalism. News magazines have bolstered their sagging bottom lines with an endless stream of cover stories touting the latest breakthroughs in medicine.

But is this news all that it is cracked up to be? Have the reporters properly weighed the importance of the studies they're touting? Have they asked the tough questions of the researchers and their sponsors to figure out the significance of the results? Have they presented the data in a fashion that is meaningful to healthcare consumers? And in an age when most clinical trials are sponsored by private companies, have they fully informed their readers of the researchers' conflicts of interest?

Too often, the answer to these questions is no. Take recent reports from the American Society of Clinical Oncology, which met in mid-May in Orlando. One leading paper reported on a Veterans Administration review of the experience of over 40,000 women in the south central US. "The women taking statins were half as likely to have breast cancer as women who were not taking the drugs," the paper reported [15]. Put that way, it sounds like a dramatic reduction. But elsewhere in the story, it was reported that 12 percent of the women were taking the cholesterol-lowering medications and that only 1.4 percent of the total group contracted breast cancer. Only by massaging the numbers could one figure out that physicians would need to put 700 women on statins to eliminate one cancer case (in medical parlance, this is called number needed to treat). It sounds a lot less impressive that way. But the number needed to treat would be a lot more meaningful to women, especially those on tight budgets wondering if it is worth $1,000 a year for a prescription.

Reporting of surrogate endpoints instead of primary endpoints is another way that readers get misled. Reports on cancer drug trials often fall into this trap. A "lifesaving" drug that shrinks tumors by 50 percent sounds a lot better than a chemotherapy agent that prolongs life by two months. The same can be said for bone density and fractures, blood pressure and strokes, and cholesterol levels and heart attacks. While there may be a minor yet statistically significant reduction in the primary endpoint, the trial sponsors prefer to promote the more dramatic-sounding secondary endpoint. Too many reporters prominently feature the less meaningful number, while leaving out or delaying until late in the story the real bottom line [16].

Reporting of Surrogate Endpoints is another way that Readers Get Misled

Sadly, the media have only lately come around to taking seriously the issue of conflicts of interest in medical science. Last July, the National Heart, Lung, and Blood Institute's National Cholesterol Education Project updated its guidelines for cholesterol management. The update, touted in the front page of every major US paper [17], called for a dramatic reduction in the cholesterol levels now considered optimal for people who have never had heart disease but are considered moderately at risk. Prescribing physicians using these guidelines will likely put millions more Americans on these drugs in the next few years.

Yet three days after the report came out, reporters at Newsday broke the story that eight of nine physicians on the National Cholesterol Education Project panel had financial ties to statin manufacturers, which had the most to gain from the new guidelines. Writing in the Washington Post, former New England Journal of Medicine editor Jerome Kassirer asked, "Why should we swallow what these studies say?" [18] The ensuing uproar contributed to a change in policy at the New York Times, which last fall circulated a memo to all reporters encouraging them to always report conflicts of interest of quoted sources in science stories, a policy that leading science and medical journals have had in place for many years [19].

In recent years the pharmaceutical and biotechnology industries have responded to complaints about the high cost of drugs by claiming they are needed to finance the medical miracles that are just around the corner. Meanwhile, the increase in life expectancy in the US has slowed and still remains far below other advanced industrial countries. The number of new drugs coming out of industry labs, despite a slight uptick last year, is actually down from a decade ago. In a health-care environment that is increasingly cost-constrained, it shouldn't be too much to ask that medical reporters get beyond the hype and hope when reporting on the latest "breakthrough."

Maria Simbra: Whatever News Managers want, Viewers Get — As Medical Reporters are Pressed to Feed the Media Beast

Reporters are surpassing doctors as a source of medical information. It's no secret health news sells. Producers and news directors take advantage of this to attract an audience for their newscasts. And viewers respond.

In a survey by Rodale Press, 39% of the respondents said they turn to TV for health and medical information, and 37% said they would ask a health professional [20].

So as audience-appointed proxies for "health professionals," television medical reporters have a daunting task. They must be accurate, authoritative, and compassionate. They also need to understand the terminology, physiology, epidemiology, study design, and statistical analysis to keep health news in context for the viewer.

But typically, this doesn't happen. The medical industry churns out volumes of information for medical reporters to quickly sift through every day. There's a lack of special training for medical journalists (the general assignment reporter can expect to get thrown into the medical beat from time to time). Usually local news reports are under 90 seconds. The pressure for ratings compounds the problem.

Medical news is often simplified, or worse, sensationalized, because of industry pressures. Because health news sells, it can be and will be promoted—and in the process, distorted.

What is a medical reporter to do? Well, alone, there's not much a reporter can do. Like medical errors, the problems with medical journalism are system wide. At the root is a clash of cultures.

Medicine tends to be very methodical, slow, and subject to change. But the media want information that's definitive, they want it now, and, boy, it better be sensational. Also, people who go into journalism and ascend to management tend to be more inclined toward writing and creative interests. They may not understand (or may be openly hostile toward) the scientific process.

Figure 2: TV reporters rarely cover medicine exclusively—one day it's finance, the next it's health (Illustration: Giovanni Maki)

For TV reporters who are committed to the medical beat, educational opportunities are available through organizations such as the Association of Health Care Journalists (www.ahcj.umn.edu) and the National Association of Medical Communicators (www.ibiblio.org/namc). Journalists can learn how to interpret studies and present evidence-based balance in order to help viewers understand and make up their own minds about the latest developments in medicine, rather than just show the gee-whiz side of new technology.

Unfortunately, it's rare to find a TV reporter who exclusively covers medicine. Stations view this as a luxury. It is more common for medical reporters to also be general-assignment reporters or anchors, and they have other priorities with their combination jobs.

It's also rare to find management that's supportive of continuing education for their reporters. Even with the large profit margins at many TV stations, news directors generally do not provide financial support and ask that reporters interested in attending educational meetings use their own vacation time to do so. Furthermore, news directors, producers, and promotions staff don't seem to be themselves interested in learning about medical reporting.

An article in JAMA says that viewers are acting on and making personal medical decisions based on health information in the mass media [21]. This trend has led some TV medical reporting experts, such as Gary Schwitzer (formerly of CNN, now at the University of Minnesota, and a contributor to this PLoS Medicine debate) and Dr. Timothy Johnson (ABC News), to call for credentialing of medical journalists. After all, some meteorologists are credentialed. Are personal health decisions less important than the weather?

There's a disconnect between what station management values, what the reporters need, and what the viewers get. Right or wrong, the audience looks to TV medical reporters to educate and guide them on medical issues. It's an important responsibility that medical reporters and the mass media in general need to take seriously.

Melissa Sweet: Remember the Commercial Imperative when Examining Media Coverage of Health

Many people make the mistake of using the terms "journalists" and "the media" interchangeably. They speak, in the same breath, of the terrible failings of journalists and the media in covering health or other issues. In so doing, they fail to make a distinction between the craft or profession of journalism and the competitive industry that is the media. They fail to understand that the goals and drivers of journalism are often in conflict with those of the media industry.

The foremost goal of the media industry is, not surprisingly, to make profit. Many journalists are too idealistic to admit, even to themselves, that their job is to make money for their employers. Some believe they are there for the public interest, or even to interest the public. Some simply love to tell a yarn, to get the buzz that comes with uncovering a great story and breaking news. Some no doubt also come to enjoy the reflected glory of associating with the famous and the powerful. Indeed, many journalists have become celebrities themselves. Not coincidentally, this has benefits for their employers—nothing sells like celebrity.

But only a brave, naïve, or foolhardy journalist would publicly admit these days to believing that one of their roles is to help provide a voice for those who otherwise have difficulty having their voices heard, such as the disadvantaged. It is not a career-enhancing move at a time when many media proprietors have decided that a key to improving profits lies with their so-called AB audiences.

For those not up-to-date with marketing jargon, AB is shorthand for the affluent professionals so beloved by cashed-up advertisers. The theory goes that media outlets that attract audiences at the AB end of the socioeconomic scale are more likely to win advertisers or, even better, to get away with charging them premium rates. A senior manager at one of Australia's major newspaper groups recently explained why his company is focusing on boosting AB readership rather than total circulation [22]. "A good circulation result is one which attracts the readership we need and advertisers want," said Mark Scott, Editor-in-Chief of Fairfax's metropolitan newspapers, which include the respected broadsheet, The Sydney Morning Herald.

"Sure, The Daily Telegraph [a tabloid] sells many more copies than The Sydney Morning Herald," said Scott, "but their ad rates are lower because the SMH [Sydney Morning Herald] has that AB audience." Scott said Fairfax's Sunday title The Sun-Herald is significantly more profitable at its present circulation level of about 513,000 than it was when it was selling 600,000 copies. "We have held that AB audience so our advertising revenue is up and our costs are lower."

So what has this to do with how the media report health? Scott explained that his newspapers do extensive market research so they know what the AB market wants to read and how they want it presented. "We create our papers with those readers in mind and shape our marketing and promotions to reinforce their values and interests." In other words, the allocation of scarce resources in ever more stretched newsrooms is driven by what market researchers tell media managers about what AB audiences want to know about.

This has implications for how the media cover all the areas that affect peoples' health—politics, economics, and education, for example—as well as the coverage of health issues themselves. I haven't seen the market research, but it's not hard to guess what interests AB groups. They might want to know how to stay as healthy, smart, and good-looking as possible for as long as possible. They might want to know which biotech companies are good investments, and might be particularly interested in private health care. They are probably less interested in the needs of indigenous people, prisoners, the homeless, asylum seekers, or the poor, and it's probably a fair bet to say that they are also less interested in the ways in which disadvantaged groups have worse access to health care and prevention efforts.

Some might think this is overly cynical. Perhaps AB people are not all self-centred; perhaps they care about broader issues than those that directly affect their own lives and personal well-being. Nor can the compliance of journalists be assumed. In the chaotic and anarchic world of journalism, there are many who try to do far more with their jobs than to make their bosses wealthy—even if they have to try and "sell" their stories to their news managers on the grounds that the stories will be of interest to the ABs. Many other factors also shape and influence news production. And a truly compelling story is likely to get a run, even if not of direct relevance to the wealthy.

Nonetheless, it is important to remember the commercial imperative when examining media coverage of health. Many initiatives aimed at influencing health coverage target journalists, who are only one component of the media industry. Other powerful forces also shape how health is covered. An analogy can be drawn with efforts to improve the quality and safety of health care, another chaotic in-dustry. Measures aimed at individual clinicians may be helpful in reducing medi-cal errors, but it is also important to look at the broader system in which clinicians work.

Australia's National Strategy for Quality use of Medicines: Responsibilities of the Media

The media are responsible for the following.

- Ethical and responsible reporting on health-care issues
- Reporting on medicines accurately and attempting to have errors corrected if they occur
- Being aware of the variety of available information sources on medicines and the limitations of each source
- Being aware of the impact of media reports on the use of medicines in the com-munity

- Being aware of issues relevant to the broad context of medicine use, including risks of medicine use, non-drug alternatives, and the cost of medicine use to individuals and society

- Encouraging dissemination of messages that enhance the quality of medication use

Katherine A. Baverstock: The Media can Play a Special Role in Providing a Voice for People to Express their Experiences of Illness

A registered pharmacist for the last 15 years, I was trained in the biomedical model of health, to measure and note signs and symptoms, make assessments, and advise about treatments on the basis of available scientific evidence.

Becoming interested in the portrayal of medicines in the media whilst working in outback Australia (which is grossly underserved by health professionals), I began my doctoral project within this quantitative biomedical tradition. As I found during my literature review, research arising from this tradition assesses media writing about medicines for "quality." Such research focuses on certain categories of quantitative information about the medicine, such as the indication, associated risks and benefits, outcomes of treatment, contraindications, and cost, that would allow readers to analyse the evidence for themselves and decide whether they should use the medicine.

The research in this area seems to be advocating a position for the health journalist as an educator. Australia's Quality Use of Medicines Strategy [23] has the objective of optimising the use of medicines within the Australian community. It lists the media as a partner in the strategy, together with consumers, health professionals, government, and the pharmaceutical industry. Similar to the other partners, the media have special responsibilities to ensure the quality use of medicines, as described in Box 2. Although many of these responsibilities sit comfortably within the codes of ethics observed by working journalists, some of these responsibilities made me uncomfortable as a health professional. Should journalists be viewed as de facto health educators with the same responsibilities as those of us in the registered health professions?

As I progressed in this quantitative framework, I began to feel more and more uncomfortable with the narrow examination of the newspaper stories I had collected for my research. As my analysis continued, it became apparent that the newspaper stories contained themes far richer and more interesting than quantitative information about how drugs work. The stories were an intriguing insight into how the community viewed issues surrounding medicines and the use of medicines. Even more interesting were the narratives about experiences with medicines. I decided to transfer my research to a communications faculty, and explored a far different perspective of medicines in the media. One of my first realisations was that the media are much more than the newspapers, television, and radio focussed on by so many biomedical researchers. They also include new media (the Internet), other print media, and small-scale media, such as leaflets and posters, and even the messages on the pens given out by pharmaceutical representatives.

I would like to propose that rather than act as educators, the media can play a special role in providing a voice for people to express their experiences of illness and their interactions with the technologies of health. The advent of the Internet has democratised the media because this medium is accessible to everyone. The Internet can cross national boundaries and counteract isolation—not only geographic isolation, but also the isolation that may be caused by the experience of chronic illness and not knowing anyone who has lived your experience. People who were unable to have their stories heard within the traditional medical consultation now have a forum where they can be heard and have their stories validated.

The Internet has Democratised the Media

There is much research published within the sociological and anthropological literature examining the narrative surrounding health and illness within various types of media. Research now needs to examine how patients use information they find within the media, and whether it does make a difference to the medical encounter. Will an informed and questioning client leave us feeling threatened?

Within the traditional health setting, lengthy communication between medical professionals and clients is often not possible. Many health professionals receive scant training in communication and counselling. The use of media technologies allows our clients to tell their story, a biography that may be ever-changing because of the experience of chronic illness. I would argue, that rather than being much maligned by health professionals, the media should be viewed as a tool that allows healing by facilitating the telling of stories.

Competing Interests

The Integrity in Science Project, of which MG is the director, is funded in part by several foundations with a pro-environmentalist concern about industry influence over the scientific process and government advisory process. MS has previously worked at The Sydney Morning Herald. KB is on the Executive Committee of the Australasian Medical Writers Association.

References

1. Lantz JC, Lanier WL (2002) Observations from the Mayo Clinic national conference on medicine and the media. Mayo Clin Proc 77: 1306–1311. Available: http://www.mayoclinicproceedings.com/inside.asp?AID=227&UID= . Accessed 4 February 2005.

2. Schwitzer G (2003) How the media left the evidence out in the cold. BMJ 326: 1403–1404. Available: http://bmj.com/cgi/content/full/326/7403/1403 . Accessed 4 February 2005.

3. Kovach B, Rosensteil T (2001) The elements of journalism. New York: Three Rivers Press. 208 p.

4. Schwitzer G (2004) A statement of principles for health care journalists. Am J Bioeth 4: W9. Available: http://www.ajobonline.com/journal/j_articles. php?aid=663 . Accessed 4 February 2005.

5. Schwitzer G (2000) The seven words you shouldn't use in medical news. Available: http://www.tc.umn.edu/%7Eschwitz/The7words.htm . Accessed 4 February 2005.

6. Schwitzer G (2004) Ten troublesome trends in TV health news. BMJ 329: 1352.

7. Kaiser Health Poll Report (2004) Health care priorities. Menlo Park (California): Kaiser Family Foundation. Available: http://www.kff.org/HealthPollReport/dec_2004/Care/. Accessed 4 February 2005.

8. Coghan A (2004 October 9) Do you believe in miracles? New Scientist 2468.

9. Mudur GS (2004 December 27) Ethics blown to winds. The Telegraph—Calcutta. Available: http://www.telegraphindia.com/1041227/asp/knowhow/story_4139179.asp . Accessed 7 June 2005.

10. Moynihan R, Bero L, Ross Degnan D, Henry D, Lee K, et al. (2000) Coverage by the news media of the benefits and harms of medications. N Eng J Med 342: 1645–1650.

11. Cassels A, Hughes MA, Cole C, Mintzes B, Lexchin J, et al. (2003) Drugs in the news: An analysis of Canadian newspaper coverage of new prescription drugs. CMAJ 168: 1133–1137.

12. Smith D, Wilson A, Henry D (2005) Monitoring the quality of medical news reporting: Early experience with 'media doctor'. >Med J Aust. In press.

13. Australian Press Council (2001 April) Reporting guidelines. General press release No. 245. Available: www.presscouncil.org.au/pcsite/activities/guides/gpr245.html . Accessed 31 February 2005.

14. Woloshin S, Schwartz LM (2002) Press releases: Translating research into news. JAMA 287: 2856–2858.

15. Brown D (2005 May 15) Statin role weighed in cancer rate study: Women using drug had fewer cases. Washington Post; Sect A: 16.

16. Schwartz LM, Woloshin S, Welch HG (2005 May 10) Overstating aspirin's role in breast cancer prevention. Washington Post; Sect F: 1.

17. Kolata G (2004 July 12) Experts set lower levels for cholesterol. New York Times; Sect A: 1.

18. Kassirer J (2004 August 1) Why should we swallow what these studies say? Washington Post; Sect B: 3.

19. Okrent D (2004 October 31) Analysts say experts are hazardous to your newspaper. New York Times; Sect 4: 2.

20. Ebencamp B (1998 November 9) The Dateline doctor is 'in'. Brandweek 39(42): 20.

21. Eggener S (1998) The power of the pen: Medical journalism and public awareness. JAMA 279: 1400.

22. Day M (2005 March 24) Words of wisdom come up against marketing strategies. The Australian 26:

23. Australian Government Department of Heath and Aging (2002) The national strategy for quality use of medicines. Commonwealth of Australia. Available: http://www.health.gov.au/internet/wcms/publishing.nsf/Content/nmp-pdf-natstrateng-cnt.htm/$FILE/natstrateng.pdf . Accessed 31 May 2005.

Communication Gap: The Disconnect between what Scientists Say and what the Public Hears

Charles W. Schmidt

Mojib Latif probably didn't anticipate the public reaction his research would attract last year. Writing in the 1 May 2008 issue of Nature, he and his colleagues from the Leibniz Institute of Marine Sciences and the Max Planck Institute in Kiel, Germany, predicted that increases in mean global temperatures could pause into the next decade, even though greenhouse gas levels were still rising in the atmosphere. That lull in warming, their models showed, was temporary, and due to complex interactions between the atmosphere and periodic cooling cycles in the oceans.

A meteorologist and oceanographer, Latif emphasized that these cyclical variations could occur even in the face of long-term climate trends. But to his surprise, skeptics seized on the findings as evidence that mean global temperatures aren't really rising. The website newsbusters.org, for instance, which bills itself as "dedicated to documenting, exposing, and neutralizing liberal media bias," compared

Latif's findings to "the Pope suddenly [announcing] the Catholic Church had been wrong for centuries about prohibiting priests from marrying." To Latif, the implication that climate change is a hoax was preposterous. "Making inferences about global warming from my short-term climate prediction is like comparing apples and oranges," he says.

Latif was caught in a familiar media trap. Research often delivers statistically nuanced findings that the lay public as well as journalists and other science communicators can find hard to understand. And just as political messages can be twisted into snippets of misinformation, scientific findings, too, are vulnerable to distortions and misrepresentations that stick in the public mind, especially if they fit ideologic biases.

These distortions are becoming all too common in today's new media environment. Although the World Wide Web offers invaluable access to information, it also gives an audience to anyone with an ax to grind. According to a commentary in the June 2009 issue of Nature Biotechnology authored by 24 experts in communication, law, and journalism, media fragmentation and the rise of ideologically slanted websites are perpetuating gridlocked opinions in science, just as they are in politics.

One of those authors is Matthew Nisbet, an assistant professor of communication at American University in Washington, DC. He says people who aren't inclined to pay close attention to an issue will learn about it from media outlets that reinforce their own social, political, or religious views. This and other types of "mental shortcuts," he says, make it possible for individuals to draw quick conclusions about complex topics that fit their own preconceptions.

Given these trends, communication experts are calling for fundamental changes in how scientists interact with the media because debates over climate change, health, energy, and technology are simply too important to lose to misinformation. As always, scientists are encouraged to communicate clearly using language that nonspecialists can understand. But now they're also being urged to step beyond the confines of the laboratory and to become more engaged in efforts to educate the public.

"The ultimate goal [in science communication]," says Nisbet, "is civic education—enabling and motivating more people into thinking, talking, and participating in collective decisions about, for example, what to do about climate change, or how to fund and oversee biotechnology." Scientists need to somehow communicate scientific uncertainties while going head-to-head against oversimplified inaccuracies in the media. The question is how best to do that.

Reworking the Angle

Nisbet in particular seeks to move beyond the traditional "deficit model" that currently dominates science communication. The deficit model assumes that if nonspecialists only understood the scientific facts, they would see eye-to-eye with the experts. Ignorance is what drives controversies in science, the model postulates. And by filling that deficit with knowledge, scientists can help make these controversies disappear.

But does that assumption really hold true? Not necessarily, Nisbet says. Disputes over climate change, for instance, remain strong despite the sustained efforts of scientists to communicate about the issue through the media. An October 2009 survey by the Pew Research Center for the People & the Press suggests public opinions about climate change line up more on political than scientific grounds.

According to that survey, 75% of Democrats see solid evidence that the average temperature on Earth has been getting warmer over the past few decades, compared with just 35% of Republicans. That disparity, Nisbet says, reflects opposing media influences geared toward their respective audiences. Both Republicans and Democrats tend to rely on news outlets that affirm their own social values, he says. And those outlets—together with input from like-minded friends and colleagues—can be more influential than the science itself.

Tellingly, the Pew survey also indicates that, compared with survey responses from April 2008, 8% fewer Democrats and 14% fewer Republicans reported seeing solid evidence of warming, which suggests confidence in the research is declining across party lines. The surveyors do not comment, however, on the reasons for that decline or whether it might reflect contradictory coverage of climate change in the press.

Nisbet is well known for his research on framing, or defining scientific issues in ways that audiences can understand in part by appealing to their core values. Climate change skeptics already do this successfully by predicting economic doom from curbing greenhouse gas emissions, he says. "You need to use metaphors and narratives that make the issue personally relevant," Nisbet explains. "It's got to be understandable and interesting to audiences that don't understand the technical details."

Teaming with evangelical leaders has enabled some scientists to frame climate change in terms of religious morality, which helps to engage conservative Christians on the issue. Among them are Eric Chivian, director of the Center for Health and the Global Environment at the Harvard Medical School, and Richard Cizik, founder and president of the recently formed New Evangelicals, who famously joined forces in 2007 to educate law makers and the public about environmental threats. Cizik is quoted in the 18 November 2009 online edition of the U.K. Guardian as saying that younger generations of evangelicals in particular "have an intensity level that even some in the environmental community don't have. They believe [environmental stewardship] is their God-given calling."

But Sharon Dunwoody, a professor of journalism and mass communication at the University of Wisconsin–Madison, cautions that frames might be labeled as spin by audiences who feel they're being manipulated. A climate change activist, for instance, might think it's effective to frame climate change in terms of dying polar bears. But a skeptic who doesn't think polar bears are at risk from climate change might feel manipulated by that frame and view it as spin.

To that, Nisbet says, "'Spin' is a problematic term since people use it in multiple ways and really never define what they mean by it. They usually just throw it out there as a way to express criticism without actually explaining what their criticism might be, or what their preferred alternative is."

Maintaining Credibility

Framing can pose other tough challenges for scientists; it requires them to know and understand what elements will engage a given target audience. And that begs insights into human nature that might not come readily to those more comfortable with data. Nisbet says talking points for use in framing can be obtained from research techniques familiar to social sciences research, such as interviews, focus groups, and surveys. Results from these investigations can be translated into practical advice for scientists who interact with different audiences via media formats such as web and video, he says.

Earl Holland, assistant vice president for research communications at The Ohio State University, argues that scientists are preoccupied with the day-to-day grinds of publishing and research, and therefore shouldn't be obliged to consider public perceptions of their work so explicitly. He suggests, moreover, that those activities might compromise a scientist's integrity.

Scientists often have the trust of the public going for them—they're typically held in high esteem, Holland says. What elevates scientists over those who spread misinformation, he explains, is credibility, and that credibility lies in part on the notion that scientists make impartial judgments based on data. But when they align themselves with a particular side in a debate, that impartiality is put to the test, he says.

"As soon as scientists take up an advocacy role, regardless of the position or topic, they lose credibility as unbiased sources," Holland asserts. "Some say that's too much to ask, but I say that just like journalists have to rein in their own political beliefs when reporting, scientists have to avoid catering to policy arguments. They're still highly regarded, but if they just get in there and punch it out with their opponents, they risk losing integrity."

Holland's view is that university news offices and what he describes as "support networks for the scientific community" bear responsibility for couching how research findings enter into policy debates—not the scientists themselves. That's not a universal view, however; many scientists see no problem with advocacy, as long as it's guided by expertise and experience.

Bruce Lanphear, a professor at BC Children's Hospital and Simon Fraser University in Vancouver, British Columbia, says debates over whether scientists should get involved in policy are mostly semantic. "There's a certain school of thought that our job as epidemiologists is simply to report results in journals while others translate those findings for the public—I don't subscribe to that," he says. "I view my job as also helping to translate findings in ways that don't mislead the public but that also help people understand why something is important."

Lanphear is best known for research that links low-dose exposure to lead and other toxicants to developmental effects in children. As a medical doctor, he says his efforts to raise awareness about industrial toxicants in commerce are consistent with the Hippocratic Oath. "Activism is a direct extension of what I was trained to do as a doctor," he says. "I feel an obligation to present data in ways that prevent dangerous exposures in the population."

Lanphear appears unfazed by charges of alarmism, and he acknowledges there remain many unanswered toxicologic questions about lead, pesticides, and other chemicals. But their known risks also compel regulatory changes to minimize exposure, he says. In communicating about low-dose chemical risks, Lanphear aims to create a sense of urgency, which he says is a prerequisite to environmental legislation.

"That's what it comes down to: community outrage," Lanphear says. "We knew lead was toxic as far back as 1909. Why did it take so long to restrict how we use it? Because of inertia, lobbyists, and the tax revenues it was generating. It took outrage and lawsuits to move the legislation. A sense of urgency holds feet to the fire."

Aiming for Clarity

People might look to science for clear-cut statements that can help them make decisions about their health and lifestyle, says Louis Guillette, Jr., a professor of biology at the University of Florida at Gainesville. But fields such as climate research, genomics, and toxicology are all grappling with enormous data sets and models that generate probabilistic instead of definitive findings. Most genetic tests, for instance, can't accurately predict if someone will get a disease; they can only suggest that someone has perhaps a 15% chance of getting the disease under certain environmental conditions. Likewise, climate models can simulate temperature changes, but they can't predict exactly where or when impacts will occur.

Individuals looking for clarity with respect to environmental threats might want a scientist to say, for instance, that a chemical will cause a specific effect at a precise real-world dose, but laboratory experiments don't allow for that, adds Guillette. Instead, experiments deliberately exclude confounding factors such as age, sex, or hormonal status to isolate a single variable's effect on a particular outcome. In the real world, these variables work simultaneously, along with a host of other chemical exposures, to produce effects that vary by individual.

It's important to provide the public with a baseline context for understanding what's meant by "risk," experts say. For instance, it's meaningless to say that family history of a disease makes a person 10 times more likely to succumb to that disease. It is clearer to say that if 1 in 100,000 people in the general population has the disease, then family history increases the risk to 1 in 10,000. That still may be a noteworthy difference—but perhaps not cause for undue alarm.

It's also important to specify what groups are being compared when talking about changes in risk so it's clear whether those changes are being described in absolute or relative terms. For example, consider preeclampsia, which affects an estimated 4% of pregnancies. If an environmental exposure increases the absolute risk of preeclampsia by 30%, that would mean going from 4% to 34%. In contrast, a relative increase of 30% would mean going from 4% to 5.2%.

All these statistical details make it impossible for scientists to speak in absolutes, so they communicate instead in terms of statistical probabilities that ideally apply under most real-world scenarios. Scientists take these nuances for granted, but they make a world of difference to anyone who has to intepret what new findings mean on a practical level. That's an essential issue, because research must somehow reconcile data with society's desire for clarity on scientific issues.

Joann Rodgers, senior advisor for science, crisis, and executive communications at Johns Hopkins Medicine and past president of the National Association of Science Writers, says environmental health findings are particularly hard to convey because, in addition to their complexity, they evoke emotional responses; climate change, pollution, and many other environmental threats affect millions of people. "Environmental issues give rise to a lot of activism," Rodgers says. "We tend to see that also in other fields, but there seems to be an extraordinary dose of mythologizing and ranting about science in the environmental health realm."

Dunwoody emphasizes that, as sources in the media, scientists get to decide what they're going to say. But she adds they should also be insightful about how those messages are received, given the need to dispel misinformation in the public arena. "The way you portray something dictates the take-home messages people walk away with," she says. "You've got to be careful."

Communication and Marketing as Tools to Cultivate the Public's Health: A Proposed "People and Places" Framework

Edward W. Maibach, Lorien C. Abroms and Mark Marosits

ABSTRACT

Background

Communication and marketing are rapidly becoming recognized as core functions, or core competencies, in the field of public health. Although these disciplines have fostered considerable academic inquiry, a coherent sense of precisely how these disciplines can inform the practice of public health has been slower to emerge.

Discussion

In this article we propose a framework—based on contemporary ecological models of health—to explain how communication and marketing can be used to advance public health objectives. The framework identifies the attributes of people (as individuals, as social networks, and as communities or populations) and places that influence health behaviors and health. Communication, i.e., the provision of information, can be used in a variety of ways to foster beneficial change among both people (e.g., activating social support for smoking cessation among peers) and places (e.g., convincing city officials to ban smoking in public venues). Similarly, marketing, i.e., the development, distribution and promotion of products and services, can be used to foster beneficial change among both people (e.g., by making nicotine replacement therapy more accessible and affordable) and places (e.g., by providing city officials with model anti-tobacco legislation that can be adapted for use in their jurisdiction).

Summary

Public health agencies that use their communication and marketing resources effectively to support people in making healthful decisions and to foster health-promoting environments have considerable opportunity to advance the public's health, even within the constraints of their current resource base.

Background

Communication is rapidly coming to be recognized as a core function, or core competency, in the field of public health. Several developments over the past few years illustrate this fact. In 2003, the Institute of Medicine identified communication as a core public health competency and called for efforts to enhance the communication skills of the public health workforce.[1] Over the past five years the National Cancer Institute—the largest biomedical research funding agency in the U.S.—has significantly increased the size of its health communication research portfolio after identifying health communication as vital to future progress in cancer control.[2]

In 2005, the Directors-General of National Public Health Institutes (NPHIs)—technical assistance units established within national health ministries—identified health communication as a core function of NPHIs,[3] and the Pan American Health Organization committed to "better utilize or increase, if needed, the numbers of ... communication experts" working in its member organizations.[4] Between 2004 and 2006, several U.S. schools of public health launched Masters in Public Health (MPH) degree programs in public health communication[5-

7]—which added significant new training capacity on top of the one extant program[8]—and the U.S. Association of Schools of Public Health published a draft set of communication competencies that are proposed to be required of every Masters in Public Health (MPH) graduate from accredited U.S schools of public health.[9]

Although marketing has not been formally recognized as a core public health function or competency—possibly because negative associations toward the concept by some in public health as a result of its roots in the business sector—many leading public health organizations are seeing its relevance to public health purposes and building their capacity in this discipline. Health Canada first established it Social Marketing Unit in 1981 and continues to expand its social marketing expertise.[10] The U.S. Centers for Disease Control and Prevention established the National Center for Health Marketing in 2004,[11] and a number of U.S. states—Arizona, California, Ohio and North Carolina, at a minimum—have recently established social marketing units. The National Health Service in the UK is currently considering a proposal to integrate social marketing as a core strategy in managing the health of the British population,[12] and public health organizations in the pacific region are working to enhance their marketing capacity.[13]

Health communication and social marketing have been vibrant areas of academic research and professional practice for several decades,[14,15] with both areas of inquiry yielding dedicated journals,[16,17] numerous books,[18-21] and myriad peer-reviewed manuscripts published in public health journals.[22-24] What has been slower to emerge, however, is a coherent sense of precisely how these disciplines can inform the practice of public health.

In this article we propose a framework through which to understand how to effectively harness the tools of communication and marketing in the practice of public health. We do so by first proposing a simple framework for public health action, and then by demonstrating the relevance of communication and marketing within the proposed framework.

Discussion

The Context: Ecological Models of Health

The Ottawa Charter[25] was a turning point in public health in that it prefaced a sea change in how public health professionals think about promoting health.[26] Its legacy—and that of leading epidemiology and population health theorists in the early 1990s[27-30]—can be seen clearly in contemporary ecological models of health.[31-34]

The concept of ecology "pertains broadly to the interrelations between organisms and their environments."[35] We interpret ecological models of health as positing, in essence, that the health of populations is influenced by: (a) the attributes of the people in the population; (b) the attributes of the environments—or places—in which members of the population live, work, go to school, shop and so forth; and (c) important interactions between the attributes of people and places. These attributes and their interactions typically influence health through their impact on health behavior and through direct effects on physical functioning and well-being.[36-42]

Health, and its behavioral, social, and environmental determinants, is nothing if not complex. A recent effort by Sallis and colleagues to create an ecological model of "active living"—i.e. physical activity—provides an excellent example of an attempt to capture this complexity.[43] Their model identifies seven broad categories of individual and environmental variables (intrapersonal, social cultural environment, natural environment, information environment, perceived environment, policy environment, and access to and characteristics of behavior settings) that influence active living behavior in each of four domains of active living (transportation, recreation, household activities, occupational activities).

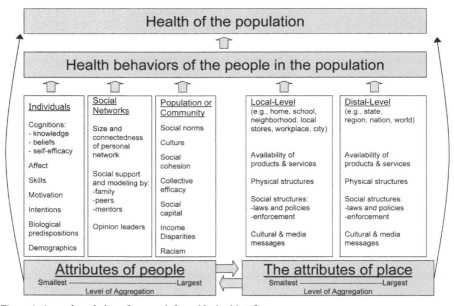

Figure 1. A people and places framework for public health influence.

In the spirit of Einstein's famous dictum—"Everything should be made as simple as possible, but not simpler"- we propose a streamlined ecological model of public health action that we call the People & Places Framework. By design, our framework principally calls attention to the attributes of people, and the attributes of places, that are known to influence the health behavior, and health, of populations. These two orthogonal factors—people and places—each operate across two or three relevant levels of analysis. Our framework describes the relevant attributes of people as operating in individual, social network, and community or population levels of analysis, and the relevant attributes of place as operating in local and distal levels of analysis). The framework is illustrated in Figure 1 and is described below. To simplify the visual presentation, we laid out the people and place factors side-by-side rather than orthogonally.

Throughout the remainder of the paper, we refer to these levels of analysis as "fields of influence" because our objective here is to describe a framework for public health action rather than a theory or theoretical framework for research purposes.

People-Based Fields of Influence

Renaissance era author John Donne's famous quote—"no man is an island, entire of itself; every man is a piece of the continent"—was prescient in its foreshadowing of contemporary theories of social science. These theories make clear that people exist within various levels of aggregation.[44] Building on earlier work, we propose that three levels of social aggregation, specifically the individual-level, social network-level, and group-, community- or population-level, offer a useful and parsimonious means of categorizing people-based fields of influence.[45]

Individual-level factors that influence health and health behavior have been the subject of intense research activity for many decades, particularly in various fields of psychology, communication research, and epidemiology. There has been—and will continue to be—lively debate regarding which individual-level factors are most relevant with regard to influencing health behavior and health.[46] Our point here, however, is not to take a position on that debate, but rather simply to affirm the importance of individual-level factors as an important field of influence on health behavior and health. For purposes of illustration, the literature points to the following as relevant individual-level attributes: cognitions (e.g., self-efficacy and outcome expectancies),[47] affect (e.g., depression),[48] skills (e.g. contraceptive skills),[49] motivation,[50,51] intentions,[52] biological predispositions (e.g., sensation seeking),[53] and demographic factors (e.g., marital status, education, income, employment status).[54,55] Most of these attributes are amenable to change through external intervention.

Much is also known about the relevant attributes of social networks with regard to health behavior and health.[56] Insights into the influence of social networks come from fields as diverse as sociology, communication, psychology, and business and organizational studies. Again, our purpose here is not to promulgate a specific theory or definitive list of attributes, but rather to affirm the importance of social networks as a field of influence on health behavior and health. The literature suggests that the relevant attributes of social networks, at a minimum, include: size and connectedness of a person's social network,[57] diversity of ties in the social network,[58] the degree to which the various relations in a social network (e.g., parents, friends, teachers and mentors) provide social support[59-62] and positive modelling,[63] and the presence of positive health opinion leaders in the social network.[64-67]

Even though Durkheim's seminal work over a century ago illustrated the importance of population attributes on health (in particular on suicide rates), the relevant attributes of groups, communities and populations with regard to health behaviors and health are perhaps the least well understood.[68] Culture and social norms are important, well documented attributes of communities and populations, although it can be argued that these are attributes operate at the individual and social network levels as well.[69] A rapidly emerging literature suggests that other important attributes of groups, communities and populations include social capital,[70] social cohesion,[71] and collective efficacy,[72-74] although additional work is needed to explicate and operationally define each of these attributes. Additionally, a large and rapidly growing body of literature is elucidating how socio-economic disparities—particularly the income gap between the most well-off and least well-off members of a community—and racism exert an important negative influence on health.[75-78]

Place-Based Fields of Influence

Needless to say, people and places are inextricably linked. Tom Farley and Deborah Cohen open their book Prescription for a Healthy Nation with a trenchant quote from Winston Churchill to illustrate this point: "We shape our buildings, and thereafter they shape us."[79] The influence of place—including our homes, schools, worksites, roads, food markets and restaurants, neighbourhood, cities, and so on—manifests itself on our health behavior, and health, in myriad complex ways. Cohen, Farley and Scribner developed a simple, elegant way to categorize these place-based influences into four factors: [80]

- *The availability of products and services.* Increased availability of health enhancing products and services (e.g., primary health care, fresh produce) tends to promote population health, while increased availability of health detracting products and services (e.g., liquor stores) has a tendency to undermine population health.

- *The physical structures in our environment.* Structures that as a natural by-product of their design encourage healthful actions (e.g., sidewalks, walking paths, easily accessible stairwells) or discourage unhealthful actions (e.g., reduced serving sizes) or outcomes (e.g., automobile airbags) tend to promote population health. Conversely, structures that as a natural by-product of their design promote unhealthful actions (e.g., super-sized meals, televisions) or enable actions that lead to morbidity or mortality (e.g., poor roadway design) tend to undermine population health.

- *The social structures (i.e., laws and policies) in our communities, and the extent to which they are enforced.* Laws and policies that require (e.g., seatbelt and child safety restraint laws) or encourage (e.g., enhanced access to fruits and vegetables in schools) healthful action, and those that discourage unhealthful actions (e.g., high tobacco taxes) tend to promote population health. Conversely, laws and policies that intentionally or inadvertently enable unhealthful behavior (e.g., permissive alcohol sales regulations) tend to undermine population health.

- *The media and cultural messages in our environment.* Media and cultural messages which model and recommend healthful practices (e.g. advertising which promotes fruit and vegetable intake) tend to promote population health, while media and cultural messages which model or promote behaviors ill-conducive to health (e.g. advertising which promotes intake of foods high in fats and sugars) tend to undermine population health.

These place-based factors operate both locally (e.g., within our own home, and in our city), and more distally (e.g., from actions taken in our state capital, in our nation's capital, and by multi-national corporations and multi-national governmental organizations).[81,82] Decisions made (or not made) in local places exert influence in a variety of pervasive ways over the behavior and health of people in that one location.[83] Conversely, the decisions made in distal places—e.g., Hollywood, Wall Street, Washington, DC—often have the potential to influence people's behavior and health over large geographic regions. Therefore, our proposed framework differentiates local and distal environments as distinct fields of influence.

The remainder of this paper focuses on describing the relevance of communication and marketing to public health practice through the lens of the People & Places Framework.

Definitions of Communication and Marketing

The distinction between communication and marketing is poorly understood throughout the field of public health.[84,85] They are often seen as interchangeable.

[86] We believe, however, that the concepts are distinct and that the distinctions are meaningful for public health. Each method offers a different and complementary approach through which to advance public health objectives.

Finnegan and Viswanth[87]—based on earlier writing by Gerbner[88]—provide a useful and concise definition of the act of communication as "the production and exchange of information and meaning by use of signs and symbols." Healthy People 2010—a publication that presents the current U.S. federal health objectives—defined health communication as "the art and technique of informing, influencing and motivating individual, institutional and public audiences about important health issues."[89] This definition is laudable for its inclusion of the full range of audiences implied by an ecological framework. Borrowing from the strengths of each definition, we define health communication as "the production and exchange of information to inform, influence or motivate individual, institutional and public audiences about health issues."

The American Marketing Association defines marketing as "an organizational function and a set of processes for creating, communicating, and delivering value to customers and for managing customer relationships in ways that benefit the organization and its stakeholders."[90] Inherent in this definition is the notion of the marketing exchange. The organization delivers value to the customer, usually in the form of products or services, in exchange for the customer's resources, usually in the form of money, effort and/or time, and which go on to benefit the organization. This definition makes clear that marketing involves the process of communication, but only as integrated function focused on creating and delivering value to customers through products and services.

Marketing and communication do overlap, both in concept and in how they are applied in public health. Marketing communication, or promotion, involves the use of communication to support the marketing process. Specifically, marketing communication is used to inform prospective customers, and business partners, about the availability, benefits, and costs associated with the organization's products and services, and to manage relationships with those key stakeholders. Moreover, the practice of public health communication has been greatly influenced by marketing methods, especially the use of marketing research and adoption of a consumer-orientation. Despite these areas of overlap, we believe that marketing and communication are sufficiently distinct—with distinctions that are directly relevant to effective public health practice—as to necessitate that one activity not be considered a sub-set of the other. The definitions above were provided with the specific intent of clarifying confusion in the literature where communication has often been mistaken for marketing, and vice versa.

The Relevance of Communication and Marketing in the People & Places Framework

One metric by which to gauge the relevance of communication and marketing to public health practice is the extent to which they are capable of creating—or contributing to—beneficial changes in each of the five fields of influence. Figure 2 illustrates our contention that communication and marketing each have potential to contribute to beneficial changes in all five fields of influence, and Figure 3 identifies the specific uses, or roles, of communication and marketing as they have been explored in public health to date. We explore each of these specific uses of communication and marketing below.

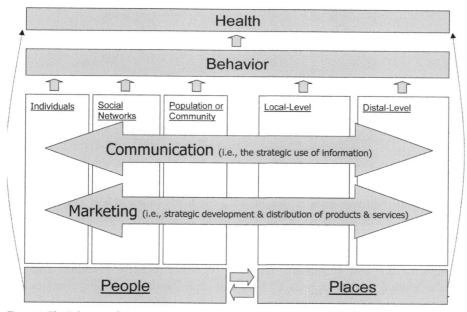

Figure 2. The Relevance of communication and marketing in the People & Places Framework.

Using Communication to Create Change in People-Based Fields of Influence

Individuals

Often referred to as "health communication," the use of communication methods to provide individuals with important health information has been a part of public health practice for decades, if not centuries. In the early 1700s, for example, Cotton Mather mounted a communication campaign in Boston to promote smallpox inoculation.[91] Informing people about immunizations remains an important public health communication priority today.[92-94]

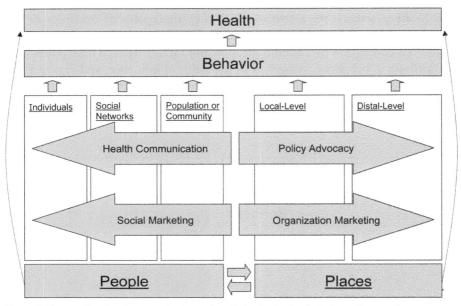

Figure 3. The specific roles of communication and marketing in the People & Places Framework.

A rich set of theories—mostly drawn from the fields of social and cognitive psychology—have been used successfully in developing health messages for individuals.[95,96] These theories include Social Cognitive Theory,[97] Elaboration Likelihood Model,[98] Stages of Change Theory,[99] and Theory of Reasoned Action,[100] and Persuasion Theory.[101] More recently, Fischhoff and colleague's "mental models" approach,[102] and other newly developing theories based in the emerging findings of neuroscience have provided new insights into effective health communication.[103]

The type and availability of communication vehicles that can be used to convey public health information to individuals has grown dramatically over time.[104] Some of these communication vehicles—e.g., brochures, small group counselling sessions, interactive DVDs, email and text messages—are well-suited to providing information to individuals on a one-to-one, or a one-to-few, basis. These communication vehicles can be effectively tailored to respond to individual attributes of the person receiving the information.[105] Other communication vehicles—e.g., TV, radio, newspapers, movies, websites—are well-suited to providing information on a one-to-many, or mass, basis. It is worth noting, however, that when we use communication vehicles on a "one-to-many" basis, we are typically attempting to influence individual-level attributes of people (e.g., self-efficacy) en mass, rather than attempting to influence attributes of the population per se (e.g., collective efficacy). The latter use of communication, as explained below, is a relatively unexplored opportunity in public health.

The dominant communication question of interest among health researchers and practitioners focused on the individual field of influence is: Can we use messages to influence people in beneficial ways? The answer to this question appears to be a qualified "yes." Case study evidence,[106] meta-analysis,[107] and systematic literature reviews[108-110] have each recently concluded that public health communication initiatives are, on the whole, effective in changing people's behavior, but usually only modestly so. To succeed, public health communication initiatives must be heard and remembered against the din of other competing messages in the media.[111] Many health communication campaigns have failed, however, because they did not achieve adequate "reach and frequency" and were not able to reliably expose members of the target audience to campaign messages. [112]

That the average public health communication campaign is only modestly effective, however, stands to reason when viewed in the context of an ecological model of health. Public health efforts to influence a single field of influence—in this case, individuals—will, on average, have only limited success because, in most cases, the other fields of influence also play significant roles in shaping the relevant behaviors and health outcomes. There are clear exceptions to this rule, however. Sudden Infant Death Syndrome (SIDS) campaigns in various nations around the world stand as an example of where communication efforts to create change in the individual field of influence (in this case by encouraging parents to place their babies to sleep on their backs) have been sufficient to create dramatic behavior change and improvements in health outcomes.[113] Presumably, communication to individuals in these cases was sufficient to create large-scale and sustained behavior change because parents are highly motivated to protect the health of their newborns, few social network, group, or environmental barriers stood in the way of their behavior change, and the behavior being recommended is quite easy to perform. The "truth" youth anti-smoking campaign is another apt exception to the rule. [114]

Social Networks

The potential influence of other people—rather than the potential influence of messages—has been the dominant question of interest among researchers and practitioners focused on the social network field of influence. Diffusion of Innovation theory[115,116] (as developed over the course of five decades by Everett

Rogers and recently launched into popular culture by Malcom Gladwell's book The Tipping Point[117]) has been particularly influential and helpful in highlighting for public health audiences the importance of social networks, although this research has tended to be explanatory rather than interventional in nature. Related areas of research have focused on activating existing relationships within social networks or developing new social networks in ways that enhance the provision of useful health information, positive sources of influence, and social support. The essential question is: Can we influence social networks so that they promote health?

Activating people within existing social networks to serve as agents of behavior change has proven to be a productive approach for cultivating health enhancement. Popular peers,[118,119] spouses,[120] parents of adolescents,[121] lay health workers and health care providers[122] have all been shown to have important behavioral influence on others.

Relatively less-studied is the question: Can we use communication to activate people to serve as agents of positive health influence within their social networks? The largest US health communication campaign to date, the Youth Anti Drug Media Campaign, is currently attempting to activate parents to take actions that are known to reduce the likelihood that their children will use drugs.[123] The initiative thus far has had only limited success in eliciting the recommended parenting behaviors.[124] An earlier effort, conducted largely through outreach to producers, directors and writers in Hollywood successfully promoted the designated driver concept as a way to reduce driving under the influence of alcohol. [125]

Interpersonal influence between peers, family members, and other members of social networks (i.e., "word of mouth" influence)—and interventions that attempt to harness this influence—has historically occurred primarily through face-to-face interaction. The introduction of the telephone in the 20th century added a new vehicle through which interpersonal influence could be expressed. Now, the internet is creating significant new possibilities for word of mouth influence. [126] The internet allows people to expand and strengthen their social networks. [127] Most recently, the growth of "social media" on the internet—places where social networks form in a manner not bounded by geographical constraints—has added a new and rapidly growing dimension to this field of influence. For example, MySpace—which lets people meet and interact with others who share similar interests and share content they create themselves such as blogs, photos, and videos—is currently the most popular destination on the Web.[128] The implications for harnessing this growing social influence process to advance the public's health are only now beginning to be considered.[129]

Groups, Communities and Populations

Understanding the influence of group, community and population attributes on health is a rapidly blossoming area of public health inquiry. Research focused on identifying viable means to influence these relevant attributes of communities and populations, however, is still in early stages of development. Important exceptions include the long-standing traditions of community organizing[130] and coalition building,[131] and the more recently established community-based participatory research model.[132,133]

The question of interest here is: Can we use communication to cultivate the attributes of community or population that promote health? Wallack has begun to articulate an answer to this question by identifying civic journalism and photovoice as promising approaches for using the mass media to build social capital in communities.[134] Civic journalism is the use of journalism to engage the community in the process of civic life.[135] Its methods—involving a variety of types of data gathering from, and information presentation to, members of the community—are intended to increase community debate and public participation in problem solving.[136] The preliminary evidence indicates that these methods offer an effective means for engaging community members in addressing important problems in their community.[137]

An interesting example of civic journalism was implemented during the most recent US presidential primary campaign. Rock the Vote, a national youth vote organization, partnered with CNN to sponsor a nationally-televised debate where Democratic presidential candidates responded to questions posed directly by young citizens. Young viewers of this event experienced greater identification with the candidates and enjoyed a heightened level of political efficacy as compared to young viewers of a traditional journalist-led debate format.[138] In other words, the positive impact of this exercise in political engagement was heightened simply by allowing members of a politically disenfranchised group (rather than a paid professional) to pose the questions to candidates.

Photovoice is a process that engages members of a community—typically members of a marginalized community—in using photography to document a public health problem that disproportionately affects them, from their own perspective.[139,140] This method seeks to encourage and enable members of the community to act on their own behalf. To the extent that it succeeds in doing so, this method can have a beneficial impact on important attributes of the community field of influence. A second and equally important objective of the method—engaging policy makers and other community leaders in the issue of concern so that they will effect the changes as recommended by members of the afflicted community—is perhaps better thought of as a place-based change strategy (see the "Using Communication to Shape the Place-Based Fields" section below).

Using Marketing to Create Change in the People-Based Fields of Influence

Individuals

Typically called "social marketing," the use of marketing to elicit health behavior change from individuals has been an active area of practice and research for the past several decades.[141,142] Much of what is called "social marketing" by practitioners and academics is not marketing, however, because neither products nor services are developed, distributed, or promoted. Rather, most of what is referred to as social marketing in public health involves exclusively the provision of information, and is therefore more correctly characterized as communication.[143]

The question of interest is: Can we develop and deliver products or services that will elicit the behavior we seek from members of our target audience? An excellent example, cited in a recent review by Grier and Bryant, illustrates how a social marketing program can reduce the incidence of driving under the influence of alcohol.[144] To address the problem of high rates of alcohol-impaired driving among young men in rural areas, the Wisconsin Department of Transportation conducted qualitative research with members of this group. In focus group interviews, the young men indicated they would not be dissuaded from drinking with their friends in bars after work, but they expressed concern about the risks associated with driving themselves home at the end of the evening. In response, the Department of Transportation developed a fee-based taxi service—The Road Crew—to safely transport people who have been drinking (or plan to drink) so that they do not drive themselves. In its first year, the marketing program proved popular with members of its target audience (over 17,000 rides were provided), and it earned widespread support from the communities where the program is offered, in part, because it reduced alcohol-related crashes by 17%.[145] Other examples of successful social marketing initiatives include the distribution and sale of condoms[146] and other contraceptives,[147] oral rehydration therapy,[148] bed nets to families in areas afflicted by high levels of malarial infestations,[149] and the distribution of point-of-use safe water products to prevent diarrhoeal disease in areas without adequate water sanitation facilities.[150]

Social Networks

A less explored use of social marketing involves developing and delivering products or services that target key members of social networks whose actions can benefit other members of their social network. The question of interest is: Can we use marketing to enhance or influence social networks so that they promote health? Kelly and colleagues' Popular Opinion Leader (POL) HIV prevention intervention provides an interesting example.[151] POL interventions attempt to influence a given geographically-bounded social network or community. The methodology involves recruiting approximately 15% of the members of a social network over time—specifically, those people who are most popular and trusted by others in the social network—into HIV prevention and advocacy training that is administered through multiple small-group sessions. When successfully implemented, the program results in significant community-wide rates of HIV risk reduction by virtue of the social influence brought to bear by the popular opinion leaders in the community.[152,153]

Groups, Communities and Populations

Public health professionals have only recently begun to consider the potential of social marketing to influence important attributes of groups, communities and populations. In theory, products and services that make it easier for citizens and community organizations to successfully come together around a common purpose and engage in community change efforts should promote both collective efficacy and social capital.[154-156] The question, therefore, is: Can we develop and deliver products or services that promote the community-level attributes that enhance health?

The Gatehouse Project in Australia provides an intriguing example.[157] To promote greater social inclusion and sense of school connectedness among the entire student population of 12 secondary schools, the project's personnel provided school officials with training and feedback, and a student curriculum, aimed at improving the school's social climate. These activities had a significant positive impact. Two years after the completion of the intervention, community-wide rates of substance use, anti-social behavior, and sexual intercourse were 25 percent lower in intervention schools as compared to control schools.

Using Communication to Shape the Place-Based Fields of Influence

The past several decades have been a time of considerable foment with regard to the uses of communication to positively influence environments. Policy advocacy—often referred to as "media advocacy"—has emerged as an important communication-based public health intervention modality. The key question here is: Can we use communication to promote beneficial changes in the places that influence peoples' health? We address this question as it pertains to both local-and distal-level places in a single discussion below, because the approaches are similar regardless of level of analysis.

Media advocacy has been defined as "the strategic use of mass media in combination with community organizing to advance healthy public policies."[158] Media advocacy involves framing public health issues, and creating news, so that members of a community will take notice, and take action, to force policy makers to revise the policies that are giving rise to the problem.

There is growing evidence supporting the effectiveness of this approach, especially at the local level.[159,160] The largest systematic effort to test policy advocacy methods to date—ASSIST (American Stop Smoking Intervention Study), a policy change-oriented tobacco control intervention conducted in 17 US states—demonstrated increased coverage of tobacco control issues in ASSIST states, including greater coverage of tobacco policy issues, although the increases in media coverage were smaller than was expected.[161]

Policy advocacy methods can also be used to target private sector policy makers who make myriad important decisions that affect the health of their stakeholders and the public at large (e.g., the CEO of Wal-Mart and other major corporations). For example, flight attendants and their union played an important role in getting smoking banned from airliners, the first ban on smoking in the workplace in the US.[162] Northwest Airline responded with a decision to prohibit smoking on all North American flights, several years in advance of being required to do so by law.[163]

Currently, public health advocacy efforts targeting the soft drink industry appear to be having positive influence. In recent years both Coca-Cola and Pepsi-Cola adopted policies to prevent their sodas from being sold in elementary schools in the US. More recently, the American Beverage Association (ABA), whose members include virtually all soft drink manufacturers, collaborated with American Heart Association and the William J. Clinton Foundation to create a voluntary set of policies that will, if embraced by ABA members, further limit soda sales in schools.[164] ABA's target is to have the policies honoured by their members in 100 percent of US schools by the beginning of the 2009–2010 school year.

Using Marketing to Shape the Place-Based Fields of Influence

Organization marketing (which in the literature is frequently referred to as business marketing or business-to-business marketing)—the process of marketing to potential customers in businesses, government agencies, and non-profit organizations—is an important use of marketing that is distinct both from consumer marketing and from traditional forms of social marketing. Andreasen[165] and Maibach and colleagues[166,167] have recently proposed the need for public health professionals to embrace organization marketing for its potential to positively influence environments and create "upstream" (i.e., place-based) changes conducive to the public's health. The key question is: Can we use marketing to promote beneficial changes in the places that influence peoples' health? A number of recent examples illustrate the potential.

The Popular Opinion Leader (POL) intervention for HIV prevention, as discussed above, has proven to be a highly effective in reducing population risk for HIV infection.[168] To encourage its broader adoption and use, Kelly and colleagues developed a web-based means of marketing the POL intervention to HIV prevention organizations in communities around the world. To evaluate this marketing approach, they specifically targeted HIV prevention organizations in 78 nations.[169] The marketing program was highly successful in that approximately 70 percent of the organizations that received the marketing offer adopted the POL intervention in their communities, or trained other agencies to use it.

To encourage other organizations (e.g., county health departments, school districts) to adopt proven disease-prevention programs, rather than use unproven programs, several US federal and non-profit health agencies created Cancer Control PLANET. PLANET is an online marketplace designed to facilitate the selection of evidence-based cancer prevention programs that are available for adoption by other organizations.[170] To enhance PLANET's value to potential customers, these agencies are currently taking active steps to expand their online library of proven programs. The US Centers for Disease Control and Prevention's DEBI (Diffusing Evidence-Based Interventions) Project is a conceptually similar effort to market evidence-based HIV prevention programs.[171]

Another excellent example is a newly-launched organizational marketing initiative by the New Jersey Health Care Quality Institute which is attempting to market evidence-based approaches to health enhancement—programs and modifications to the built environment—to New Jersey's mayors and municipal health task forces. The objective is to enable mayors and municipal task forces to, in turn, market the programs to employers, school officials, senior care managers, and community-based organizations in their cities. The logic model underlying this organization marketing strategy is illustrated in Figure 4.

The Importance of Cultivating Change in Multiple Fields of Influence

Inherent in the logic of ecological models of health is the premise that, to have the largest impact on behavior and health, public health professionals should seek to create change, as feasible, among multiple levels of influence.[172] Confirmation of this premise is nicely illustrated in the context of food micronutrient fortification programs.

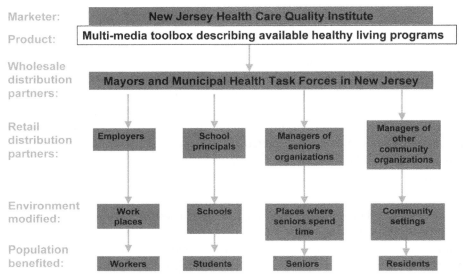

Figure 4. Distribution channels for the New Jersey Mayors Wellness Campaign.

Food micronutrient fortification strategies have long been the preferred strategy to ensure that people's diets include an adequate micronutrient levels precisely because of the assumption that "fortification requires minimal consumer involvement and little to no change in dietary habits."[173] A recent review of fortification programs, however, concluded that "the primary factor leading to long-term sustainability of food fortification is consumer awareness of the nutrient deficiency and consumer demand for and perceived benefits of the fortified food." This illustrates that the domains of influence reinforce one another, and that cultivating change in both people- and place-based fields of influence enhances the odds of achieving population-based health gains.

Of course, public health resources are inherently scarce and they must be stewarded wisely.[174] Organizations in the public health sector cannot afford to, nor would they be wise to, invest indiscriminately in attempting to create change in all fields of influence for every public health problem. We believe that public health organizations should develop strategic plans that consider and balance the following four factors in determining how to focus their efforts. These factors are: (1) the organization's current and potential resources; (2) the relative importance of each field of influence in creating or sustaining the problem being addressed; (3) the likely impact (and other potential benefits) associated with various programmatic options that the organization is capable of implementing; and (4) the likely costs of implementing the various programmatic options under consideration. This approach is grounded in well-established methods for health promotion program planning and management,[175] as well as in more recent thinking about how best to focus programmatic efforts against public health challenges with dimensions that are both people- and place-based.[176] Describing various methods for considering these factors is beyond the scope of this paper.

Communication and Marketing are Assets in Dissemination of Evidence-Based Public Health Programs

Over the past few decades, there has been a growing recognition of the importance of the dissemination of evidence-based "best practices" in public health programs, practices, and policies.[177] Thus far, however, the notion of evidence-based public health has been more promise than practice. Communication and marketing methods offer great potential in helping to bridge the divide between the promise and the practice of evidence-based public health.[178]

Conceptually, the challenges are fairly straight-forward: encouraging practitioners and policy makers to factor the evidence-base into their decision-making; and making it easy for them to effectively do so.[179] To fully harness the value of the evidence-based public health paradigm, however, we must successfully address these dissemination challenges with many different types of practitioners and decision-makers. Most obviously, this includes the people who shape public health and health care programs and policies. But it also includes the people who influence programs and policies in a wide variety of other aspects of the public sector (including education, housing, transportation, environment, and economic development), and in the non-profit and for-profit sectors (e.g., childcare, education, elder care). Successfully addressing these dissemination challenges will require a combination of methods including communication outreach, marketing, advocacy, illustrating with successful examples, technical assistance, and enabling the adaptation of evidence-based models to new circumstances.[180,181]

The Robert Wood Johnson Foundation's portfolio of Active Living initiatives provides an illustrative example.[182] Together, these programs seek to increase routine physical activity by disseminating evidence-based policy and environmental changes to American communities. Their methods include funding research studies to identify environmental factors and policies which influence physical activity; stimulating collaboration among professional associations to support elected and appointed government officials' efforts at promoting active living for their constituents; providing technical assistance to community partnerships to create and implement demonstration projects); and creating a "blueprint" that can be used by multiple organizations, associations and agencies to inform and support their change efforts. To highlight the need for change and the potential for success, each of the Active Living initiatives also conveys four key dissemination messages: (1) Physical activity has been engineered out of daily life; (2) As a result of inactivity, America is facing an obesity epidemic and related health problems; (3) By changing the places were we live and work, we can return physical activity to daily routines and reverse current health trends; (4) There is public support for creating activity-friendly places and this work is underway in some communities.[183]

Maximizing the Impact of Existing Communication and Marketing Resources

Although they may not think in these terms, most public health organizations currently make investments in—and have additional potential resources for—communication and marketing. Public health organizations should strive to enhance the impact of these investments because doing so can improve their agency's overall impact, even within current levels of funding.

With regard to communication, most public health organizations have actual resources in the form of communication expertise, information content, and some capacity to package and deliver that information to a variety of important audiences. Some public health organizations are well-positioned to use communication to target people-based fields of influence—based on their resources and capacity to reach people directly affected by health problems—while others are not. Conversely, based on their capacity to reach decision-makers at the local or distal level with credible information, some organizations are well positioned to use communication to target place-based fields of influence. Organizations should identify their current communication assets and determine how best to focus them.

Public health organizations should conduct a similar self-assessment with regard to marketing. An organization should identify: what products and services it currently offers people and other organizations; its capacity to improve those products and services—or to develop different products and services—based on feedback from current and potential customers; its capacity to deliver or distribute products and services to new priority populations; and finally, its capacity to promote its products or services to the people and organizations it wishes to serve.

Organizations are generally best served by developing programs that build on the strengths of their existing resources and core competencies, and by avoiding programs that require them to develop and sustain unrelated new resources. Once an organization is clear about the programs and information it wishes to deliver to its various customers, it can consider how its capacity can be extended through partnerships with other organizations. Partnering with other organizations—organizations that have a compelling reason to collaborate—is an important strategy both for enhancing impact, and for sustaining the initiative. Organizations can also build new resources and competencies, but doing so concurrent with developing new programs that requires those resources is challenging.

The Need for Training

The public health workforce worldwide is currently under-trained in the critical functions of communication and marketing.[184] Schools of public health and other public health institutions must take seriously the need to identify necessary competencies in these disciplines, and to develop and deploy training approaches that meet the needs of both current and future public health professionals. While these training resources are likely to emerge sooner rather than later in nations of the developed world, we mustn't lose sight of the fact that similar training resources are even more desperately needed in nations of the developing world. International health organizations should rapidly develop and deploy a strategic plan to improve the communication and marketing competency of the public health workforce worldwide, especially in developing countries. The success or failure of public health initiatives often hinges on effective marketing and communication.

Summary

- Communication and marketing are important tool kits for improving the public's health.

- These tool kits are uniquely well suited to advancing health in a manner consistent with an ecological model—as recommended by the Ottawa Charter—because each has the potential to influence people and places (i.e., environments).

- We suggest a practical framework by which to understand—and harness—the potential of communication and marketing to advance public health.

- Public health organizations should strive to enhance their competence in communication and marketing, because doing so can improve their impact even within current levels of funding.

- The public health workforce worldwide is currently under-trained in these critical competencies. International health organizations should rapidly develop and deploy a strategic plan to improve the communication and marketing competency of the public health workforce worldwide, especially in developing countries.

Competing Interests

The author(s) declare that they have no competing interests.

Authors' Contributions

Ed Maibach conceived and wrote the first draft of the manuscript. Lorien Abroms and Mark Marosits provided extensive input, feedback and editing on all sections of the paper.

Acknowledgements

The authors wish to thank Don Matheson and Tracey Bridges for helpful feedback in response to the first presentation of these ideas. Our thanks also go to our students Laurel Cassidy, Fran Fiocci, Nancy Freeborne, Ruth Hoffman, Memi Miscally, and Ellen Sowala and to our colleague Moshe Engelberg for their critical feedback of an early draft, and to Michael Slater and Ken Resnicow for helpful peer reviews.

References

1. Institute of Medicine: Who Will Keep the Public Healthy? Educating Public Health Professionals for the 21 st Century. Washington, DC, National Academies Press; 2003.

2. Hesse B: Why communication science is vital to progress against diseases in the 21 st century. In Presentation to the Symposium on State-of-the-Science Health Communication Research: Advancing the Science, Extending the Research, and Improving the Effectiveness of Health Communication. Bethesda, Maryland; May 10, 2006

3. Koplan J, Puska P, Jousilahti P, et al.: Improving the world's health through national public health institutes. Bulletin of the WHO 2005, 83:154–158.

4. [http://www.paho.org/English/GOV/ce136-05a-e.pdf]

5. [http://www.gwumc.edu/sphhs/departments/pch/phcm/index.cfm]

6. [http:/ / www.public-health.uiowa.edu/ cbh/ prospectivestudents/ mphsub-track-comm.html]

7. [http:/ / www.usc.edu/ schools/ medicine/ departments/ preventive_medicine/ divisions/ behavior/ education/ mph/ assets/ pdf/ HealthCommTrack2004-05. pdf]

8. [http:/ / www.tufts.edu/ med/ education/ phpd/ mph/ concentrations/ health-communication.html]

9. [http://www.asph.org/UserFiles/FinalVersion2.1.pdf]

10. Health Canada [http:/ / www.hc-sc.gc.ca/ ahc-asc/ activit/ marketsoc/ socmar-hcsc/ experience_e.html]

11. [http://www.cdc.gov/healthmarketing/aboutnchm.htm]

12. National Social Marketing Center [http://www.nsms.org.uk] It's our health! Realizing the potential of effective social marketing London: National Consumer Council; 2006.

13. Social Marketing Down Under website [http://www.socialmarketing.co.nz/]

14. Rogers E, Storey D: Communication campaigns. In Handbook of Communication Science. Edited by: Berger C, Chaffee S. Thousand Oaks, CA, Sage; 1986:814–846.

15. Bloom P, Novelli W: Problems and challenges in social marketing. Journal of Marketing 1981, 45:79–88.

16. Journal of Health Communication: International Perspectives, Philadelphia, Taylor and Francis; Health Communication, Lawrence Earlbaum Associates.

17. Social Marketing Quarterly, Philadelphia, Taylor & Francis

18. Hornik R: Public Health Communication: Evidence for Behavior Change. City, Lawrence Earlbaum Associates; 2002.

19. Andreasen A: Marketing Social Change. San Francisco, Jossey-Bass; 1995.

20. Maibach E, Parrott R: Designing Health Messages: Approaches from Communication Theory and Public Health Practice. Thousand Oaks, CA, Sage; 1995.

21. Kotler P, Roberto N, Lee N: Social Marketing: Improving the Quality of Life. Thousand Oaks, CA, Sage; 2002.

22. Lefebvre C, Flora J: Social marketing and public health intervention. Health Education Quarterly 1988, 15:299–315.

23. Grier S, Bryant C: Social marketing in public health. Annual Review of Public Health 2005, 26:319–339.

24. Noar S: A 10-year retrospective of research in health mass media campaigns: Where do we go from here? Journal of Health Communication 2006, 11:21–42.

25. [http://www.who.int/hpr/NPH/docs/ottawa_charter_hp.pdf]

26. Nutbeam D: What would the Ottawa Charter look like if it were written today? [http://www.rhpeo.org/reviews/2005/19/index.htm] Reviews of Health Promotion and Education Online 2005.

27. Rose G: The Strategy of Preventive Medicine. Oxford, England, Oxford University;

28. Stokols D: Establishing and maintaining health environments: Toward a social ecology of health promotion. American Psychologist 1992, 47:6–22.

29. Susser M: The logic in ecological: I. The logic of analysis. American Journal of Public Health 1994, 84:830–835.

30. Susser M, Susser E: Choosing a future for epidemiology: II. From black box to Chinese boxes and eco-epidemiology. American Journal of Public Health 1996, 86:674–677.

31. McLeroy KR, Bibeau D, Steckler A, Glanz K: An ecological perspective on health promotion programs. Health Education Quarterly 1988, 15:351–77.

32. Salis J, Cervero R, Ascher W, Henderson K, Kraft K, Kerr J: An ecological approach to creating active living communities. Annual Review of Public Health 2006, 27:1–14.

33. Etches V, Frank J, Di Ruggiero E, Manuel D: Measuring population health: A review of indicators. Annual Review of Public Health 2006, 27:29–55.

34. Brownson RC, Haire-Joshu D, Luke DA: Shaping the context of health: A review of environmental and policy approaches in the prevention of chronic diseases. Annual Review of Public Health 2006, 27:341–370.

35. Stokols D: Establishing and maintaining health environments: Toward a social ecology of health promotion. American Psychologist 1992, 47:6–22.

36. Berkman LF, Syme SL: Social networks, host resistance and mortality: A nine-year follow-up study of Alameda County residents. American Journal of Epidemiology 1979, 109:186–204.

37. Marmot MG, Smith GD, Stansfeld S, Patel C, North F, Head J, White I, Brunner E, Feeney A: Health inequalities among British civil servants: the Whitehall II study. The Lancet 1991, 337:1397–93.

38. Cohen S, Doyle WJ, Skoner DP, Rabin BS, Gwaltney JM Jr: Social ties and susceptibility to the common cold. JAMA 277(24):1940–4. 1997 Jun 25

39. Cohen D, Scribner R, Farley T: A structural model of health behavior: A pragmatic approach to explain and influence health behaviors at the population level. Preventive Medicine 2000, 30:146–154.

40. Resnicow K, Vaughan R: A chaotic view of behavior change: a quantum leap for health promotion. Int J Behav Nutr Phys Act 2006, 3:25.

41. Baranowski T: Crisis and chaos in behavioral nutrition and physical activity. Int J Behav Nutr Phys Act 2006, 3:27.

42. Brug J: Order is needed to promote linear or quantum changes in nutrition and physical activity behaviors: a reaction to 'A chaotic view of behavior change' by Resnicow and Vaughan. Int J Behav Nutr Phys Act 2006, 3:29.

43. Sallis J, Cervero R, Ascher W, Henderson K, Kraft K, Kerr J: An ecological approach to creating active living communities. Annual Review of Public Health 2006, 27:1–14.

44. Emmons K: Health behaviors in a social context. In Social Epidemiology. Edited by: Berkman L, Kawachi I. New York, Oxford University Press; 2000:242–266.

45. Flora J, Maibach E, Maccoby N: The role of media across four levels of health promotion intervention. In Annual Review of Public Health. Volume 10. Palo Alto, CA, Annual Reviews Press; 1989:181–201.

46. Noar S, Zimmerman R: Health behavior theory and cumulative knowledge regarding health behaviors: Are we moving in the right direction. Health Education Research 2005, 20:275–290.

47. Bandura A: Health promotion by social cognitive means. Health Education & Behavior 2004, 31:143–64.

48. Isen A: An influence of positive affect on decision making in complex situations: Theoretical issues with practical implications. Journal of Consumer Psychology 2001, 11:75–85.

49. Brown SS, Eisenberg L, Eds: The Best Intentions: Unintended Pregnancy and the Well-Being of Children and Families. Washington, D.C.: National Academy Press; 1995.

50. O'Donnell MP: A simple framework to describe what works best: improving awareness, enhancing motivation, building skills, and providing opportunity.

American Journal of Health Promotion 20(1): suppl 1–7 following 84, iii, 2005 Sep-Oct.

51. Ryan R, Deci E: Self-determination theory and facilitation of intrinsic motivation, social development, and well-being. American Psychologist 2000, 55:68–78.

52. Fishbein M: The role of theory in HIV prevention. AIDS Care 2000, 12:273–278.

53. Palmgreen P, Donohew L, Lorch E, Hoyle R, Stephenson M: Television campaigns and adolescent marijuana use: Tests of sensation seeking targeting. American Journal of Public Health 2001, 91:292–296.

54. Institute of Medicine: Speaking of Health: Assessing health communication strategies for diverse populations. Washington, DC: National Academies Press; 2002.

55. Marmot MG, Smith GD, Stansfeld S, Patel C, North F, Head J, White I, Brunner E, Feeney A: Health inequalities among British civil servants: the Whitehall II study. The Lancet 1991, 337:1397–93.

56. House JS, Landis KR, Umberson D: Social relationships and health. Science 1988, 241:540–5.

57. Berkman L, Glass T: Social integration, social networks, social support and health. In Social Epidemiology. Edited by: Berkman L, Kawachi I. New York: Oxford University Press; 2000.

58. Cohen S, Doyle WJ, Skoner DP, Rabin BS, Gwaltney JM Jr: Social ties and susceptibility to the common cold. JAMA 1997, 277:1940–4.

59. Berkman L, Glass T: Social integration, social networks, social support and health. In Social Epidemiology. Edited by: Berkman L, Kawachi I. New York: Oxford University Press; 2000.

60. House JS, Landis KR, Umberson D: Social relationships and health. Science 1988, 241:540–5.

61. Cohen S: Psychosocial models of the role of social support in the etiology of physical disease. Health Psychology 1988, 7:269–297.

62. Coker A, Smith P, Thompson M, McKeown R, Bethea L, Davis K: Social support protects against the negative effects of partner violence on mental health. Journal of Women's Health & Gender-Based Medicine 2002, 11:465–476.

63. Bandura A: Health promotion by social cognitive means. Health Education & Behavior 2004, 31:143–64.

64. Rogers E: Diffusion of Innovation. 5th edition. New York: Free Press; 2003.

65. Kelly J: Popular opinion leaders and HIV prevention peer education: Resolving discrepant findings, and implications for the development of effective community programs. AIDS Care 2004, 16:139–150.

66. Valente T, Hoffman B, Ritt-Olson A, Lichtman K, Johnson A: Effects of a social-network method for group assignment strategies on peer-led tobacco prevention programs in schools. American Journal of Public Health 2003, 93:1837–1843.

67. Durantini M, Albarracin D, Mitchell A, Earl A, Gillette J: Conceptualizing the influence of social agents of behavior change: A meta-analysis of the effectiveness of HIV prevention interventionists for different groups. Psychological Bulletin 2006, 132:212–48.

68. Durkheim E: Suicide: a study in sociology. Glencoe, IL: Free Press; (1987,1951)

69. Kreuter M, McClure S: The role of culture in health communication. Annual Review of Public Health 2004, 25:439–55.

70. Kawachi I, Kennedy BP, Glass R: Social capital and self-rated health: a contextual analysis. Am J Public Health 1999, 89:1187–93.

71. Kawachi I, Berkman L: Social cohesion, social capital, and health. In Social Epidemiology. Edited by: Berkman L, Kawachi I. New York: Oxford University Press; 2000.

72. Cohen D, Finch B, Bower A, Sastry N: Collective efficacy and obesity: The potential influence of social factors on health. Social Science & Medicine 2006, 62:769–778.

73. Bandura A: Self-Efficacy: The Exercise of Control. Edited by: . New York: WH Freeman & Co; 1997:477–525.

74. Sampson RJ, Raudenbush SW, Earls F: Neighborhoods and violent crime: a multilevel study of collective efficacy. Science 1997, 277:918–24.

75. Ram R: Further examination of the cross-country association between income inequality and population health. Soc Sci Med 2006, 62:779–91.

76. Zimmerman FJ, Bell JF: Income inequality and physical and mental health: testing associations consistent with proposed causal pathways. J Epidemiol Community Health 2006, 60:513–21.

77. LaVeist TA: Race, Ethnicity, and Health. San Francisco: Jossey-Bass; 2002.

78. National Institute of Public Health (FHI): Discrimination—A threat to public health. [http://www.fhi.se/shop/material_pdf/r200622_discrimination_eng.pdf] 2006.

79. Farley T, Cohen D: Prescription for a Healthy Nation: A New Approach to Improving Lives by Fixing our Everyday World. Boston: Beacon Press; 2005.

80. Cohen D, Scribner R, Farley T: A structural model of health behavior: A pragmatic approach to explain and influence health behaviors at the population level. Preventive Medicine 2000, 30:146–154.

81. Booth S, Mayer J, Sallis J, Ritenbaugh C, Hill J, et al.: Environmental and societal factors affect food choice and physical activity: Rationale, influences, and leverage points. Nutrition Reviews 2001, 59:S21–39.

82. Andreasen A: Social Marketing in the 21 st Century. Thousand Oaks, CA: Sage; 2006.

83. Farley T, Cohen D: Prescription for a Healthy Nation: A New Approach to Improving Lives by Fixing our Everyday World. Boston: Beacon Press; 2005.

84. McDermott L, Stead M, Hastings G: What is and what is not social marketing: The challenge of reviewing the evidence. Journal of Marketing Management 2005, 21:545–553.

85. Maibach E, Rothschild M, Novelli W: Social marketing. In Health Behavior and Health Education. 3rd edition. Edited by: Glanz K, Rimer B, Marcus Lewis F. San Francisco, Jossey-Bass; 2002:437–461.

86. Maibach E: Explicating social marketing: What is it, and what isn't it. Social Marketing Quarterly 2002, 8:1–7.

87. Finnegan J, Viswanath K: Communication theory and health behavior change: The media studies framework. In Health Behavior and Health Education. 3rd edition. Edited by: Glanz K, Rimer B, Marcus Lewis F. San Francisco, Jossey-Bass; 2002:361–388.

88. Gerbner G: Field definitions: Communication theory. In 1984–85 U.S. Dictionary of Graduate Programs. Princeton, NJ, Educational Testing Service; 1985.

89. US Department of Health & Human Services: Healthy People 2010: Understanding and Improving Health. Washington, DC: USDHHS; 2000.

90. American Marketing Association [http://www.marketingpower.com/mg-dictionary-view1862.php] 2006.

91. Paisley W: Public communication campaigns: The American experience. In Public Communication Campaigns. 3rd edition. Edited by: Rice R, Atkin C. Thousand Oaks, CA: Sage; 2001:3–21.

92. Ball L, Evans G, Bostrom A: Risky business: Challenges in vaccine risk communication. Pediatrics 1998, 101:453–458.

93. Dittmann S: Vaccine safety: risk communication–a global perspective. Vaccine 2001, 19:2446–56.

94. Gellin B, Maibach E, Marcuse E: Do parents understand immunizations? A national telephone survey. Pediatrics 2000, 106:1097–1102.

95. Noar S: A 10-Year retrospective of research in health mass media campaigns: Where do we go from here? Journal of Health Communication 2006, 11:21–42.

96. Maibach E, Parrott R: Designing Health Messages: Approaches from Communication Theory and Public Health Practice. Thousand Oaks, CA: Sage; 1995.

97. Bandura A: Social Foundations of Thought and Action: A Social Cognitive Theory. Englewood Cliffs, NJ: Prentice Hall; 1986.

98. Petty R, Rucker D, Bizer G, Cacioppo J: The elaboration likelihood model of persuasion. In Perspectives on persuasion, social influence and compliance gaining. Edited by: Seiter J, & Gass G. Boston:Allyn & Bacon; 2004:65–89.

99. Maibach E, Cotton D: Moving people to behavior change: A staged social cognitive approach to message design. In Designing Health Messages. Edited by: Maibach E & Parrott R. Thousand Oaks, CA: Sage; 1995:41–64.

100. Fishbein M, Middlestadt S: Using the theory of reasoned action to develop education interventions: Applications to Illicit Drug Use. Health Education Research 1987, 2:361–71.

101. Cialdini R: Harnessing the science of persuasion. Harvard Business Review 2001, 79:72–79.

102. Fischhoff B: Why (cancer) risk communication is hard. Journal of the National Cancer Institute 1999, 25:7–13.

103. McComas K: Defining moments in risk communication research: 1996–2005. Health Communication Research 2006, 11:75–91.

104. Maibach E: The influence of the media environment on physical activity: Looking for the big picture. American Journal of Health Promotion 2007, 21:(S)353–62.

105. Campbell MK, Quintiliani LM: Tailored interventions in public health. American Behavioral Scientist 2006, 49:775–93.

106. Hornik R: Public Health Communication: Evidence for Behavior Change. Hillsdale, NJ: Lawrence Earlbaum; 2002.

107. Snyder L, Hamilton M: A meta-analysis of US health campaigns on behavior: Emphasize enforcement, exposure, and new information, and beware the secular trend. In Public Health Communication: Evidence for Behavior Change. Edited by: Hornik R. Hillsdale, NJ: Lawrence Earlbaum; 2002:357–384.

108. Noar S: A 10-year retrospective of research in health mass media campaigns: Where do we go from here? Journal of Health Communication 2006, 11:21–42.

109. Rimer BK, Glassman B: Is there a use for tailored print communications in cancer risk communication? J Natl Cancer Inst Monogr 1999, 25:140–8.

110. Suggs S: A 10-year retrospective of research in new technologies for health communication. Journal of Health Communication 2006, 11:61–74.

111. McGuire WJ: Public communication as a strategy for inducing health-promoting behavioral change. Prev Med 1984, 13:299–319.

112. Hornik R: Public health communication: Making sense of contradictory evidence. In Public health communication: Evidence for behavior change. Edited by: Hornik R. Mahwah, NJ: Lawrence Earlbaum Associates; 2002:1–19.

113. Mitchell E: The changing epidemiology of SIDS following the national risk reduction campaigns. Pediatr Pulmonol Suppl 1997, 16:117–9.

114. Sly DF, Hopkins RS, Trapido E, Ray S: Influence of a counteradvertising media campaign on initiation of smoking: the Florida "truth" campaign. American Journal of Public Health 2001, 91:233–8.

115. Rogers E: Diffusion of Innovation. 5th edition. New York: The Free Press; 2003.

116. Singhal A, Dearing J, editors: Communication of Innovations: A journey with Ev Rogers. Thousand Oaks, CA: Sage; 2006.

117. Gladwell M: The Tipping Point. New York: Little, Brown and Company; 2000.

118. Kelly J: Popular opinion leaders and HIV prevention peer education: Resolving discrepant findings, and implications for the development of effective community programs. AIDS Care 2004, 16:139–150.

119. Valente T, Hoffman B, Ritt-Olson A, Lichtman K, Johnson A: Effects of a social-network method for group assignment strategies on peer-led tobacco prevention programs in schools. American Journal of Public Health 2003, 93:1837–1843.

120. Park EW, Tudiver F, Schultz JK, Campbell T: Does enhancing partner support and interaction improve smoking cessation? A meta-analysis. Ann Fam Med 2004, 2:170–4.

121. Simons-Morton B, Hartos J, Leaf W, Preusser D: Do recommended driving limits affect teen-reported traffic violations and crashes during the first 12 months of independent driving? Traffic Injury Prevention 2006, 7:1–10.

122. Lancaster T, Stead L: Physician advice for smoking cessation. Cochrane Database Syst Rev (4):CD000165. 2004 Oct 18

123. Kelder S, Maibach E, Worden J, Biglan A, Levitt A: Planning and initiation of the ONDCP National Youth Anti-Drug Media Campaign. J Public Health Manag Pract 2000, 6:14-26. javascript:PopUpMenu2_Set(Menu10848479)

124. Hornik R, Maklan D, Cadell D, Barmada C, Jacobsohn L, et al.: Evaluation of the National Youth Anti-Drug Media Campaign: 2003 Report of Findings. [http://www.nida.nih.gov/PDF/DESPR/1203report.pdf]

125. Montgomery KC: The Harvard Alcohol Project: Promoting the designated driver on television. In Organizational Aspects of Health Communication Campaigns: What Works?. Edited by: Backer T, Rogers E. Newbury Park, CA: Sage; 1993.

126. Silverman G: The secrets of word-of-mouth marketing. New York: Amacom; 2001.

127. Jeffrey Boase, John HorriganB, Barry Wellman, Barry , Lee Rainie: The Strength of Internet Ties. Washington, DC: Pew Internet & American Life Project; 2006.

128. WOMMA Research Blog [http://www.womma.org/research/studies/myspace_knows_y.htm]

129. Lefebvre C: The implications of social media for social marketing and public health. In Presentation at the Quarterly Seminar Series in Public Health Communication & Marketing, September 27, School of Public Health and Health Services. The George Washington University, Washington, DC; 2006.

130. Chervin DD, Philliber S, Brindis CD, Chadwick AE, Revels ML, et al.: Community capacity building in CDC's Community Coalition Partnership Programs for the Prevention of Teen Pregnancy. J Adolesc Health 2005, 37(3 Suppl):S11-9.

131. Wolff T: The future of community coalition building. Am J Community Psychol 2001, 29:263.

132. Kreuter MW, Lezin N: Social capital theory. Implications for community-based health promotion. In Emerging Theories in Health Promotion Practice and Research. Edited by: Diclemente RJ, Crosby RA, Kegler MC. San Francisco: Jossey-Bass; 2002.

133. Minkler M, Wallerstein NB: Community and group models of behavior change. In Health Behavior and Health Education. Edited by: Glanz K, Rimer BK, Lewis FM. San Francisco: Joesey-Bass; 2002.

134. Wallack L: The role of mass media in creating social capital: A new direction for public health. In Health and Social Justice: Politics, Ideology, and Inequity in the Distribution of Disease. Edited by: Hofrichter R. San Francisco, Jossey-Bass; 2003:594–625.

135. Merritt D: Public Journalism and Public Life. Mahwah, NJ: Erlbaum; 1995.

136. Friedlan L, Sotirovic M, Daily K: Public journalism and social capital. In Assessing Public Journalism. Edited by: Lambeth B, Meyer P, Thorson E. Columbia, MO:University of Misouri Press; 1998. (pages ?)

137. Denton F, Thorson E: Effects of a multi-dimensional public journalism project on political knowledge and attitudes. In Assessing Public Journalism. Edited by: Lambeth B, Meyer P, Thorson E. Columbia, MO:University of Misouri Press; 1998. (pages ?)

138. Mckinney M, Banwart M: Rocking the youth vote through debate: Examining the effects of a citizen versus journalist controlled debate on civic engagement. Journalism Studies 2005, 6:153–63.

139. Wang C: Photovoice: A Participatory action research strategy applied to women's health. Journal of Women's Health 1999, 8:185–192.

140. Wang C, Burris M: Photovoice: Concept, methodology, and sse for participatory needs assessment. Health Education Quarterly 1997, 24:171–186.

141. Andreasen A: Marketing social change: Changing behavior to promote health, social development and the environment. San Francisco: Jossey-Bass; 1195.

142. Kotler P, Roberto E, Lee N: Social marketing: Strategies for changing public behavior. Thousand Oaks, CA: Sage; 2002.

143. Hill R: The marketing concept and health promotion: A survey and analysis of recent health promotion literature. Social Marketing Quarterly 2001, 2:29–53.

144. Grier S, Bryant C: Social marketing in public health. Annual Review of Public Health 2005, 26:319–339.

145. Rothschild M, Mastin B, Karsten C, Miller T: The Road Crew final report: A demonstration of social marketing to reduce alcohol-impaired driving by individuals aged 21 through 34. [http://www.dot.wisconsin.gov/library/publications/topic/safety/roadcrew.pdf] Wisconsin Department of Transportation Technical Report, Madison, Wisc 2003.

146. Eloundou-Enyegue P, Meekers D, Calves A: From awareness to adoption: The effects of AIDS education and condom social marketing on condom use in Tanzania (1993–1996). Journal of Biosocial Science 2005, 37:257–268.

147. Harvey P: Let every child be wanted: How social marketing is revolutionizing contraceptive marketing around the world. Oxford: Greenwood Publishing; 1999.

148. Kenya PR, Gatiti S, Muthami LN, Agwanda R, Mwenesi HA, et al.: Oral rehydration therapy and social marketing in rural Kenya. Soc Sci Med 1990, 31:979–87.

149. Hanson K, Kikumbih N, Schellenberg J, Mponda H, Nathan R: Cost-effectiveness of social marketing of insecticide-treated nets for malaria control in the United Republic of Tanzania. Bull World Health Organ 2003, 81:269–76.

150. Population Services International: Disinfecting Water, Saving Lives: Point-of-Use Safe Water Products Prevent Diarrhea and Improve Family Health. [http://www.psi.org/child-survival/safe-water.html]

151. Kelly J, Murphy D: Randomised, controlled, community-level HIV-prevention intervention for sexual-risk behavior among homosexual men in US cities. Lancet 1997, 350:1500–1506.

152. Kelly J, Somlai A, Benotsch E, McAuliffe T, Amirkahnian Y, et al.: Distance communication transfer of HIV prevention interventions to service providers. Science 2004, 305:1953–55.

153. Kelly J: Popular opinion leaders and HIV prevention peer education: Resolving discrepant findings, and implications for the development of effective community programmes. AIDS CARE 2004, 16:139–150.

154. Kreuter MW, Lezin N: Social capital theory. Implications for community-based health promotion. In Emerging Theories in Health Promotion Practice and Research. Edited by: Diclemente RJ, Crosby RA, Kegler MC. San Francisco: Jossey-Bass; 2002.

155. Bandura A: Self-Efficacy: The Exercise of Control. New York: WH Freeman; 1997:477–525.

156. Wallack L: The Role of mass media in creating social capital: A new direction for public health. In Health and Social Justice: Politics, Ideology, and Inequity in the Distribution of Disease. Edited by: Hofrichter R. San Francisco, Jossey-Bass; 2003:594–625.

157. Patton GC, Bond L, Carlin JB, Thomas L, Butler H, et al.: Promoting social inclusion in schools: a group-randomized trial of effects on student health risk behavior and well-being. Am J Public Health 2006, 96:1582–87.

158. Wallack L: The role of mass media in creating social capital: A new direction for public health. In Health and Social Justice: Politics, Ideology, and Inequity

in the Distribution of Disease. Edited by: Hofrichter R. San Francisco, Jossey-Bass; 2003:594–625.

159. Holder H, Treeno A: Media advocacy in community prevention: News as a means to advance policy change. Addiction 1997, 92:S189–199.

160. Asbridge M: Public place restrictions on smoking in Canada: Assessing the role of state, media, science and public health advocacy. Social Science & Medicine 2004, 58:13–24.

161. Stillman F, Cronin K, Evans D, Ulasevich A: Can media advocacy influence newspaper coverage of tobacco: Measuring the effectiveness of the ASSIST media advocacy strategies. Tobacco Control 2001, 10:137–144.

162. Pan J, Barbeau E, Levenstein C, Baibach E: Smoke-free airlines and the role of organized labor: A case study. American Journal of Public Health 2005, 95:398–4404.

163. Lopipero P, Bero L: Tobacco interests or the public interest: 20 years of industry strategies to undermine airline smoking restrictions. Tobacco Control 2006, 15:323–332.

164. American Heart Association: Alliance for a Healthier Generation and industry leaders set healthy school beverage guidelines for U.S. schools. [http://www.americanheart.org/presenter.jhtml?identifier=3039339] AHA News 2006.

165. Andreasen A: Social marketing in the 21 st century. Thousand Oaks, CA: Sage; 2006.

166. Maibach EW, Van Duyn MAS, Bloodgood B: A marketing perspective on disseminating evidence-based approaches to disease prevention and health promotion. [http://www.cdc.gov/pcd/issues/2006/jul/05_0154.htm] Prev Chronic Dis [serial online] 2006 Jul [August 8, 2006]

167. Dearing J, Maibach E, Buller D: A convergent diffusion and social marketing approach for disseminating proven approaches to physical activity promotion. American Journal of Preventive Medicine 2006, 31(4S):S11–23.

168. Kelly J, Murphy D, Sikkema K, McAuliffe T, Roffman R, et al.: Randomised, controlled, community-level HIV-prevention intervention for sexual-risk behavior among homosexual men in US cities. Lancet 1997, 350:1500–1505.

169. Kelly J, Somlai A, Benotsch E, McAuliffe T, Amirkhanian Y, et al.: Distance Communication Transfer of HIV Prevention Interventions to Service Providers. Science 2004, 305:1953–1955.

170. Cancer Control PLANET [Internet] [http://cancercontrolplanet.cancer.gov/index.html] Bethesda (MD): National Institutes of Health;

171. [http://www.effectiveinterventions.org/interventions/sista.cfm]

172. Sallis J, Owen N: Ecological models of health behavior. In Health Behavior and Health Education. 3rd edition. Edited by: Glanz K, Rimer B, Marcus Lewis F. San Francisco: Jossey-Bass; 2002.

173. Darnton-Hill I, Nalubola R: Fortification strategies to meet micro-nutrient needs: Successes and failures. Proceedings of the Nutrition Society 2002, 61:231–241.

174. Lomborg B, ed: How to spend $50 billion to make the world a better place. Cambridge: Cambridge University Press; 2006.

175. Green L, Kreuter M: Health promotion planning: An education and ecological approach. 3rd edition. Mountain View, CA: Mayfield Publishing Co; 1999.

176. Booth S, Mayer J, Sallis J, Ritenbaugh C, Hill J, et al.: Environmental and societal factors affect food choice and physical activity: Rationale, Influences, and Leverage Points. Nutrition Reviews 2001, 59:s21–s39.

177. Brownson R, et al.: Evidence-based public health. Oxford: Oxford University Press; 2003.

178. Maibach EW, Van Duyn MAS, Bloodgood B: A marketing perspective on disseminating evidence-based approaches to disease prevention and health promotion. [http://www.cdc.gov/pcd/issues/2006/jul/05_0154.htm] Prev Chronic Dis [serial online] 2006 Jul [August 8, 2006]

179. Dearing J, Maibach E, Buller D: A convergent diffusion and social marketing approach for disseminating proven approaches to physical activity promotion. American Journal of Preventive Medicine 2006, 31(4S):S11–23.

180. Berwick D: Disseminating innovations in health care. JAMA 2003, 289:1969–75.

181. Dearing J, Maibach E, Buller D: A convergent diffusion and social marketing approach for disseminating proven approaches to physical activity promotion. American Journal of Preventive Medicine 2006, 31(4S):S11–23.

182. Lavizzo-Mourey R, McGinnis JM: Making the Case for Active Living Communities. American Journal of Public Health 2003, 93:1386–1388.

183. [http://www.activeliving.org/downloads/core_messages.pdf]

184. Institute of Medicine: Who Will Keep the Public Healthy? Educating Public Health Professionals for the 21 st Century. Washington, DC, National Academies Press; 2003.

Mass Media Theory, Leveraging Relationships, and Reliable Strategic Communication Effects

Colonel John R. Robinson

Words matter. It has never been clearer than in this information age that people respond to written and verbal messages in an endless mixture of ways and that the ways a sender presents information impacts the emotional response and behavior of a receiver. Because words increasingly matter, the United States military's interest in strategic communication, its potential, effects and limitations, is growing as well. There are many definitions for strategic communication, but a recent and simple explanation defines it as, "a way of persuading other people to accept ones' ideas, policies, or courses of action."[1] The usual military venues that conduct strategic communication are public affairs, information operations and public diplomacy. Today's U.S. military leaders are briefed daily on communication "messages" that are intended to effectively address whatever the most likely subjects, as assessed from mass media, that will be in the public consciousness. These written and verbal messages are critical to ensuring unity among the U.S. military's public communicators They provide a foundation for "one voice" and set conditions for a timely response to disinformation and breaking news.

This emphasis on messaging is nothing new or innovative. Since the dawn of modern mass media, national leaders have worked to capture its power and employ it to their advantage with large populations. The intense propaganda campaigns of the early 20th century show how past governments and militaries have used both truthful and sometimes twisted information in order to vilify enemies and mobilize publics in support of a national cause.[2] What has always been troubling and frustrating to public communicators, though, is that the effects from their "messages" are far from predictable. Regardless of how carefully messages are crafted and employed, people respond differently and sometimes, they do not seem to respond at all. The problem is not that messages crafted in words do not achieve effects, but rather, the effects are sometimes not what was intended, difficult to manage and difficult to assess. Partly because of this lack of reliability from messaging, one of the primary criticisms of strategic communication is that people can rarely guarantee the characteristics or timing of effects. With that in mind, areas of strategic communication that seem to have more reliability than written or verbal messaging are communication based on relationships. People tend to respond more positively to people who are of the same social and cultural groups. As examples, families respond to patriarchs and matriarchs, congregations respond to pastors, and teens respond to peers.

This paper will use known mass media and social theories to review how strategic communication that is based on relationships is more reliable than approaches that assume successful effects from messages alone. Figure 1 gives a list of referenced mass-media theories to be discussed. For the sake of clarity, "messages" or "messaging" in this paper always refers to written or verbal messages, rather than communication via action. The first three theories to be discussed all apply to message-centric communication. These theories will show how messages do in fact achieve effects, but that the effects are unreliable. The next four theories apply to relationships and will show how relationship-centric communication can achieve more reliable effects. In addition, this paper will address two final theories to show that there is no such thing as a relationship "magic bullet" that will always achieve desired effects. Although there are theories that show how relationship-centric communication is more reliable than message-centric communication, there are also theories that show how publics will only tolerate a limited amount of persuasion from mass media. Sometimes publics will use mass media to self-correct behavior in order to make society seem more "normal."

Relationships cannot replace the utility of planned messages for ensuring "one voice" among communicators or for minimizing response time to defeat misinformation. Finally, this paper will address how the information battlespace can change depending on a message-centric or relationship-centric perspective. In the end, words matter because messages in public communication are critical for unity of effort and timely response. However, relationships are also very important and a combination of messages and relationships must be considered to achieve successful strategic communication effects.

Verbal and Written Message-Centric Theories	Premise of Theory
Magic Bullet	Every member of an audience responds to media messages in a relatively uniform way.
Psychodynamic Persuasion Strategy	"Learn-Feel-Do" – Carefully employed information from a persuader can change the psychological structure of an individual.
Meaning Construction Persuasion Strategy	Words take on new meaning beyond the words themselves. Related to "branding."
Relationship-Centric Theories	
Media Systems Dependency	People use media because they are dependent on it in order to understand their environment.
Social Differentiation	Communication technology enables virtual subcultures to evolve according to individual interests.
Sociocultural Persuasion Strategy	"Learn-Conform-or-be-Punished" – Groups impose revised expectations on individuals, who must then conform to acceptable norms of behavior
Two-Step Flow	People are more likely to believe information from experts or authority figure persons with whom they have a trusted or perceived positive relationship.
Relationship-Centric Theories That Show Limits of Effects	
Harmony and Balance	People gravitate toward information they already believe.
Structural Functionalism	When society begins to seem chaotic, the participants of the society will take steps to reestablish social harmony.

Figure 1: List of Referenced Theories

The Search for Messaging Effects

Interestingly, the U.S. Army learned early on that message-centric public communication is not very reliable. The U.S. Army began using mass communication on an unprecedented scale during World War II and conducted significant research projects to determine media effectiveness.[3] One of these Army projects was a series of films called Why We Fight. The purpose of this film series was to enhance the motivation of Army recruits during training and orientation. Research on the series revealed it was very good at providing factual information, somewhat effective in changing specific opinions, but had no effect in motivating people to serve or causing them to resent the enemy. When combined with other research, the Why We Fight series showed that a mass communication message is unlikely to change strongly held attitudes.[4] It seems illogical then, that despite what was learned in this film series, and after years of communicating strategically, the U.S. military seems to remain heavily focused on achieving communication effects with messaging.

An indicator of how the U.S. Army came to its current approach to strategic communication occurred in the late 1990's. During this period, the missions of the U.S. military were evolving toward humanitarian and stability operations. Fire supporters at this time seemed bereft of opportunities to plan missions for lethal munitions. In the absence of lethal missions, they began planning and organizing public affairs and information operations activities as part of non-lethal fires, perhaps because fires-planning was already a well-understood management tool.[5] In other words, information for general public consumption was sometimes controlled in the same manner as non-lethal ordnance, such as smoke artillery rounds. There seemed to be assumptions at that time that using carefully prepared information alone as part of fires planning could yield timely and reliable effects. Information for public release was distilled down to the most critical themes and messages with the intent to publish them at planned times via designated media. Today, information operations and public affairs are still often categorized as non-lethal fires.

Even though it may have seemed innovative in the 1990's, the idea that written and verbal messages could be managed and employed like ordnance was not new. The "Magic Bullet" theory is an early message-centric communication theory referenced during World War I and used again in the 1930's when Paul Joseph Goebbels employed intense propaganda and messaging techniques to mobilize and maintain German public will in support of Adolf Hitler's policies. The logic behind this theory is that every member of an audience responds to media messages in a relatively uniform way, and carefully crafted information can produce immediate and direct responses.[6] Sociologists today tend to regard this theory as "naïve and simple."[7] Basically, the Magic Bullet theory only seems to be effective if an audience is already psychologically disposed to either believe the message or sincerely trust the source of the information. For example, if the theory were used by the U.S. military in Iraq, it would first have to be assumed that the population uniformly trusts information from the U.S. government. Given the complexity of Arab audiences and their varying suspicions of western motives, it is likely that any U.S. effort to employ the Magic Bullet theory in the Middle East would be a failure.

Despite the limitations of the Magic Bullet theory, researchers continue to try to find a way to tie reliable effects to messaging, because the idea of achieving valuable results with the mass distribution of words alone is just too tempting. This may be why the military today seems to employ another message-centric approach known as Psychodynamic Persuasion Strategy. The Psychodynamic Persuasion Strategy hinges on an assumption that the key to persuasion lies in effective individual learning. Many advertisers and other communicators employ this approach as though it were nothing short of common sense. The premise of Psychodynamic Persuasion Strategy is that carefully employed information from a persuader can change the psychological orientation of an individual. This theoretical reaction to information might also be described as "learn-feel-do,"[8] and is illustrated in Figure 2 (next page). Hypothetically, after exposure to carefully prepared messages, a person who has a firm suspicion of soldiers will become somewhat less suspicious and more cooperative upon learning that only a tiny percentage of American soldiers have ever committed crimes. The diagram below shows how Psychodynamic Persuasion Strategy is intended to work. Once an individual hears a persuasive message, he thinks differently, and subsequently changes his behavior.

The problem with Psychodynamic Persuasion Strategy is that researchers can not make it work reliably. Rather than learning that American soldiers are trustworthy, feeling less afraid, and then behaving in a way that is not averse to those soldiers, it is impossible to determine how the target person's suspicions of American soldiers are affected. This may be because, as researchers consistently have determined, unwanted 'boomerang' and side-effects occur because of unknown or uncontrolled variables in the target audience. These problems significantly impact the success of information campaigns, which depend to some degree on messages being interpreted in the same way as was intended by the information source. Because all individuals are different and have varying life-situations and experiences, they often react to messages differently.[10]

One other theoretical approach using messaging that deserves discussion is Meaning Construction Persuasion Strategy.[11] People experience this strategy every day in the form of catchy advertising slogans and symbols that signal memory

responses as to the real meaning behind words. One mobile phone company identifies itself using the term, "fewest dropped calls," while another asks, "can you
hear me now?" A credit card company asks, "what's in your wallet?" and a news
organization says, "we report, you decide." The Army is "Army Strong," and the
Marine Corps is, "The Few. The Proud." All of these phrases are at the heart of
modern branding techniques and they carry meanings beyond the words themselves. In effect, the words take on a new meaning, as seen in Figure 3.

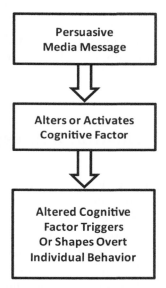

Figure 2: Psychodynamic Persuasion Strategy ("Learn-Feel-Do")[9]

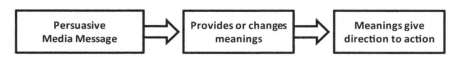

Figure 3: The Meaning Construction Persuasion Strategy[12]

When these slogans and brands work as intended, the meaning behind the
words results in positive action, such as buying a cell phone or joining the Army.
These techniques are clearly useful and effective, explaining the huge sums of
money spent on advertising yearly. Once again though, and despite the many
hours that advertisers spend brainstorming for the perfect phrase that will result
in widespread action or profit, the Meaning Construction Persuasion Strategy is
not consistently reliable. The effects of branding may be successful for one audience or culture, but ineffective with another.

In roughly the past 100 years, there are reflections of all of these message-centric communication theories and approaches in the public communication efforts of the U.S. military. Because these message-centric techniques have unreliable effects on individuals, some information campaigns seem to be based on simple hope that broad distribution of messages will achieve intended effects on at least some members of an audience. For advocates who would manage messages as non-lethal fires, messages are the ultimate area-fire weapon. Still, the effects are unpredictable. The question is why do communicators continue to emphasize messaging in military planning? The answer already mentioned is the unity of message and the timeliness that message planning affords. In addition, it seems to be ingrained in western psyche that messages in themselves achieve consistent and reliable effects, even though they do not.[13] This may be most evident by reviewing how the U.S. military tends to view something it calls "the information battlespace."

Message-Centric Information Battlespace

Depending upon the message-centric theories to which military strategic communicators subscribe will affect how they view the information battlespace. An Internet search of "information battle-space" yields many different ideas about the environment of public communication and how that environment is affected. Generally, though, the view of the information battlespace that many in the U.S. military employ is an ever-changing domain of data that is continuously impacted by a large variety of influencers.[14] These influencers include the White House and other global executive bodies, Congress, other agencies and foreign governments, various militaries and related institutions such as the Northern Atlantic Treaty Organization, the United Nations, infinite media organizations, bloggers, and so on. The way to persuade people in this constantly changing information domain is to dominate the news cycle with high-interest events, appealing visuals, and well-crafted messages in order to achieve a cognitive effect with audiences. The characteristics of an information battlespace that is nebulous and ever-changing include effects that last only as long as a subject remains in the mind, or cognitive domain, of the media and public. This means there is often constant anxiety among public communicators over which influencing agent has managed to dominate the news cycle. A videotape of Osama bin Laden that is released by al Qaeda to the general public may be considered a significant win for the enemy and the organization that first publishes that videotape, perhaps al Jazeera, is suspected as an al Qaeda sympathizer. Mass media analysts and researchers conduct endless assessments on the number of times specific "messages" are published in the press and these numbers are sometimes presented as metrics for success or non-success.

Because the mass-media theories that have been discussed thus far show that messages do not guarantee reliable effects, it is troubling that the U.S. military's strategic communication community views its information battlespace as just the opposite, a place that is constantly fluid and changing, but where effects can be reliably achieved. It is no wonder there is so much frustration. The U.S. military's constantly changing information battlespace, where messages are not reliable, might be akin to fighting the biggest tar baby ever imagined, or worse, trying to shape a world made of goo.

Theories that Point to Relationships

One place to start when researching for mass media theories that are more sophisticated than the Magic Bullet theory, and more reliable than other message-centric approaches, is to determine how and why people use media in the first place. The Media Systems Dependency theory asserts that people use media because they are dependent on it in order to understand their environment. In a sense, people establish relationships with their preferred media. Watching news and entertainment on television, listening to the radio, reading newspapers and books, and of course surfing the Internet, all contribute to an individual's complete understanding of the world.[15] At the same time, media are dependent on audiences because it is each individual who chooses which media are useful and reliable. However, if a person ever comes to believe that a media source is no longer a trustworthy source of information, he or she will choose a different media system that they perceive as more credible. The implications of the Media Systems Dependency theory for the military are very serious, because it indicates how public information must have long term credibility in order to be strategically effective. Any information accredited to the U.S. military that is somehow proven to be fallacious or biased can ruin the military's relationship with an audience for as long as it takes to reestablish trust. Given the pervasiveness of public communication in today's world, the fallout from false information grows exponentially as information is passed from media to media.[16] Public information that intentionally deceives enemies can also deceive allies, all of whom have the potential to choose other sources of information once the deception is revealed. As one source explains it, "Everything in the realm of strategic communication should be as truthful as human endeavor can make it. Tell the truth even though sometimes, for security, you can't tell the whole truth."[17]

Because people seem to establish forms of relationships with media, the Media Systems Dependency theory's approach to why people choose media has a very important connection to another useful theory know as Social Differentiation. The Social Differentiation theory contends that people increasingly choose communities of interest, rather than geographical communities. The result of willingly organizing into communities of interest is people separating into virtual subcultures based on whether they are liberal, conservative, athletic, academic, homosexual, Christian, Islamic, and so on.[18] The obvious modern-day medium between social differentiation and media is the internet, which has enabled virtual subcultures to evolve dynamically according to individual interests. For instance, a man with a strong interest in hunting will seek out other people who like hunting. He might establish new relationships with other hunters using Internet chat rooms and newsgroups and these friends will tell him where to find the finest hunting equipment, as well as the best places to hunt. Because of shared interests and lifestyles, this hunter could eventually have more developed relationships with his online hunting friends than with his own next door neighbors. Therefore, when public communicators seek to be more influential by establishing relationships with audiences, it is important to consider the norms, interests and media of various subcultures, and adjust engagement techniques accordingly.

To some degree, by taking steps to communicate with differing audiences according to what media is preferred, the U.S. military is already operating in the realm of social differentiation. Blogging, podcasting, web communication, television, radio, and installation newspapers are all used by the U.S. military to reach different subcultures. Still, if the military fails to remain a credible source of information using any particular medium it has invested in, the Media Systems Dependency theory indicates that the subcultures tied to that medium are potentially lost to the military for an undetermined period of time in lieu of other, more credible sources of information. When applied to the Middle East, the implications for the U.S. military are very severe. If subcultures perceive media that present the U.S. military's information as less credible than an adversary's media, the U.S. military potentially loses those subcultured audiences to media that report an enemy's points of view.

Critical to the ideas behind Social Differentiation theory, and the possible persuasive powers of subcultures, is the importance and influence of individual sociocultural relationships. It was mentioned at the beginning of this paper how the military sometimes seems to use the approach of Psychodynamic Persuasion Strategy in its public communications resulting in a "learn-feel-do" explanation for how people are persuaded. Even though this approach seems like common sense, researchers have an abundance of evidence to suggest that individuals are actually more persuaded by social expectations than by direct messages. Most people have heard of "peer pressure" for instance, and its influence on the behavior of teens. So, as an example, in a community where soldiers represent a key means of security or income, a person who dislikes and criticizes soldiers in that social environment might, in turn, be humiliated or belittled by other members of the local society. In this example, the individual stops criticizing soldiers because the group imposes a sort of "learn-conform-or-be-punished" approach, called the Sociocultural Persuasion Strategy, rather than a "learn-feel-do" approach.[19] As seen in the diagram below, when a group responds to information, perhaps from a persuasive leader, the values and norms for the group can change. In turn, the group imposes revised expectations on individuals, who must then conform to acceptable norms of behavior.

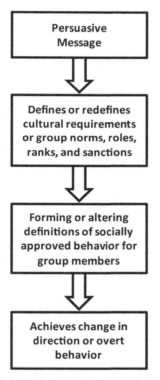

Figure 4: Sociocultural Persuasion Strategy ("Learn-Conform-or-Be-Punished")[20]

The key difference between this strategy and Psychodynamic Persuasion Strategy is that researchers have more than enough evidence to show that it works. Generally, the social groups that people interact in, whether family, schools, churches, clubs or cliques, have enormous influence over what is and is not normal, acceptable and expected behavior.[21]

Society has endless examples of how group pressure is leveraged to change behavior, from the use of Alcoholics Anonymous as an effective means of combating drinking, and "Smoke Out" day to discourage cigarette use, to heavy publicizing of the "Run for the Cure" to encourage activism on behalf of breast cancer cures.[22] Simply, the power of social and cultural groups within public communication is extraordinarily significant. When applied to how the U.S. military communicates and changes opinions among populations, community relations and civil affairs techniques become very important tools within the Sociocultural Persuasion Strategy framework. Events and actions that emphasize well-being and respect for groups have the potential to, sequentially, influence the behavior of single individuals.

Because group pressure is so persuasive on the behavior of individuals, the challenge for the U.S. military is determining how to establish, reestablish or improve linkages with key audiences or subcultures. The concept of Two-Step Flow is a theory that at least provides a starting point to persuading groups. The Two-Step Flow theory asserts that people are more likely to believe information from experts or authority figure persons with whom they have a trusted or perceived positive relationship, such as a pastor, parent, trusted journalist, or like-minded politician.[23] This theory is about engaging and networking with opinion-setters who have the capacity to impact the attitudes of secondary audiences. As an example, the late Jerry Falwell often used media to inform his Evangelical Christian followers. When something appeared in the news that was controversial to Falwell's followers, they might reserve their opinions until hearing what Falwell had to say about the subject.[24] When the Two-Step Flow is tied to Social Differentiation, it is clear that identifying the opinion-leaders for a variety of subcultures is key to impacting the behavior of larger and more general audiences. The Ayatollah Sistani, for instance, is a critical opinion-setter that the U.S. military must consider to gain a positive relationship with many Shi'ites in Iraq. Likewise, Muktadr al-Sadr is another opinion-setter for the Shiite Mehdi Militia subculture in Iraq and the U.S. military has already shown that it must decide whether to silence or persuade al-Sadr in order to change the behavior of the Mehdi Militia.

Relationship-Centric Information Battlespace

The four relationship-centric theories discussed in the section above show that strategic communication effects derived from relationships tend to be more reliable than message-centric effects. It is important to discuss how a relationship-centric information battlespace differs from the message-centric information battlespace that was discussed earlier. The information battlespace for a communication strategy that is focused specifically on relationships is less fluid. It is not a domain of ever-changing data. Rather, the battlespace for relationships is, simply, people. As seen in the Sociocultural Persuasion Strategy, people consistently respond to the pressures from their associated groups and often conform to the behaviors of a group even if they do not personally believe in that behavior. In a battlespace of people, there is less concern over dominating the information domain and a more targeted focus on information that can affect the core opinions of groups and subcultures. An individual who hears a particular message may never change behavior in the way intended by the sender, even if he hears the message repeatedly. However, if a group as a whole is persuaded, perhaps through the influence of group opinion-leaders, then the individual may be persuaded as well. Researchers have determined that, "many longer-term effects of mass media do not involve the intentional or immediate audience at all, but are the secondary responses of others."[25] Finally, analysis of an information battlespace of people is less about the number of times a message appears in the media and more about an assessment of cultural norms, behaviors and opinions on issues in response to detailed study, surveys, focus groups and other similar types of research.

Relationship-Centric Theories that Show Limits of Effects

Despite having more reliable effects, relationship-centric theories do not offer any "Magic Bullet" of their own. There are also theories that highlight realistic limitations to the potential effects of relationship-centric communication. First, related to the Two-Step Flow is the Harmony and Balance theory, which asserts that people gravitate toward information they already believe. In other words, audiences do not want to be challenged by new information or controversial ways of thinking. Audiences instead seek out other people with whom they already agree.[26] Most Rush Limbaugh listeners, for instance, listen to him because they have already decided in favor of the things that he says, not necessarily because Rush Limbaugh is autonomously empowered to significantly change the opinions of large audiences. The implication behind Harmony and Balance theory for the U.S. military is that it cannot be assumed that subculture members who have controversial leaders are simple-minded or easily swayed. Rather, it is more likely that subculture members have identified with a group and leader that already reflect their acceptable norms and beliefs. Referring back to al-Sadr and the Mehdi Militia in Iraq, some people might say that al-Sadr can mobilize the Mehdi Militia because he speaks forcefully for a community that has suffered oppression in Iraq. However, Harmony and Balance explains that many Shiites in and around Baghdad are sympathetic to al-Sadr's political and religious opinions because they already share similar views.

A second theory that reveals the limits of effects from relationship-centric communication is Structural Functionalism. The concept behind the Structural

Functionalism theory is that the organization of society is the source of its stability and each category of society's participants contributes to the attainment of social harmony.[27] When society begins to seem chaotic, the participants of the society will take steps to reestablish social harmony. When applied to mass media, Structural Functionalism indicates that audiences that are experiencing chaos will prefer media that reflect a return to social harmony. American television programming from the 1960's and 1970's are possible examples. Television audiences might have preferred "The Brady Bunch," "The Waltons," and "Happy Days" because these shows reflected ideal families with normal behavior. Applied to the chaos of current Iraqi society, Structural Functionalism would assert that many Iraqis will prefer media that point to a return to an Iraqi view of social harmony. In other words, some Iraqis might prefer media that identify with traditional values and strict interpretations of Islam, reflecting a desire to return to historically stable governments in Islamic history. Structural Functionalism's challenge for the U.S. military is how to best present Iraqis with a path to social harmony that does not require a return to non-democratic, oppressive forms of Islamic government.

Discussion and Recommendations

The first thing that should result from reading this study is realization that messages alone are not sufficient for planning and achieving reliable strategic communication effects. Messages are critical to unity of intent among various communicators, achieving "one voice" and responding quickly in order to address breaking news and disinformation. But messaging effects are not reliably consistent or controllable. On the other hand, effects from relationship-centric communication are much more reliable. Unfortunately, at the same time that U.S. military strategic communicators seem heavily focused on gaining effects via messaging, there seems to be few mechanisms for harnessing relationships. Those that exist appear primarily in the civil affairs and public affairs (community relations) arenas, as well as various engagements with military support to public diplomacy.[28] The community relations parts of public affairs are currently very focused on enhancing the U.S. military's image in U.S. local communities through bands, capability demonstrations, speakers bureaus, and similar venues, but do not necessarily operate along synchronized paths to achieve strategic effects. In order to become more effective, the U.S. military's strategic communication efforts should evolve in planning and execution to include effects via relationships, both personal and public. These identified relationships should include government, community, media and opinion leaders that have the capacity to impact audiences on a local, national and international level. Planning should also address the sociocultural norms that drive these audiences, as well as reasonable goals for impacting audience behaviors. Because public affairs is the only strategic communication capability that communicates directly to U.S. citizens, the community relations capabilities of U.S. military public affairs should be expanded and refined.

The second point the reader should glean from this study is that the U.S. military's information battlespace is much more manageable and understandable if viewed from a relationship-centric rather than message-centric perspective. An information battlespace that is centered on relationships is less fluid and enables communication techniques that have more reliable effects. The attitudes and beliefs of people evolve over time. Therefore, a people-oriented information battlespace does not immediately change or justify panic just because a strategic communicator makes a mistake or an enemy proves able to publish his message. On the other hand, a message-centric battlespace is hardly manageable, precisely because it is ever-changing with new information and because the effects from messages intended to change the battlespace are themselves unreliable. As a result, the U.S. military should reexamine if its current view of the information battlespace is useful and appropriate. Choosing to view the information battlespace from a relationship-centric point of view would require communicators to think about strategic communication in entirely new ways. One, because relationships require time to evolve, the effects and expectations from strategic communication would be less immediate. Two, strategic communicators would have to operate according to information that goes well beyond what is being "said," so that decisions are also based on what is being "done." Third, analysts in a relationship-centric battlespace would have to focus less on how many times certain information appears in the mass media and more on identifying key personalities and influencers, as well as, their agendas, preferences, characteristics and personal interests.

The third point from this paper stimulates the question whether or not the U.S. military is adequately prepared to conduct successful strategic communication that is based on relationships. A military that is predominately focused on achieving victory through combat may not be correctly postured to achieve victory in the information battlespace. This means that the U.S. military must critically review its programs for language and cultural training, as well as for strategic communication training, to ensure that leaders can succeed in a non-lethal, relationship-centric information battlespace. Finally, the U.S. military must seriously review its own relationship with the U.S. State Department, determine precisely what all the military's role is in diplomacy, and enable better linkages between foreign affairs officers and other strategic communicators.

Conclusion

In summary, even though the U.S. Army learned during World War II that message-centric public communication is not a reliable means of gaining desired effects, most of its communication efforts still seem to work from a message-centric point of view. The Magic Bullet theory, Psychodynamic Persuasion Strategy, and Meaning Construction Persuasion Strategy all demonstrate that written and verbal messages have effects, but that these effects are not reliable. On the other hand, communication that harnesses relationship linkages is much more reliable. The Sociocultural Persuasion Strategy shows that groups have the power to influence individual behavior, as seen in families, churches, schools, businesses and communities. The Two-Step Flow explains that the leaders of these sociocultural groups have the ability to influence the behavior of associated communities and subcultures. Once these and the other discussed theories are fully understood, the challenge for the U.S. military is determining how to establish, reestablish or improve strategic communication with key audiences or subcultures and their leaders. Ultimately, strategic communicators have to develop both synchronized messaging and savvy management of relationships to achieve unified and reliable strategic communication. In his classic guide, How to Win Friends and Influence People, Dale Carnegie suggests that the only way to get anybody to do anything without forcing them is by making them want to do it.[29] The way to make them want to do something is by determining and offering what they need or desire. Similarly, the late Speaker of the House of Representatives, Thomas P. "Tip" O'Neil, is oft remembered for saying, "All politics is local." His own success indicates he knew that one must demonstrate true concern for the well-being of voters in order to gain their support. These classic communicators understood that extraordinary powers of persuasion very often result from having a real or perceived positive relationship with individuals or larger audiences. Perhaps it is time for the United States military to do the same.

Endnotes

1. Richard Halloran, "Strategic Communication," Parameters (Autumn 2007): 4-14.

2. Werner J. Severin and James W. Tandard, JR., Communication Theories, (White Plains NY: Longman, 2001), 110.

3. Ibid., 153.

4. Ibid., 154.

5. Steven Curtis, Robert A. B. Curris, and Marc J Romanych, "Integrating Targeting and Information Operations in Bosnia," Field Artillery, (July/August, 1998): 31.

6. Melvin L. DeFleur and Sandra Ball-Rokeach, Theories of Mass Communication, (White Plains NY: Longman, 1989), 146.

7. Ibid., 164.

8. Ibid., 278.

9. Defleur and Ball-Rokeach, 279.

10. Denis McQuail, McQuail's Mass Communication Theory, (London: Sage Publications, Ltd., 2005), 476.

11. Ibid., 290.

12. Ibid., 293.

13. Ibid., 280.

14. Mari K. Eder, "Toward Strategic Communication," Military Review (July/August 2007): 61.

15. Defleur and Ball-Rokeach, 304.

16. Halloran, 13.

17. Ibid., 14.

18. Defleur and Ball-Rokeach, 186.

19. Ibid, 282.

20. Ibid., 285.

21. Ibid., 283.

22. Severin and Tandard, 193.

23. Defleur and Ball-Rokeach, 192.

24. Dr. Corely Dennison, Dean, W. Page Pitt School of Journalism and Mass Communications, Marshall University, telephone interview by author, 9 November, 2007.

25. McQuail, 478.

26. Dennison.

27. Defleur and Ball-Rokeach, 31.

28. U.S. Joint Chiefs of Staff, Joint Functions, Joint Publication 3.0 (Washington DC: U.S. Joint Chiefs of Staff, 17 September 2006), III-15.

29. Dale Carnegie, How to Win Friends and Influence People, (New York NY: Simon and Schuster, Inc., 1981), 18.

Re-Examination of Mixed Media Communication: The Impact of Voice, Data Link, and Mixed Air Traffic Control Environments on the Flight Deck

Melisa Dunbar, Alison McGann, Margaret-Anne Mackintosh and Sandra Lozito

Summary

A simulation in the B747-400 was conducted at NASA Ames Research Center that compared how crews handled voice and data link air traffic control (ATC) messages in a single medium versus a mixed voice and data link ATC environment The interval between ATC messages was also varied to examine the influence of time pressure in voice, data link, and mixed ATC environments. For messages sent via voice, transaction times were lengthened in the mixed media environment for closely spaced messages. The type of environment did not affect data link times. However, messages times were lengthened in both single and mixed-modality environments under time pressure. Closely spaced messages also increased the number of requests for clarification for voice messages in the mixed environment and review menu use for data link messages. Results indicated that when time pressure is introduced, the mix of voice and data link does not necessarily capitalize on the advantages of both media. These findings emphasize the need to develop procedures for managing communication in mixed voice and data link environments.

Introduction

Re-examination of Mixed media Communication: The Impact of Voice, Data Link and Mixed Air Traffic Control Environments on the Flight Deck Controller Pilot Data Link Communication (CPDLC) is a newly implemented means of communication between controllers and pilots using electronic messaging. While the concept of data link is not new and has been researched for over two decades, Very High Frequency (VHF) radio remains the primary source for the transfer of information between the air traffic service provider and the aircraft. A number of studies examining incident and accident reports have identified problems arising from voice communication, including those associated with frequency congestion and communication errors. (Billings & Cheaney, 1981; Lee & Lozito, 1989; Morrow & Rodvold, 1998).

Furthermore, the increase in aircraft requiring the use of the National Airspace System (NAS) continues to exacerbate the problem of already crowded frequencies. These issues have led to a renewed effort by the Federal Aviation Administration (FAA) and the aviation industry to find relief for the overburdened system. Operational use of CPDLC in a limited South Pacific oceanic environment began in 1995 and has since expanded into other oceanic regions (FAA, 1999). The European aviation community began conducting its trials of data link in 1995 and continues to broaden its program (Eurocontrol, 2000). The use of data link in the domestic en route environment has now been called for to augment conventional radio communication in an effort to help alleviate some of the constraints of the current system and to establish the foundation for enabling subsequent technologies.

Because data link will be supplemental to voice communication, a mixed environment where pilots and controllers will be required to move from radio to data link media is anticipated (RTCA, 2000). Voice amendments to data link clearances can also be foreseen due to potential difficulties with pilot-controller negotiations via data link communication (Air Transportation Association [ATA], 1992). Early data link research concentrated on single medium voice or data link environments. Research findings have shown an increase in accuracy and consistency for data link at the cost of speed for the transfer of information (see Kerns, 1991, 1999 for a review). Still other studies have examined a limited mixed voice-data link environment. For example, when using data link for redundancy of a voice message, Talotta et al., (1988) found that the controllers workload increased. Hinton and Lohr (1988) examined an environment where specific messages, such as heading and altitude clearances, were issued through data link, whereas other specific clearances were delivered via voice communication. The participants in the study found this mix of voice and data link to be pretty "natural". Kerns (1999) reports in her research summary that a dual-media environment of voice and data link requires fewer total transmissions than the all-voice environment. While research has indicated a reluctance by pilots to use data link in the busy terminal area and for non-routine transmissions (Kerns, 1999), little research exists that examines how the two media will best coexist.

There has been relevant research that may illustrate some potential issues around a mixed media environment. Morrow and Rodvold (1993) found that the time interval between messages impacts both voice and textual data link communication. Results showed that breaking down long messages into pairs of shorter messages with a brief interval in between reduced the overall number of voice clarifications in a voice environment, yet increased the number of voice clarifications in the data link environment. No ability to review messages was available for this study requiring all clarifications to be handled on the voice channel. The study also revealed longer overall acknowledgement times for both voice and data link when there was a short interval between messages. Underscoring the importance of these findings, researchers (Cardosi, 1993; Morrow, Lee, & Rodvold, 1993) have emphasized that in the voice environment, complex messages overtax pilots' working memory and have recommended that controllers reduce the length of their messages. Creating shorter messages may increase the number of clearances that must be given in a short time period. The mixed data link-voice environment that requires the user to switch modalities and communication procedures during short intervals may magnify the problems associated with time pressure in air-ground communication.

Additionally, voice and data link communication have different procedural constraints. One such constraint is the ability to respond to the message. Because voice is more temporal and often more salient than the visual modality (Sorkin, 1987), a voice clearance may draw a more immediate response. In contrast, a suggested benefit of data link is its flexible access where the pilot can manage the communication task around other flight duties (Kerns, 1991). Additionally, sequential constraints differ for the two different media. For radio communication the entry of the clearance data is flexible and can be implemented simultaneously while receiving the voice communication. The textual data link environment, in contrast, requires a fixed sequence of discrete steps for message handling. However, the permanent nature of the data link message allows for flexibility of when the message is retrieved.

Voice and data link environments have special characteristics associated with them. Combining the two media in a mixed environment may alter the characteristics in a way that does not maintain the advantages of each medium separately. To examine whether there may be an impact of switching between voice and data link communication due to the change in modality and communication procedures, McGann, Morrow, Rodvold, and Mackintosh (1998) examined the flight deck perspective of voice and data link communication in both single medium and mixed media environments. The interval between air traffic control (ATC) messages was also varied to look at the influence of time pressure in voice, data link, and mixed ATC environments. Results from this part-task simulation indicated that voice transaction times were longer in the mixed than in the single medium environment, while data link transaction times were unaffected by the environment. Time pressure resulting from short intervals between messages increased data link transaction times in both the pure data link and mixed data link-voice environments. However, message interval influenced voice communication only in the mixed environment and only when a voice clearance closely followed a data link message. Closely spaced messages also increased the number of requests for clarification for voice messages and review menu use for data link messages. Pilots appeared to handle all communication sequentially, closing out a data link message prior to attending to the voice message. Because the voice clearance was ephemeral, pilots had trouble remembering the voice message and this resulted in more clarifications.

There were some potential weaknesses to the previous study by McGann et. al (1998). The testing environment used for the experiment was a part-task simulator. Although the realism for the flight deck environment was good, it did not have the full set of tools and displays that would be available on a commercial flight deck. In addition, in this experiment the simulator supported single pilot operations in the earlier investigation. One participant performed all aviation, navigation, and communication tasks, including data link operations. Thus, workload was likely different from what would be expected in an actual commercial aircraft with multiple crewmembers.

The present study was designed to follow up on the part-task study described above. Several differences exist between the two experiments. Unlike the earlier investigation, this experiment used two flight crewmembers involved in each experimental run. In addition, the current study involves a full-mission simulator, while the previous study was run in a part-task environment. Finally, the flight deck implementation of data link is different between the two studies. The first study had a dedicated display of data link, whereas the current study had a data link display that was time-shared with the Flight Management System Control Display Unit (FMS/CDU). There were also other interface differences associated with each of these display differences related to alerting, message access, and responses available.

The data link system that is currently envisioned is considerably different from what was originally examined in much of the previous research (Aeronautical Data Link Integrated Product Team, Human Factors Working Group, 1999). Therefore, the goal of this research was to re-examine the issues involved in shifting modalities in a mixed media, domestic, en route environment using a current implementation of data link and recommended procedures in a high fidelity simulation. Specifically, we were interested in comparing voice, data link, and mixed ATC environments under time pressure caused by short intervals between messages. Additionally, we hoped to get an early look at how pilots handle more urgent messages in the voice, data link, and mixed environments. We expected that voice communication would be most impacted by the mixed environment and that closely spaced messages would result in more communication problems and longer transaction times and clearance entry times.

Method

Participants

Ten airline pilots (all male) were paid to participate as flight crew members in this study. All participants were either currently type-certified on the B747-400 or retired for less than one year. Average total flight time for the participants was 11,100 hr, ranging from 3,500 to 20,000 hr. Average total flight time on the B747-400 was 987 hr, ranging from 405 to 2,000 hr.

Simulation Facilities

Crews flew in the Boeing 747-400 (B747-400) simulator at the Crew-Vehicle Systems Research Facility (CVSRF) at NASA Ames Research Center. The NASA B747-400 Simulator was built by CAE Electronics and is certified to the FAA Level D certification requirements. Advanced avionics on the B747400 simulator include two flight management computers (FMCs), three multi-function control display units (MCDUs), Future Air Navigation System (FANS 1/A) data link capability, a Ground Proximity Warming System Unit, and an ARINC Communications, Addressing, and Reporting System (ACARS) Management Unit. Data collection is available for user interaction with all subsystems, including the autopilot system and communication devices.

In addition, the CVSRF is equipped with an ATC Simulation. The ATC system simulated a multi-aircraft, multi-ATC environment. (For a more detailed description of the aircraft simulation facility, see Sullivan and Soukup, 1996).

Data Link Functionality

The simulator was equipped with FANS 1/A data link capability as exists on the 747-400 today (The Boeing Company, 2000). This is an FMC-integrated data link utilizing either of the forward CDUs as an interface. An ATC function key on the CDU keyboard allowed both the Captain and the First Officer access to the ATC data link information on their respective CDUs. Each of the forward CDUs can also be used to interact with the FMC for data input or output (e.g., altitude, route, or speed data). Generally, the Pilot-Not-Flying (PNF) would display the most recent ATC data, while the Pilot-Flying (PF) would remain on an FMC function page.

Upon receipt of a data link message, the visual alert ATC Message was displayed on the upper Engine Indicating Crew Alerting System (EICAS) indicating the presence of a message in the queue. A single aural chime accompanied the alert. The visual alert would disappear once the message was acknowledged by a flight crewmember.

An ATC function key was available to both pilots as a hard key on the CDU keyboard. This key was used to access a new message or the ATC Index page if no new messages were in the queue. A method of accessing ATC messages through a menu structure was also available; however, this method was used less frequently since it required, on the average, an extra keystroke by the pilot for message access.

Once a message was accessed, it was displayed on the CDU/CRT (Figure 1). The message page consisted of one or two pages of message content, the text ATC UPLINK at the top, a time stamp representing the time a message was sent, and a page number over the pages available for the message. In addition, the message Acknowledgement options were displayed at the bottom of the message. The Acknowledgement options included "ACCEPT," "REJECT," and "STANDBY," and once acknowledged a verify prompt appeared and a second button press was required to downlink the response to ATC. All of these options were selected by using the line select keys closest to the appropriate response.

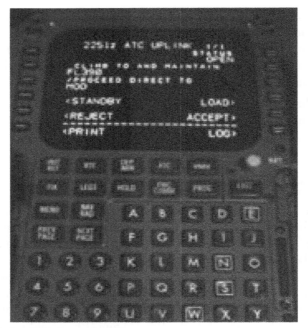

Figure 1. CDU display of a single page data link message.

For a limited number of clearances, there was also a "load" prompt and an "arm" prompt, which would enable the direct entry of the message contents into the FMC. Due to a simulator limitation, crews were instructed to ignore the "load" and "arm" prompts and to enter all information manually.

Other capabilities included in the data link system were the ability to review previous messages and the ability for the pilot to construct and transmit downlink messages to the controller. The menu used to access all ATC activities was titled the ATC Index Menu. This menu page was used to access the ATC Log, ATC Request, and ATC report pages. These other data link capabilities required input through the ATC menu structures displayed on the right and left sides of the display. The ATC Log allowed for an alternative method to access messages upon their arrival into the cockpit, and also was used to access messages that had been previously viewed. The ATC Request and ATC report pages were also used to construct downlink messages to the controller.

Instructions and Training

Participants were given an overview of the experiment and the FAA's current plans for expanding CPDLC in the near future. They were told that the focus of the study was on air-ground communication in the different experimental conditions. They were not briefed on the differences in message interval until after the experiment.

Although all participants were already FANS 1/A qualified, all crews participated in a short briefing and training on the data link system. Based on the recommendation of the aviation community, crews were asked to follow some general procedural guidelines (RTCA, 2000). Specifically, the PNF was asked to handle the ATC communication tasks as is done today, but both pilots were requested to read ATC uplink clearances directly from the display. Crews were also advised as to the relative priority of the different communication media: ATC voice communication was to be handled with the highest priority, followed by ATC data link communication, and finally company communication should be considered the lowest priority. Crews were also instructed that they should respond to ATC messages using the same communication medium (voice or data link) in which they were received. Finally, due to a simulator limitation, crews were asked not to use the "load" or "arm" prompts and to enter clearance data and create reports manually.

After the briefing, the crews participated in a short 30-minute training scenario, in which the crews flew the simulator and operated data link. The procedural guidelines, message alerting, display, and response techniques were explained and demonstrated in detail. Also, the ability to review and downlink data link clearances were demonstrated and practiced.

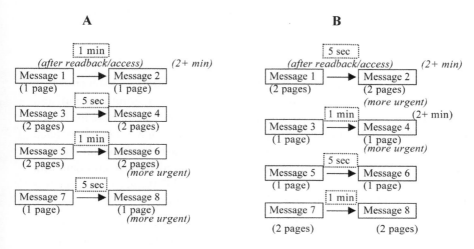

Figure 2. Target messages. All messages contained two commands and all crews flew a version of both Scenario A and Scenario B in pure voice, pure data link, and mixed environments.

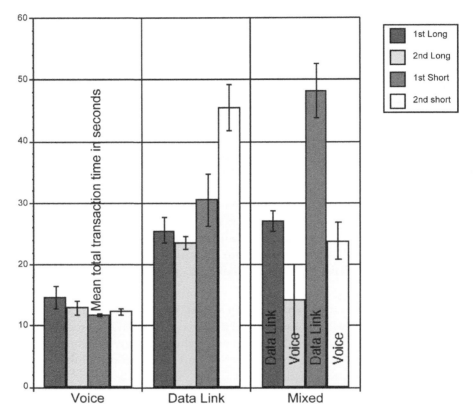

Figure 3. Mean total transaction times for messages by medium, interval and order with ± 1 SEM bars.

Procedure

Participants flew a total of six short flights 20–30 min in duration. Each crew flew two legs with voice communication, two legs with data link communication, and two legs with a mix of voice and data link communication. Crews were initialized en route over Salt Lake Center with flight plans to Chicago or San Francisco. Each leg was scripted with a different set of clearances with the help of current and former controllers. Experimenters transmitted the pre-recorded voice and data link messages from the ATC control room, and a retired TRACON controller was available to respond via radio to any pilot communication.

Analyses focused on four pairs of messages (a total of eight target messages) in each scenario. Each of the target messages under investigation contained two commands. The interval between the paired messages was varied: either 5 s or 1 min after the pilot accessed the data link clearance or after the readback of the voice clearance. Because the previous study by McGann et al. (1998) only found problems in the mixed environment when a voice message closely followed data link, and because it is recommended that controllers use voice communication for urgent amendments (RTCA, 2000), we focused on that sequence only. Thus for the mixed environment, data link was always followed by voice. The order of legs, communication medium, and interval was counterbalanced.

FANS 1/A formatting was such that two-element data link clearances could result in either one- or two-page messages. Therefore, for the data link messages, page length (1 vs. 2 pages) was also counterbalanced. Finally, urgency was also varied. Although all target messages defined as normal urgency by the RTCA Minimum Operational Performance Standards (MOPS) document (1993) (no urgent or distress messages were sent), clearances were sent that stopped climbs or descents or asked crews to expedite a turn. The context in which these clearances were sent added a level of urgency, and these messages were systematically varied to allow us to examine the effects of these "urgent" messages on transaction times and clearance entry times. Figure 2 demonstrates how the target messages were constructed to assess medium, interval, order, urgency, and page length in voice, data link, and mixed environments.

This study was designed to assess the effects of communication medium (voice, data link or mixed), message interval (5 s or 1 min), message order (first or second), message urgency, and data link message page length on pilot communication. Three primary measures were collected for each message: the total transaction time, the time to enter the first clearance directive into the Mode Control Panel (MCP), and number of communication problems (clarifications and errors). Following the experimental runs, flight crews filled out questionnaires about their experiences using each communication medium in the different environments. Additional questions gathered data on pilots' assessments of the data link display, functionality, and associated procedures, as well as the impact of data link in light of other flight duties.

Results

Total Transaction Time and Clearance Entry Time

Total data link transaction time included time for the pilot to access the message, read it, and acknowledge it to ATC. Total voice transaction time included time from the controller onset of the message (i.e., the time the experimenter sent the prerecorded message digitally) to the end of the pilot readback including any clarification. These data were collected from the videotapes by two coders. Total transaction times for both data link and voice messages were extended to include any communication by either crewmember with the air traffic controller about the content of the message. These are the operational measures most commonly used for transaction time (Cardosi & Boole, 1991; Kerns, 1991; McGann et al., 1998).

Clearance entry time was defined as the interval from the onset of the digitized ATC message to the time when pilots entered the new clearance data and selected the appropriate mode to initiate an aircraft change based on the new input parameter. This involved entering speed, heading, altitude, or frequency changes into their flight systems. Each clearance transmitted contained two elements, but because some clearances included a request to report reaching an altitude, only the first element entered was used for a comparison across all clearances. For voice clearances, pilots could begin dialing values before the end of the digitized ATC message.

Total transaction time and clearance entry time were each analyzed in a 3 (medium: voice only, data link only or mixed) x 2 (interval: long or short) x 2 (order: first or second message) repeated measures Analysis of Variance (ANOVA). The analysis for total transaction time revealed a significant three-way medium by interval by order interaction, $F(2, 8) = 4.80$, $p < .05$. The analysis for clearance entry time also revealed a significant three-way interaction of medium, interval, and order, $F(2, 8) = 11.82$, $p < .01$. See Figures 3 and 4 for means and standard errors for total transaction time and clearance entry times, respectively. Because the highest order interactions were found, lower level interactions and main effects will not be discussed. To interpret these results, we analyzed the data separately for each environment (voice only, data link only and mixed).

Comparison of Communication Media

Single Medium Environments

Based on the previous study, two hypotheses were generated for the single medium environments, both time pressure and message order would interact in the data link only environment causing the second message in the short interval condition to be lengthened. However, time pressure and message order would not significantly impact message timing variables in the voice only environment.

For each of the two single-medium environments (voice only and data link only), a separate 2 (interval) x 2 (order) repeated measure ANOVA was conducted on total transaction time. For messages in the data link only environment, significant main effects for interval, $F(1, 4) = 26.91$, $p < .01$, $\omega^2_A = .139$, and order, $F(1, 4) = 7.86$, $p < .05$, $\omega^2_A = .041$, were identified. Total transaction times for data link messages in the short interval pairing (M = 38.05 s, SD = 19.21 s) were significantly longer than those with a longer interval between messages (M = 24.54 s, SD = 7.58 s). Additionally, messages that were second in the pairing had significantly longer Acknowledgement times (M = 34.55 s, SD = 16.50 s) than the first message in the pairing (M = 28.04 s, SD = 15.04 s). In the voice only environment, no significant interaction or main effects were found. It took crews an average of 12.88 s (SD = 4.95 s) to acknowledge a voice message in the pure voice environment.

Similar 2 (interval) x 2 (order) repeated measure ANOVAs for the two single-medium environments were conducted on clearance entry time. In the data link only environment, a significant interval by order interaction was found, $F(1, 4) = 13.80$, $p < .05$, $\omega^2_A = .063$. The central set of bars in Figure 4 shows that the clearance entry times for the second data link message in the short interval was lengthened, while order had no effect on the long interval messages. In the voice only environment, a significant main effect for order was identified, $F(1, 4) = 17.06$, $p < .05$, $\omega^2_A = .091$. It took significantly longer to start entering clearance elements for the first message in the pairing (M = 11.68 s, SD = 6.20) compared to the second messages (M = 9.48 s, SD = 5.29).

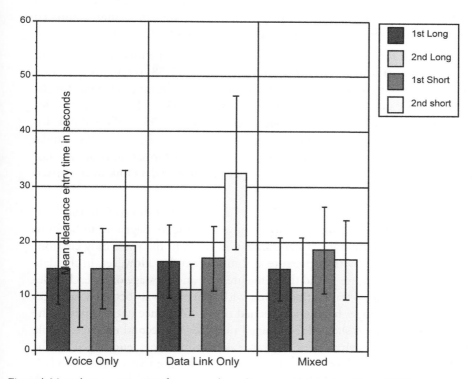

Figure 4. Mean clearance entry times for messages by medium, interval and order with ± 1 SEM bars.

Mixed Media Environments

Based on previous research, we hypothesized that the voice messages would be lengthened in the mixed environment under conditions of time pressure. For the mixed media environment, we analyzed total transaction time and clearance entry time in separate 2 (interval) x 2 (order) repeated measures ANOVAs. Recall that in the mixed condition, data link was always the first in a pair of messages followed by a voice amendment. This sequence was chosen for study based on the previous finding that data link followed by voice was the only problematic sequence (i.e. not voice followed by a data link message). Thus, the order of the messages also distinguishes the clearance medium (data link vs. voice). In the analysis for total transaction times, there were main effects for both interval, $F(1, 4) = 45.00$, $p < .01$, $\omega^2_A = .216$, and order, $F(1, 4) = 20.56$, $p < .05$, $\omega^2_A = .109$. The data link clearances (first message in each pair) resulted in longer transaction times (M = 37.65 s, SD = 18.18 s) compared to the voice clearances (second message in the pair; M = 19.15 s, SD = 11.24 s). It seems that pilots interrupted the data link clearance to attend to the voice message before closing out the data link message. Interval had a large effect on total transaction times (accounting for 21.6% of the variance, $\omega^2_A = .216$), in that a short interval between messages (M = 36.04 s, SD = 20.71) significantly lengthened total transaction times compared to long intervals between the two messages (M = 20.76 s, SD = 9.15 s).

The analysis for clearance entry time for messages in the mixed environment revealed a significant main effect for interval, $F(1, 4) = 7.58$, $p = .05$, $\omega^2_A = .040$, with crews taking significantly longer to enact the first clearance element for the messages with a short inter-message interval (M = 17.64 s, SD = 7.49) than for the messages with a long inter-message interval (M = 13.35 s, SD = 7.78). Interestingly, no main effect for order was found, $F(1, 4) = 5.59$, $p = .08$. Unlike total transaction time, crews started entering clearance information equally as fast independent of whether the message was sent via voice or data link in the mixed environment.

In summary, the modality by which a message was sent from ATC to the flight crew affected the time it took crews to acknowledge the message and to begin to enact the control instructions. Total transaction times in the voice only environment were unaffected by time pressure and message order. However, in the data link only environment, we found that time pressure and message order each independently affected total transaction times, with short intervals between messages and subsequent messages having lengthened times. Clearance entry times in the voice only environment showed lengthened times for the second message. While in the data link only environment, clearance entry times were lengthened for the second message in the short interval sequence. When the two message modalities were used in the same flight segment (data link followed by voice), it took crews significantly longer to acknowledge a data link message compared to a voice message (order effect). Also, time pressure affected both modalities, with longer total transaction times and longer clearance entry times in the short interval sequence.

Single-Medium vs. Mixed Environments

To further analyze the impact of the mixed environment on communication, we conducted separate analyses to directly compare each medium (voice and data link) in the single and mixed environments. Comparing mixed and single-medium conditions once again required matching transactions in terms of message order. Since in the mixed environment the data link message was always first in the pair of messages, only the first in each pair of messages in the pure data link environment was used in this comparison. We analyzed data link total transaction times in a 2 (environment: pure DL vs. DL in mixed) x 2 (interval) x 2 (page length: 1 vs. 2-page messages) repeated measures ANOVA. This analysis revealed a significant main effect for interval, $F(1, 4) = 14.22$, $p < .05$, $\omega^2_A = .076$. As was found in the previous analyses of the data link messages, total transaction times were longer in the short interval pairing (M = 39.38 s, SD = 21.11 s) compared to long interval messages (M = 26.32, SD = 8.42 s). No main effects for environment or page length nor any interactions were found.

In addition to total transaction time, we analyzed data link clearance entry times in a 2 (environment: pure DL vs. DL in mixed) x 2 (interval) x 2 (page length: 1 vs. 2-page messages) repeated measures ANOVA. This analysis revealed a main effect for page length, $F(1, 4) = 83.39$, $p < .001$, $\omega^2_A = .340$. Page length had a large effect on total transaction times, accounting for 34% of variance. The mean clearance entry time for 1-page messages (M = 19.88 s, SD = 5.91 s) was significantly longer than for 2-page messages (M = 13.58 s (SD = 5.75 s). No main effects for environment or interval nor any interactions were found.

A similar analysis for transaction times was conducted for the voice messages. In this case, voice was always the second in the pair of messages in the mixed environment. Therefore, only the second in each pair of messages in the pure voice environment were used for this comparison. We analyzed voice transaction times in a 2 (environment) x 2 (interval) repeated measures ANOVA. The analysis revealed a significant environment x interval interaction, $F(1, 4) = 7.60$, $p < .05$, $\omega^2_A = .040$. Post-hoc analyses indicated that the voice message following the short interval in the mixed-modality environment had a significantly longer total transaction time than the other three message types.

We analyzed voice clearance entry times in a 2 (environment) x 2 (interval) repeated measures ANOVA. It took significantly longer to start implementing clearance information for voice messages in the mixed environment (M = 14.24 s, SD = 8.56 s) compared to the pure voice environment (M = 9.48 s, SD = 5.29), $F(1, 4) = 20.72$, $p < .01$, $\omega^2_A = .110$.

In summary, we found that the type of environment (pure versus mixed modality) influenced the length of acknowledgement times and time to begin enacting clearance elements for voice messages, but not for data link transactions. For messages sent aurally, total transaction times were significantly longer for messages in the mixed environment when under time pressure (short interval in mixed environment). Clearance entry times were lengthened in the mixed environment compared to the pure voice environment, independent of time pressure. Type of environment did not affect data link timing variables. However, we did find that data link total transaction times were lengthened under time pressure, and time to begin entering clearance information was lengthened for one-page messages compared to two-page messages.

Urgent Messages

As explained earlier, the messages used to convey urgency were not defined as urgent or distress by the MOPS message set, but clearances were sent that stopped climbs or descents or asked crews to expedite a turn. The messages defined as urgent were always the second in the pair of messages, and thus were always voice messages in the mixed environment. This follows the recommended procedure that any non-routine message should be communicated via the voice channel (RTCA, 2000). To examine the impact of urgent messages on total transaction time, we extracted the transaction times for only the urgent messages and conducted a 3 (medium) x 2 (interval) repeated measures ANOVA. The analysis revealed a significant medium x interval interaction, $F(2, 8) = 30.05$, $p < .01$. See Figure 5 for mean transaction times. Simple effects analyses revealed that total transaction times for the second message in a short interval sequences were lengthened in the data link only ($\omega^2_A = .417$) and in the mixed ($\omega^2_A = .057$) environments. However, the impact of the interval manipulation was much stronger in the pure data link environment (accounting for 41.7% of the variance in total transactions times) than in the mixed environment (interval accounting for 5.7% of the variance). Unlike the other two environments, interval had no effect on total transaction times for urgent messages in the voice only condition.

The same analysis was run for clearance entry time, in which we extracted the clearance entry times for the urgent messages and conducted a 3 (medium) x 2 (interval) repeated measures ANOVA. This analysis also revealed a significant medium x interval interaction, $F(2, 8) = 8.39$, $p = .01$. See Figure 6 for means and standard errors. Simple effects analyses revealed that a short interval message significantly lengthened clearance entry times in the pure voice ($\omega^2_A = .066$) and pure data link environments ($\omega^2_A = .082$). However, interval had no effect in the mixed environment.

In summary, urgent messages (ones that contain an amendment to the preceding message) sent via data link suffered both lengthened total transaction time and clearance entry time under conditions of time pressure. The results for messages sent via the voice channel are less clear. For total transactions times, voice messages were lengthened when they quickly followed (short interval) a data link message (mixed environment). However, the clearance entry times for voice messages were lengthened in the voice only environment combined with a short interval.

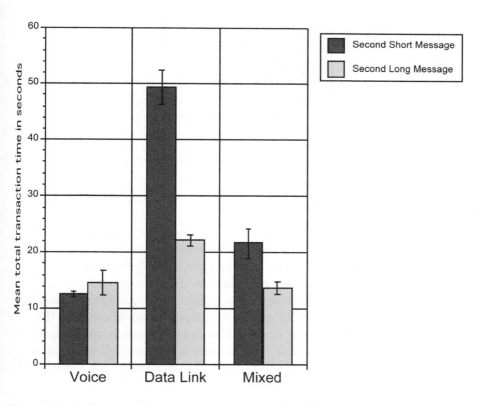

Figure 5. Mean total transaction times for urgent messages by medium and interval with

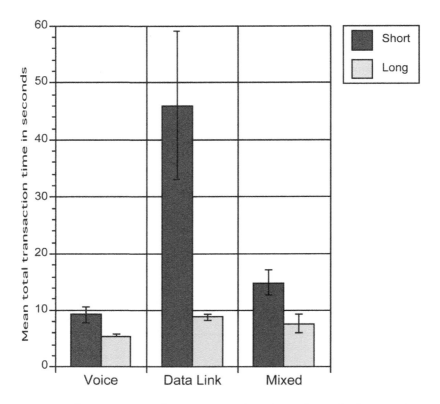

Figure 6. Mean clearance entry times for urgent messages by medium and interval with ± 1 SEM bars.

Errors and Clarifications

Communication problems, such as requests for clarification, were also examined. We hypothesized that the mixed communication environment and short inter-message intervals would produce more communication problems. Communication problems were defined as actions performed by the crew to clarify an ATC message. There were two kinds of actions. First, pilots could call ATC to clarify a voice or data link message (e.g., by asking for a repeat or confirmation). This definition was used in earlier studies of air and ground communication problems (Morrow et al., 1993, McGann et al., 1998). Second, for data link only, pilots could use the review log to clarify message content. Conceptually, use of the review log is similar to voice clarification because the crew performs an action to check or clarify the message. Operationally, they are different because voice clarification ties up the radio frequency whereas review log usage involves only the crew and not the controller.

For this analysis, we wanted to compare the number of voice clarifications across all conditions. However, there were no voice clarifications in the data link only condition, presumably because pilots had the data link review menu available to them, and also there were no clarifications in the short interval messages in the pure voice condition. Therefore, the voice only environment was dropped from the statistical analysis investigating the impact of interval. Overall, there were 18 voice clarifications and 41 data link "clarifications" (messages reviewed through the review log) in the 240 target messages under investigation. See Table 1 for frequencies of the clarifications across each medium and interval level. A 2 (environment: data link only vs. mixed) x 2 (interval) repeated measures ANOVA was conducted on the total number of clarifications made by each crew (voice clarifications and data link review menu usage). As predicted, a significant main effect for interval was found, $F(1, 4) = 90.00$, $p < .001$, $\omega^2_A = .681$. The short interval significantly increased the number of clarifications.

Table 1. Frequency of message clarificatioon types for each level of medium and interval.

	Voice Only		Data Link Only		Mixed	
	Short	Long	Short	Long	Short	Long
Voice Clarifications	0	6	0	0	7	5
Data Link Clarifications	No review log available	No review log available	18	9	9	5
Total Clarifications	0	6	18	9	16	10

In order to investigate the impact of medium, the number of clarifications made per crew were summed across the two levels of the interval manipulation. A one-way repeated measure ANOVA was conducted on the number of messages clarified in each of the three mediums (voice only, data link only, and mixed). No significant effect was found, $F(2, 8) = 2.08$, $p = .187$. It is interesting to note that only six messages or 10% of all clarifications occurred in the pure voice medium (M = 1.2 clarifications per crew, SD = .84). The data link only environment accounted for 46% of the clarifications (M = 5.2 clarifications, SD = 1.48), while 44% occurred in the mixed environment (M = 5.4 clarifications, SD = 6.07). The large amount of variance in the mixed environment may be masking possible differences between environments.

Additionally, we examined the types of voice communication problems since they may indicate which cognitive processes are impacted by the mixed media environment and time pressure. Voice clarification type included 1) a request to repeat the clearance, 2) a request for confirmation, and 3) incorrect readbacks. Of all radio clearance clarifications, 67% of clarifications occurred in the mixed environment and 33% occurred in the pure voice environment. (Only once in the mixed condition was a data link clearance clarified via the voice frequency.) There were no pilot readback errors in this study. In the mixed condition, pilots asked the controller for confirmation of a clearance half of the time and the other half of the time requested ATC to repeat the clearance. For the pure voice condition, requests for confirmation of a clearance occurred most frequently (83%) and there was only one request for a repeat of the clearance (17%). These results suggest that crews experienced more difficulty hearing or remembering voice messages in the mixed ATC environment than in the voice-only environment.

Two types of communication errors were coded from the videotapes by two coders. We expected that the mixed environment and short inter-message interval would produce more errors. First, in four cases, crews missed responding to an entire voice message. All of these missed clearances occurred in the mixed environment, three with a short inter-message interval and one with a long inter-message interval. Experimental procedure was to re-send the entire pre-recorded message. In one case, the crew discussed that they would attend to the voice message after finishing the data link message they were working on, but in fact they never did follow up.

Second, in seven cases, crews failed to implement one element of a clearance message. Four times they failed to report reaching an altitude, twice they failed to implement a speed change, and in the final case they failed to engage LNAV, the appropriate mode for the heading change they intended to implement. Six of these seven errors of omission occurred in the mixed environment and one in the pure data link environment. See Table 2 for a breakdown of the errors of omission.

Table 2. Breakdown of Clearance Entry Errors.

ATC ENVIRONMENT	OMMISSION ERROR
Mixed Voice, Short Interval	4-Report Reaching, 1-Speed
Mixed Data Link, Short Interval	1-Speed
Pure Data Link, Short Interval	1-Heading (failed to engage LNAV)

Taken as a whole, the results of clarifications and errors analyses suggests that voice messages in the mixed environment were most likely to be problematic, especially under time pressure. Voice messages in the mixed environment had a clarification rate four times that of voice messages in pure voice environment (taking into account that there were half as many messages sent in the mixed environment). In addition, most of the missed clearances and messages with implementation errors occurred for voice messages in the mixed environment. Data link messages in both environments (data link only and mixed) had equal rates of clarifications (via the review log), and both suffered when time pressure was present. Crews had by far the fewest problems handling messages in the voice only environment. Total clarification rate in the mixed environment was 4.5 times higher than the voice only environment and was 4.3 times higher in the data link only environment compared to the voice environment.

Messages Acknowledged Out of Order

It is interesting to note that time pressure caused by a short interval between messages sometimes resulted in messages being acknowledged out of order. That is, the second message in a short interval sequence was sometimes acknowledged prior to a response for the first message. Messages were acknowledged out of order in 17 cases (across 240 opportunities). Thirteen of these cases occurred in the mixed environment and four of these cases were from the pure data link environment.

Subjective Data

Questionnaire Data

After the simulation, participants responded to a questionnaire and all questions were rated on a five point scale. When asked about the use of data link crews indicated feeling that data link improves the effectiveness of air-ground communication (M = 4.10, SD = .99) and that they would be satisfied with the data link system as a safety enhancement in the en route phase of flight (M = 4.70, SD = .48). Pilots also felt that while the data link display was pretty easy to read (M = 4.10, SD = 1.29), the head-down time required for detecting, reading, and responding to a data link message was only moderately acceptable (M = 3.50, SD = 1.18). Additionally, pilots indicated that overall the review menu was easy to use (M = 4.10, SD = .99). They felt that the review menu was pretty effective for providing a reference to clearances during the pure data link scenarios (M = 4.50, SD = .53), but only moderately useful during the mixed data link and voice scenarios (M = 3.30, SD = 1.25).

When comparing the pure medium environment with the mixed media environment, pilots reported that handling voice messages in the mixed environment was more difficult than handling voice messages in the pure voice environment

(M = 2.80, SD = 1.14). Likewise, crews indicated that data link messages in the mixed environment were more difficult to handle than they were in the pure data link environment (M = 2.10, SD = .88).

Finally, pilots were asked about the specific data link procedures used in the study and they reported that they were comfortable with the procedures (M = 4.60, SD = .52) and that the procedures were effective for ensuring complete understanding of ATC message content by both crew members (M = 4.50, SD = .85). Furthermore, the crews felt that the procedures were effective in promoting timely and efficient handling of ATC communication (M = 4.60, SD = .70) and that the procedures did not interfere with other crew duties related to normal flight operations (M = 1.90, SD = .88).

In summary, flight crews reported positive attitudes about their ability to use this implementation of data link for air-ground communication in the domestic, en route phase of flight. They reported that the data link functionality and procedures used in this study supported safe and efficient communication with air traffic control. However, pilots did recognize the diminishing value of the data review log and increased difficulty with both types of messages in the mixed environment.

Discussion

This study extends a previous study by McGann et al., 1998, to better understand how a mixed voice and data link environment affects crew communication. Specifically, the factors of communication modality (voice, data link or mixed), message interval (5 s or 1 min), message order (first or second), message urgency, and data link message page length on pilot communication were evaluated. The principal measures collected were total transaction time, the time to enter the first clearance directive into the Mode Control Panel (MCP), and number of communication clarifications and errors.

While the former study was run in a part-task simulation, the present study allowed us to examine a current data link system (FANS 1/A) in a full-mission environment. Also, this experiment considers the use of data link by two crew members, whereas the previous study examined only a single crewmember. Some differences existed between the data link implementations utilized. The previous study evaluated a dedicated display data link, while this experiment investigated a data link time-shared with the FMC/CDU. There were also variables studied in this research that were not considered in the previous study: message urgency and message length. Thus, this was not a direct replication. However, this study was intended to represent a mixture of voice and data link that is a plausible scenario for near-term data link implementation.

Medium

It was predicted that closely spaced messages would result in more communication problems and longer crew response times. The results from this study indicate that the time pressure present in closely spaced messages differentially impacted voice and data link.

Direct comparison of the single-medium environments in this study allowed us to determine a baseline of communication performance for both voice and data link. Data link transaction times were significantly longer than voice transaction times. This is partly due to the data link implementation requiring discrete procedural steps to open and acknowledge data link clearances. However, despite the longer transaction times, it appears that crews usually implement the clearance data prior to acknowledging a data link message. Therefore, data link clearances are often enacted prior to their acknowledgement to ATC. Voice and data link transaction times and clearance entry times were also differentially impacted by time pressure. A short interval between messages significantly lengthened both transaction times and clearance entry times for data link messages, but closely spaced messages had no impact on voice transaction times in the single medium environment. However, an order effect was present in the clearance entry times in the pure voice environment. Thus, the pure voice environment was robust enough to handle a short interval between messages with no impact on Acknowledgement times, but time pressure does appear to affect clearance entry time in both data link and mixed environments.

The finding that voice and data link transactions were differentially affected by time pressure replicates the results from the previous study by McGann et al. (1998). Both voice and data link have particular characteristics associated with them. When considering Acknowledgement time, voice is the faster and more flexible of the two media while data link has the advantage of message permanence, but is slower and more sequential in nature. However, the timing of the input of data link clearance elements suffers in short interval messages. Since the data indicate that it is the second message in the short interval sequence that is lengthened, this finding is possibly due to the lack of time to complete the data entry for two messages in rapid succession.

It is also interesting to note that data link total transaction time was always impacted by interval, regardless of whether the data link message was in the pure data link environment or the mixed environment. The sequential nature of the textual data link, which requires a variety of visual and manual tasks, seems to be incompatible with time pressure when responding to a clearance message.

Environment

Based on the findings of the previous study, we expected that voice transaction times would be lengthened in the mixed environment relative to the pure voice environment. Moreover, while we expected that data link messages would be affected by a short inter-message interval, we did not expect the mixed environment to impact data link transaction times or clearance entry times. In fact, we found that both voice and data link transaction times and clearance entry times were lengthened in the mixed environment.

Pilots in the part-task study handled messages sequentially in the mixed environment, completing a data link message before attending to a subsequent voice message, whereas crews in the present study seemed to interrupt the data link message to attend to the subsequent voice message. Recall that the part-task study had a single pilot participant for each of the data collection runs. Despite the different strategies used in the two studies, voice transaction times were lengthened in the mixed environment for both simulations. Procedurally, both crew members were required to read the data link messages from the display, and this could explain why in the present study the PNF did not close out the data link clearance before attending to the voice message in the mixed environment and why the second message in the pure data link environment had longer transaction times compared to the first. These data reflect crew comments that it was more difficult to handle voice messages, in the mixed environment than in the single medium environment.

With regard to message clarification, there were voice communication problems in the voice condition, but not in the data link condition. Some examples of these include clarification based on the verbal information provided to the crew. As was found in the previous simulation, data link reduced the need for verbal communication with the controller to resolve problems and misunderstandings, largely because messages were permanently stored and available for pilot review. When review log usage was taken as a measure of message clarification, there were more uses of the review log in data link than there were clarifications in the voice environment. This suggests that the textual messages were not easier to remember, they were simply more available for review. Although frequency congestion was reduced in the data link condition relative to the voice condition (6 out of 40 messages were clarified verbally), pilots clarified via voice more in the mixed environment (11 out of 20 voice messages were clarified verbally). Apparently, the value of a review log is diminished when voice and data link messages are mixed.

Pilots cannot rely on their data link review log for confirmation of the most recent clearance when many clearances are transmitted by voice. In fact pilots commented that the review menu was only moderately useful in the mixed scenarios. Hence, one of the primary benefits of data link communication, permanent message storage, may be reduced in the mixed environment. In addition, more voice clarification may be required for both verbal clearances and those presented over data link.

Finally, the mixed environment also resulted in more errors than either the pure voice or pure data link environments. Crews were requested to respond to a message in the medium in which it had arrived, so a data link message would necessitate a data link Acknowledgement while a voice message would be responded to in voice. However, the controller was always available during each run, so it was possible to respond to a data link message over the voice channel. In four cases, crews missed hearing the entire voice message in the mixed environment. Crews never missed a voice message in the pure voice environment, even with the time pressure caused by closely spaced messages. Additionally, in seven cases, crews missed implementing one element of a clearance message. All of these errors of omission occurred in messages separated by a short interval. Six of these errors were in the mixed environment while one was in the data link environment. These errors may have occurred because crews sometimes acknowledged closely spaced message out of order. It appears that in switching back and forth between messages, some elements were overlooked.

Urgent Messages

This study also investigated how messages of increased urgency were handled by crews in the voice, data link, and mixed ATC environments. For the purposes of this study, urgent messages were defined as amendments to a previous message. The results indicate that while voice in a pure environment was robust enough to handle time pressure, even urgent voice messages took longer to acknowledge and implement in the mixed environment under conditions of time pressure. Because there was no differential alerting for data link messages, urgent amendments in the data link environment were not readily identifiable and therefore took longer to acknowledge and implement because of the short inter-message interval. Procedurally this raises an important issue because it is often suggested by many within the aviation community that urgent amendments should be handled via voice. However, these data suggest that an urgent voice amendment to a data link clearance is not handled in as expedient a manner as an urgent voice amendment in a pure voice environment.

Page Length

We found no page-length effect for total transaction time whereas 2-page messages actually resulted in shorter clearance entry times than 1-page messages. Further examination revealed that with two-page messages, crews began clearance entry with the first element 17 of 20 times, while for one-page messages they began with the first clearance element only 12 of 20 times. (These elements were comparable in their content.) One explanation for this result may be that the density of the one-page data link messages was greater than that of the two-page messages causing it to be more difficult to read and leading to longer clearance entry times. The one page messages had all elements of a two element clearance on a single page, usually resulting in about four lines of text for the clearance instruction. Two page messages had those clearance elements split between the two pages. In addition, there may have been some crews who moved more quickly through the data entry of the first element in the two-page messages in the anticipation of the second page. While this may provide a more timely response, it could lead to more confusion regarding that first element due to less careful processing. This finding needs to be investigated further.

Conclusion

Inefficiencies in an overloaded voice radio communication system have galvanized the aviation community to advance the use of data link communication between controllers and pilots to create additional capacity on the voice channel. The implementation of CPDLC throughout the NAS will involve a mixed environment, requiring pilots and controllers initially to switch attention between textual data link and voice media. Some research shows that data link can help reduce transfer of information problems including missed or blocked transmissions (Kerns, 1999). Other studies have shown that a dual-media system requires fewer overall transmissions than the single medium voice system (Talotta, Shingledecker, & Reynolds, 1990).

The results of the present study illustrate what may occur when mixing voice and data link environments under conditions of time pressure. The simulation revealed longer transaction times and longer clearance entry times in the mixed environment than in the pure voice environment. Additionally, flight crews missed entering more clearance data with mixed voice-data link communication than with either of the single medium conditions. Finally, relative to the pure voice environment, there were more voice clarifications in the mixed environment. When comparing the mixed environment to the pure data link environment, however, the numbers of clarifications (as measured by review log usage in data link) are the same proportionately given that there are more data link messages in the pure data link environment. Again, this seems to be an indication of the added difficulties of shifting between the voice and data link media. Clarifying message content over voice with the controller contributes to frequency congestion and adds workload to the controller.

However, the use of the review log may be problematic since it may not reflect voice amendments and could therefore be inaccurate. In the mixed condition, they are using both methods in an apparent attempt to compensate for some of the possible confusion.

Our research findings substantiate the conclusions from the previous part-task simulation demonstrating that when time pressure is introduced, the mix of voice and data link does not necessarily capitalize on the efficiency of voice and the precision of data link. To ensure the development and use of an effective system, we need to address the human performance concerns for all users in the complex mixed media environment.

Acknowledgements

This work was funded through a joint National Aeronautics and Space Administration/Federal Aviation Administration Interagency Agreement DTFA01-X-0245, under a cooperative agreement with San Jose State University (NCC 2-1095).

The authors would like to thank Diane Carpenter, Rod Ketchum, and Jerry Jones for all of their development support, Tom Kozon for his help with data management and analysis, and George Mitchell and Steve Lester for their invaluable ATC expertise and help in running the scenarios.

References

1. Aeronautical Data Link Integrated Product Team, Human Factors Working Group. (1999). Controller-pilot data link communications: Roadmap for human factors activities. Washington, DC: Federal Aviation Administration.

2. Air Transport Association. (1992). Research agenda for data link: Proposed for inclusion in the ATC/flight deck integration section of the national plan for aviation human factors. Washington, DC: Author.

3. Billings, C. E., & Cheaney, E. S. (1981). Information transfer problems in the aviation system. (NASA Tech. Paper 1875). Moffett Field, CA: National Aeronautics and Space Administration, Ames Research Center.

4. The Boeing Company. (2000). Air Traffic Services Systems Requirements and Objectives (Ref D926U087 Rev. A). Seattle, WA: Author.

5.　Cardosi, K. M. (1993). An analysis of en route controller-pilot communications (Rep. No. DOT/FAA/RD–93/11). Washington, DC: Department of Transportation, Federal Aviation Administration.

6.　Cardosi, K. M. & Boole, P. W. (1991). Analysis of pilot response time to time-critical air traffic control calls (Rep. No. DOT/FAA/RD-91/20). Washington, DC: Department of Transportation, Federal Aviation Administration.

7.　Eurocontrol. (2000). PETAL-II interim report, v.1.3 (Document number DED2/OPR/ET1/ST05/2000/P2/18). Brussels, Belgium: Eurocontrol.

8.　Federal Aviation Administration (Flight Technologies and Procedures Division—AFS400) and Fans Interoperability Team (FIT). (1999). Operator guide to CPDLC operational approval. Washington, DC: U.S. Department of Transportation, Federal Aviation Administration.

9.　Hinton, D. A. & Lohr, G. W. (1988). Simulator investigation of digital data link ATC communications in a single pilot operation (NASA Tech. Paper No. 2837). Hampton, VA: National Aeronautics and Space Administration, Langley Research Center.

10.　Kerns, K. (1999). Human factors in air traffic control/flight deck integration: Implications of data-link simulation research. In D. J. Garland, J. A. Wise & V. D. Hopkin (Eds.), Handbook of aviation human factors (pp. 519-546). New Jersey: Lawrence Erlbaum Associates, Inc.

11.　Kerns, K. (1991). Data-link communication between controllers and pilots: A review and synthesis of the simulation literature. The International Journal of Aviation Psychology, 1(3), 181–204.

12.　Lee, A. T. & Lozito, S. (1989). Air-ground information transfer in the national airspace system. In R. S. Jensen (Ed.), Proceedings of the Fifth Symposium on Aviation Psychology (pp. 425-432). Columbus, OH: The Ohio State University.

13.　McGann, A., Morrow, D., Rodvold, M., & Mackintosh, M. (1998). Mixed media Communication on the Flight Deck: A comparison of voice, data link, and mixed ATC environments. . The International Journal of Aviation Psychology, 8(2), 137–156.

14.　Morrow, D. G. & Rodvold, M. A. (1998). Communication issues in air traffic control. In M. Smolensky & E. Stein (Eds.), Human factors in air traffic control. New York: Academic.

15.　Morrow, D. G. & Rodvold, M. A. (1993). The influence of ATC message length and timing on pilot communication (NASA Ames Contractor Rep. No. 177621). Moffett Field, CA: National Aeronautics and Space Administration, Ames Research Center.

16. Morrow, D. G., Lee, A. T., & Rodvold, M. A. (1993). Analyzing problems in routine controller-pilot communication. The International Journal of Aviation Psychology, 3, 285–302.

17. RTCA. (2000). Minimum human factors standards for air traffic services provided via data communications utilizing the ATN, builds1 and 1a (RTCA/DO-256). Washington, DC: RTCA, Inc.

18. RTCA. (1993). Minimum operational performance standards for ATC two-way data link communications (RTCA/DO219). Washington, DC: RTCA, Inc.

19. Sorkin, R. D. (1987). Design of auditory and tactile displays. In G. Salvendy (Ed.), Handbook of human factors. New York: Wiley-Interscience.

20. Sullivan, B. T., & Soukup, P. A. (1996, July). The NASA 747-400 flight simulator: National resource for aviation safety research. Paper presented at American Institute of Aeronautics and Astronautics, San Diego, CA (AIAA-963517).

21. Talotta, N. J., Shingledecker, C., & Reynolds, M. (1990). Operational evaluation of initial data link en route services, Volume I (Rep. No. DOT/FAA/CT-90/1, I). Washington, DC: Department of Transportation, Federal Aviation Administration.

22. Talotta, N. J., Shingledecker, C., Zurinskas, T., Kerns, K., Marek, H. R., Van Campen, W., & Rosenbert, B. (1988). Controller evaluation of initial data link air traffic control services: Mini study 1. (Rep. No. DOT/FAA/CT-88/25, I). Washington, DC: Department of Transportation, Federal Aviation Administration.

Copyrights

Index